ESSENTIALS
of Cost Management

Essentials Series

The Essentials Series was created for busy business advisory and corporate professionals. The books in this series were designed so that these busy professionals can quickly acquire knowledge and skills in core business areas.

Each book provides need-to-have fundamentals for those professionals who must:

- Get up to speed quickly, because they have been promoted to a new position or have broadened their responsibility scope.
- Manage a new functional area.
- Brush up on new developments in their area of responsibility.
- Add more value to their company or clients.

Other books in this series include:

Essentials of Accounts Payable, by Mary S. Schaeffer

Essentials of Capacity Management, by Reginald Tomas Yu-Lee

Essentials of Cash Flow, by H.A. Schaeffer, Jr.

Essentials of CRM: A Guide to Customer Relationship Management, by Bryan Bergeron

Essentials of Credit, Collections, and Accounts Receivable, by Mary S. Schaeffer

Essentials of Intellectual Property, by Alexander I. Poltorak and Paul J. Lerner

Essentials of Trademarks and Unfair Competition, by Dana Shilling

Essentials of XBRL: Financial Reporting in the 21st Century, by Miklos A. Vasarhelyi, Liv A. Watson, Brian L. McGuire, and Rajendra P. Srivastava

Essentials of Corporate Performance Measurement, by George T. Friedlob, Lydia L.F. Schleifer and Franklin J. Plewa, Jr.

For more information on any of the above titles, please visit www.wiley.com.

ESSENTIALS
of Cost Management

Catherine Stenzel

Joe Stenzel

WILEY

This book is printed on acid-free paper.

Copyright © 2003 by John Wiley & Sons, Inc., Hoboken, New Jersey. All rights reserved.

Published simultaneously in Canada

No part of this publication may be reproduced, stored in a retrieval system, or transmitted in any form or by any means, electronic, mechanical, photocopying, recording, scanning, or otherwise, except as permitted under Section 107 or 108 of the 1976 United States Copyright Act, without either the prior written permission of the Publisher, or authorization through payment of the appropriate per-copy fee to the Copyright Clearance Center, Inc., 222 Rosewood Drive, Danvers, MA 01923, 978-750-8400, fax 978-750-4470, or on the web at www.copyright.com. Requests to the Publisher for permission should be addressed to the Permissions Department, John Wiley & Sons, Inc., 111 River Street, Hoboken, NJ 07030, 201-748-6011, fax 201-748-6008, e-mail: permcoordinator@wiley.com.

Limit of Liability/Disclaimer of Warranty: While the publisher and author have used their best efforts in preparing this book, they make no representations or warranties with respect to the accuracy or completeness of the contents of this book and specifically disclaim any implied warranties of merchantability or fitness for a particular purpose. No warranty may be created or extended by sales representatives or written sales materials. The advice and strategies contained herein may not be suitable for your situation. You should consult with a professional where appropriate. Neither the publisher nor author shall be liable for any loss of profit or any other commercial damages, including but not limited to special, incidental, consequential, or other damages.

For general information on our other products and services, or technical support, please contact our Customer Care Department within the United States at 800-762-2974, outside the United States at 317-572-3993 or fax 317-572-4002.

Wiley also publishes its books in a variety of electronic formats. Some content that appears in print may not be available in electronic books.

ISBN: 0-471-22734-X

Printed in the United States of America.

10 9 8 7 6 5 4 3 2 1

We dedicate this book to management accountants everywhere.

Contents

	Preface: Cost and Value	ix
1	Cost Management: Control and Profitability	1
2	Traditional Cost Types, Terms, and Practices	33
3	Cost Accounting Structures: Standards, Budgets, and Controls	59
4	Operational Resource Accounting	101
5	Process and Resource-Based Cost Management	145
6	Tactical Management of Costs and Resources	181
7	Strategy-Based Systems and the Future of Cost Management	217
	Suggested Readings	261
	Index	265

Preface: Cost and Value

In the last half of the twentieth century, executives and managers grew increasingly frustrated with precise, detailed general ledger and cost management systems that were often irrelevant to operations management and day-to-day decision making. Income statements and balance sheets pointed either to the past or to a single point in time but had little to say about managing the current or future operations.

Only recently have more successful cost management alternatives surfaced: activity-based costing, performance measurement, and strategic cost management are a few of the better known paradigms. The boom economy of the 1990s provided organizations with an environment of relative freedom in which to experiment with a variety of these new approaches to manage cost. Then, just as we seemed to be getting somewhere, recession set in. At this writing, early in 2002, no one seems to know what will happen next. Yet the need to manage cost remains constant in all economic conditions, as no aspect of business and organization life is quite so enduring as cost. In good economic times, the focus on cost diminishes to varying degrees, but it never disappears. During difficult economic times, the importance of cost ascends.

Coming to Terms

Considering the pervasive and perennial nature of cost, every manager should thoroughly understand its management. The term "cost" is so much a part of the fabric of our business and personal lives that we don't realize just how much it occupies our attention and drives our behaviors. Personal habits and beliefs about cost are so deeply embedded in our value systems that we rarely articulate them to others. We take for granted that everybody knows what cost is, and we assume that everyone understands the term the way we do. Nothing could be farther from the truth. That's where the trouble starts.

The focus of the financial professional exacerbates these misunderstandings and communication failures. First, traditional standard cost systems support bookkeeping and financial statement consistency and comparability; however, their usefulness to nonfinancial managers is questionable. Second, financial professionals must answer directly to shareholders, whether public or private. The shareholder's interest in financial outcomes creates a historical focus on information that does little to support day-to-day management or long-term planning. Finally, financial professionals simply do not always know the other common lexicons within business language: operations, market, human capital, and value. Financial professionals would do well to learn these other dialects thoroughly.

Organizations graced with broadly educated, creative, operations-friendly financial professionals who see the big picture still face cost management communications challenges. Within any enterprise, small or large, all managers must come to a common understanding of the essential nature and dynamics of cost and cost management, and how these impact performance. Conflicts and misunderstandings arise when leaders and managers conduct daily operations under different cost management conceptual frameworks. A commonly understood framework and a working vocabulary that matches business conditions and management style are more important than the specific "brand" of cost and performance system. While every manager is held accountable for budgetary prudence, actions that support one manager's budgetary success may undermine the next manager's fiscal performance. Take, for

Preface

example, the perennial battle between the sales manager compensated on sales-dollar volume without regard for product complexity, and the counterpart manufacturing manager, who must build complex products but is measured in terms of performance in cycle time, minimizing cost, and eradicating waste. A common understanding of cost behavior and dynamics would do much to alleviate such counterproductive dynamics.

Like No Other—Except One

The cost management discipline has immense range. And though *Essentials of Cost Management* covers only the peaks of that range, much like "Cliff Notes" for *War and Peace*, condensed versions are often just the ticket. For readers wanting more, this discussion is available in expanded and enhanced form under the title, *From Cost to Performance: A Guide to Creating Value*. This hardbound edition, also available from John Wiley & Sons, Inc., (June 2003) extends cost management's conceptual underpinnings, executive insights, and strategic connections.

You will find that both books are like no other cost management book yet written. Neither is an academic text for business students nor an exhaustive theoretical tome for college faculty. Importantly, neither book is an advertisement for one method, one philosophy, or any other magic bullet that will save your organization. There are too many good methods available to advocate any one. You will, instead, benefit from an unbiased, up-to-date explanation on a range of perspectives in the fields of cost and performance management.

We advocate *blended approaches*, a theme you will see throughout both books. The increasingly unique profile of all organizations argues for blending. The old saw, "business is business," does not express our view of reality. Although organizations have certain elements in common—people, assets, money (usually), and a purpose for being—many more differences than similarities abide within each company. What works in one company fails miserably in another. That's why you've been seeing so much in the business press about knowledge management, intellectual capital, and learning organizations. Differences in intangible assets such as these are a factor behind the staggering rate of recent, significant corporate failures. One business model does not work for all—over the long haul, one model doesn't even work for one business. Money is important, but it isn't everything. It is the unique nonfinancial assets—not reflected in traditional financial reporting—that set companies apart. Managing the costs and value of nonfinancial assets is necessary now, even though the frameworks for doing so are just emerging and being tested.

To successfully manage cost, you will need to engage the hard and creative work of all successful cost managers. This hard and creative work includes evaluating, testing, changing, intuiting, and *blending* the array of available cost management tools and techniques. And, yes, every executive and manager is a cost manager, whether in the form of nonfinancial assets not yet quantified, or traditional budgets, capital projects, and the entire organization's profit-and-loss statement.

That's where this book, *Essentials of Cost Management*, and its expanded version, *From Cost to Performance*, can support you. Whether you use one or both of these volumes as an occasional reference, an intense study course, or as a refresher, we have fashioned content and substance to assist you in your decision making in your day-to-day management and in your long-term vision and planning.

Defining Essential Value

What is cost management? Ask ten executives and you will get ten answers. Still, one common theme will emerge: Cost is what gets subtracted from revenue, and that calculation equals profit. (For now, we

Preface

lump expenses into cost and do not draw the accounting distinction.) All roads diverge after that commonly understood calculation. The work of this book will be to draw out the *essentials* of cost and cost management—the essentials beyond revenue minus cost equals profit. This book uses *value* as the common thread that knits together the fabric of cost management essentials.

In recent years, writers and consultants have discovered and even started to market "value." Value propositions. Value management. Value equations. Economic Value Added. Even though value has always been in the business vocabulary, we trace the modern discovery of value back to the early days of activity-based costing (see Chapter 5) when we were all busy identifying so-called nonvalue-added (NVA) activities, thereby adding two more letters to that scarlet letter "A." Woe unto you in those days if you were found to be NVA!

The chopping and pruning quickly led to the discovery that cutting costs by eliminating NVA activities wasn't always a very smart thing to do, especially if you didn't understand the interdependence of activities across the organization and the value this created. Even less smart was eliminating the activity, but keeping the resource! Predictably, costs remained the same.

Then along came a spider that whispered, "Value equals creating shareholder wealth," and we wove a nasty web around that definition of value. This myopic focus on shareholder wealth continues to lead to destructive short-term attention on financial capital measures and practically no attention to human capital constituents: employees, customers, and communities. Worse, in many companies, the short-term financial focus eroded the very shareholder wealth managers were trying to protect.

The invalid assumption in these examples and many others is an unarticulated belief about revenue and cost: Revenue is good; cost is bad. This simple characterization is not valid. By their nature, revenue and cost are neutral elements. Only management of these elements can place them in the plus or minus column.

Revenue equals cash in the door is easy to understand. Looks good. But it stays good only if part of the revenue eventually makes its way to the profit line. Enter the gunslinger in the black hat: Cost. Who and what make cost the bad guy? Valuable resources (i.e., costs) are obtained in the hopes of creating something of value. In this light, *cost is the engine of value.* Only a race of extinct dot-commers and their investors ever thought that value could be created without some cost.

So, we have come full circle. Cost is the raw material of value, the resource from which value is created. Cost is the fuel for revenue generation. Cost *management* is the successful stewardship of valuable financial and human resources that results in benefits to an organization's important constituents. Each organization has the right to decide which of its constituents it can afford to ignore or short-change.

Experienced managers have learned that they need an integrated and balanced view attending to cost *and* revenue, to the financial *and* nonfinancial, to both human *and* monetary capital. Such professionals use integrated, balanced systems that promote continuous improvement, motivate innovations and breakthroughs, and energize important constituents. Such managers are not fixated on cost cutting, meeting historical budgets, or meeting a quarterly earnings-per-share target. They neither fear taking risks nor shrink from putting their money (i.e., cost) where their mouths are.

The purpose of *Essentials of Cost Management* is to assist you in becoming a business professional who sees cost management as a value-creating opportunity, or to enhance your management in new and different ways.

Preface

How the Book Is Organized

Seven chapters tour the cost management field. The early chapters cover conventional approaches that form the foundation and rationale for the advanced perspectives and methods discussed in parts of Chapter 3 and in the last four chapters. Chapter 4 provides an important bridge between conventional and advanced practices.

Most chapters will contain In the Real World sidebars to help you assess your cost system. Throughout this book, "real world" refers to helping you mature the cost management systems in your life. We will do this in three ways:

1. Provide questions and explorations you can use to evaluate the level of maturity of your organization's cost practices.

2. Give you enough technical knowledge to ascertain the value that your accounting staff is providing to your business.

3. Let you know what you can expect from a conventional cost system and from the more advanced cost management approaches.

In addition, we will suggest Tips & Techniques related to application in practice.

In the final analysis, cost and performance management influences human behavior and makes effective use of capital resources. Therefore, we will consistently examine cost practices as they affect the behavior of real people, their attitudes, and their motivations. Behavioral impacts make or break a cost management system.

An Invitation

Finally, we invite you to contact us when the mood strikes you. We always look forward to hearing stories from the field and exploring new

Preface

ideas. You can reach us at genesis@visi.com. We'll leave a light burning for you—it's worth the cost.

Joe and Catherine Stenzel

Minneapolis, Minnesota
April 2002

CHAPTER 1

Cost Management: Control and Profitability

After reading this chapter you will be able to

- Understand the objectives of an effective cost management system (CMS)
- Explain the relationship between control and profitability
- Explain the connection points between cost and financial accounting systems
- Articulate the design features of a value-focused CMS
- Distinguish between cost and performance management systems

All executives and managers account for cost. In various ways, all business professionals manage cost, and most managers engage in capital investment decisions, forecasting, pricing, and product or service management. All these business activities are deeply embedded in the work of cost accounting. Cost-related tasks consume a significant amount of management time at all levels of the organization.

A business professional must understand the organization's cost accounting practices to competently manage a specified area and understand how personal accountabilities are calculated and tracked. An accounting instructor with considerable experience in the field always gave her MBA students the same advice, "Learn the language of accounting. It's the language of business, and if you don't learn it, some little bean counter wearing a green eyeshade will blow your grand marketing or operations idea right out of the water!"[1]

Bellwether organizations that employ advanced management systems still run their accounting systems—"keep their books"—according to basic cost accounting principles. Importantly, conventional practices shape advanced techniques; therefore, more mature methods cannot be fully understood without reference to their predecessors. As a baseline, an organization's executives must establish management/cost accounting practice foundations that serve decision making and operations, first, and financial accounting, second, before moving to advanced systems. To accomplish this, executives need the ability to distinguish system alternatives. This chapter addresses these requirements.

The Profit Imperative: Defining the Objectives of Cost Management

Profitability, variously interpreted as net income, equity value, and return on investment is a results-focused indicator watched more carefully than any other performance measurement category. But if these measurements depict results, what measurements show the dimensions of performance for the processes that lead to those results? At the core, profit has only two components: revenue and cost. To understand how a cost management system works, here are some key terms to be familiar with:

- *Cost.* An outflow of a resource, whether in cash, as a payable, a rendered service, or as a trade or barter, that is consciously made with expectation of benefit to the organization: goods, property, or services acquired.
- *Cost accounting.* The accounting profession is divided into two major branches: (1) financial and (2) management (or managerial) accounting. The later is synonymous with cost accounting.

Cost Management: Control and Profitability

The term "management" refers to the comparatively internal focus of the cost accounting field as compared with the external focus of financial accounting. The word "traditional," when used to describe cost accounting methods, refers to the standard practices that are taught in basic management accounting courses and practiced in most North American firms. The standard practices include cost systems and procedures, methods of determining costs, points of cost accountability, forecasts, cost comparisons (e.g., standard cost systems), and budgets (operational, project, and capital). The purpose of cost accounting is to assist in the wise and prudent stewardship of overall organizational resources.

- *Cost and expense distinctions.* Both costs and expenses are expenditures. For the remainder of this book, the word "expenditures" will be used to identify an organization's total outflow of assets in all forms. Chapter 2 will further clarify important distinctions between cost, expense, and expenditure. In the standard income statement of a for-profit firm, costs typically refer to the categories of material, labor, and overhead appearing above the income statement's gross margin line (revenue minus cost). See Exhibit 1.1 for an example of the income statement components for a manufacturing firm. Expenditures typically called *operating expenses* are displayed below the gross margin line. On the income statement, the material, labor, and overhead items are called *cost of goods sold* (COGS). Operating expenses consist of monetary or asset outlays for general, administrative, selling, marketing, and other functions deemed to be indirectly related to production. Operating expenses are commonly abbreviated as SG&A for sales, general and administrative.

- *Cost management.* The use of cost accounting systems and methods to guide current and future operations toward specified objectives; the analysis and interpretation of cost data is critical to the decision-making process.

- *Cost management system (CMS)*. An expenditure information architecture that tracks, monitors, reports, and provides decision-quality information and insights. A CMS is less constrained by exacting professional standards and reporting formats than financial accounting; therefore, a CMS can and should be customized to match an organization's internal environment and specific cost structures.

  A CMS sets direction for resource consumption priorities and makes course corrections by emphasizing operations first and accounting practices second. A CMS specifically answers the demands of the profit imperative when it aligns employee spending behaviors with the organizational strategy. The purpose of the CMS is to *understand the nature and behavior of cost, and thereby manage valuable assets wisely through optimizing limited resources.*

  The chief CMS responsibility is to promote improvement in cost structure. The CMS should:

  - Support understanding of the nature and behavior of cost (and the humans doing the spending).
  - Promote, track, and give feedback on value creation and continuous improvement.
  - Assist management in wise use of resources.

- *Cost types.* Management accountants created cost types in an attempt to understand the nature and behavior of different resources. Cost types are designations given to categories of resource expenditures. They are based on assumptions about the ways that resources are consumed in relation to the activities to which they are applied. They are also based on the purposes for which the resources are used. Some traditional cost types include:

- *Fixed.* Costs assumed not to vary with production/service unit volume
- *Variable.* Costs assumed to vary with production/service unit volume
- *Semi-fixed/variable, also called step-fixed/variable.* Costs that vary at incremental volume levels
- *Direct.* Costs that can be clearly linked, and therefore assigned to, specific product/service units
- *Indirect.* Costs that cannot easily be linked to specific product/service units, and therefore, must be allocated to production/services based on a selected cost driver

Financial Accounting

Financial accounting is the branch of the accounting field concerned with formal, aggregate reporting of transactions related to the income statement (revenue minus expense equals profit/loss), the balance sheet (assets, liabilities, and owners' equity) and other related statements (e.g., working capital, cash flow). Standard report forms used across companies and an external, shareholder focus, characterize financial accounting. The primary statement in financial accounting is the balance sheet. See Exhibit 1.2 for an example of the balance sheet components for a manufacturing firm. This exhibit is best read as a companion to Exhibit 1.1 to compare the fundamental similarities and differences in these two essential reporting systems.

Value

When accountants talk about *value* they refer to "any preferred object or interest therein"; and *accounting valuation* is "a judgment expressing or implying preference, or relative approval or disapproval."[2] Organizations exist to become the provider of preference by conveying value

> **EXHIBIT 1.1**
>
> ## The Basic Components and Terminology of a Traditional Income Statement
>
> **Income Statement** ➡ also known as ➡ **Profit & Loss Statement, P&L Operating Statement**
>
> | | |
> |---|---|
> | Revenue | Sales |
> | Deductions from Revenue | Credits, Allowances, Discounts |
> | Net Revenue | Net Sales |
> | | |
> | Cost of Goods Sold (COGS) | Cost of Sales, Cost of Goods Purchased |
> | Material | Raw material, Direct material |
> | Labor | Direct labor |
> | Overhead | Indirect manufacturing costs |
> | | |
> | Gross Margin | Contribution Margin |
> | | |
> | Operating expenses | Sales, General & Administrative (SG&A) |
> | Sales and Marketing | |
> | General & Admin | May be broken down to functions |
> | | |
> | Net Income Before Tax (NIBT) | Net Profit Before Tax |
> | Tax | Many colorful expletives |
> | Net Income After Tax (NIAT) | Net Profit, Income |

to customers, clients, and constituents. This is as true of a spiritual organization with a humanitarian mission as it is of a large corporation focused chiefly on shareholder wealth.

The path to value is different for each organization, and value has many definitions beyond those of the accountant. In the last half of the twentieth century, the focus on value became rooted in the idea of creating shareholder value. What do customers, shareholders and employees value? What do they really want? How can we differentiate ourselves from the competitor in terms of value? Should we be as concerned about internal constituents (i.e., employees) as we are about customers and shareholders? How do all the converging interests of those with a stake in the organization's success or failure work together to create a mutually satisfying sense of value?

EXHIBIT 1.2

A Simplified Traditional Balance Sheet Format

THE BALANCE SHEET EQUATION: Assets = Liabilities + Owners' Equities

		Also known as
ASSETS		
	Current Assets	Short-term Assets
	Cash	
	Temporary Investments	Short-term investments
	Accounts Receivable	Sales receivable, A/R
	Inventories	Subcategories: Raw materials, work-in-process, finished goods
	Prepaid expenses	
	Maturing portion of Long-term Loans	Current debt; payments receivable
	Total Current Assets	
	Long-term Assets	
	Buildings	Fixed Assets, Property Plant & Equipment (PP&E)
	Land	
	Machinery & Equipment	
	(Less depreciation on above categories)	
	Loans and Mortgages	
	Total Assets	
LIABILITIES		
	Current Liabilities	
	Accounts Payable	A/P
	Wages & Salaries	Payroll, Benefits
	Debt-Current Portion	Maturing Debt, Current Debt
	Long-term Liabilities	
	Loans	
	Mortgages	
	Total Liabilities	
		STOCKHOLDER EQUITY, NET WORTH
OWNERS' EQUITIES	Paid-in capital	Stock at par value, stated value
	Additional paid-in capital	Capital surplus
	Retained Earnings	Earned surplus, based on income/loss

None of these questions has an easy answer, but one fact is certain: The first and most common cause of enterprise failure is, simply, overspending—a basic failure to manage expenditures flowing out and revenues flowing in. The solution to overspending behaviors involves little more than the skill set required to balance a checkbook. Creating value for the complex organization requires clear cost management objectives embedded in a cost management system.

Cost Management Objectives

Nearly all business professionals know the major components of a general ledger (G/L) system, or at least two of the important reports generated by it: the income statement and the balance sheet. Far fewer managers can describe a cost management system—and with good reason. An effective CMS is customized to match an organization's internal environment and specific cost structures. While an experienced financial professional, and many managers, can move from company to company and quickly understand the financial statements of each, even practiced accountants need considerably more time to understand the intricacies of different cost management systems from company to company. A CMS is less constrained by exacting professional standards and reporting formats than are financial systems, with a few exceptions like the regulated cost guidelines of government contractors.

Importantly, the CMS sets direction for resource consumption priorities and makes course corrections by emphasizing operations first and accounting practices second. A CMS specifically answers the demands of the profit imperative by aligning employee spending behaviors with the organizational strategy.

Four-Stage Model

A good context for understanding the CMS is to ask not *what it is*, but rather *how it functions*. This book acknowledges and borrows from the approach used by Robert S. Kaplan and Robin Cooper in their 1998 book, *Cost & Effect*. Their "four-stage model of cost system evolution" describes how a CMS typically evolves over the life cycle of a maturing organization. This book will use their four-stage model, adapted in Exhibit 1.3, to contrast conventional and advanced cost management systems and techniques so that readers have a practical context for using the ideas presented in this text as they apply to current practices in the reader's workplace.[3]

If a Stage I system is not adequate for routine reporting, it cannot hope to deliver information on product, customer, and operations costing. Such systems offer little in support of strategic control. Stage II systems

> **EXHIBIT 1.3**
>
> ### Four-Stage Model of Cost System Development
>
> | Stage One | Stage Two |
> |---|---|
> | • Broken
• Many errors with large variances
• Inadequate external reporting
• Inadequate product, service, and customer cost information
• Inadequate operational and strategic control | • Driven by financial reporting
• Meets audit standards
• External reports tailored to financial reporting needs
• Inaccurate and hidden product, service, and customer costs
• Strategic feedback limited and delayed |
>
> | Stage Three | Stage Four |
> |---|---|
> | • Specialized
• Shared databases but stand-alone systems with informal linkages
• Same as Stage Two
• Product, service, and customer costs in separate ABM systems
• Strategic/operational control with several separate performance measurement systems | • Integrated
• Fully linked databases
• Financial reporting systems create external reports
• Product, service, and customer costs integrated in ABM systems
• Strategic/operational control within an integrated performance measurement system |
>
> Adapted from Robert S. Kaplan and Robin Cooper, *Cost and Effect: Using Integrated Cost Systems to Drive Profitability and Performance* (Boston: Harvard Business School Press, 1998).[3]

are driven by financial reporting requirements, and they meet financial accounting standards. However, they remain severely limited in decision-quality data. They often distort both costs and profits, and they are not timely in delivering feedback.

Stage III systems are specialized, in that the cost and financial accounting systems use the same databases; however, the two systems remain isolated and specialized in application. In this stage, activity-based costing (ABC) and performance measurement systems often emerge. Stage IV systems are integrated, and present a unified reporting format supportive of operational strategy. Financial and operations data, as well as budget and actual information, are all linked.

Organizations today remain spread across the Four-Stage spectrum. A healthy number of companies have moved to Stage III; but, it remains rare to find a true Stage IV company, although many claim to be. An enterprise resource planning (ERP) implementation does not guarantee a Stage IV environment. Every executive and manager first needs to determine which stage current accounting systems are in, and then progressively move through each stage to the integrated level, whether by using the Kaplan/Cooper model or some other proven, logical method. Kaplan and Cooper caution against the high failure rate of organizations that try to jump stages.[4]

Operations Focus Is Primary

The primary focuses of an effective CMS are operations and the support of management decision making. In addition to routine bookkeeping (see Chapter 2), the CMS objectives include, but are not limited, to ten characteristics. A CMS that supports decision making must:

1. Display past, present, and future expenditures.
2. Mirror the organization's cost structure and behaviors to support ongoing improvement and control.
3. Support realistic, reliable strategic planning and explicit management intention.
4. Influence individual and team behaviors toward goal accomplishment.
5. Monitor and control resource use against mission and strategic intentions.
6. Provide warning when unhealthy financial thresholds are imminent.
7. Facilitate the repositioning of resources.
8. Hold specific individuals and groups accountable for standards of performance.

9. Assist in analyzing key discrete points of profitability: customer, process, product, and region.

10. Display a 360-degree unbiased view of the organization's cost structure, one that is understood and actually used in decision-making by all executives and managers.

1. Display Past, Present, and Future Expenditures. This characteristic means that historical, current, and prospective (i.e., forecast, simulation) expenditure data are accessible, timely, and accurate. *Accessibility* is primarily judged on ease of use. In other words, can nonfinancial managers make use of the system's data and information? *Accuracy* is based on compliance with cost system design and with data-gathering integrity. *Timeliness* is based on proximity to real-time information. In the Kaplan/Cooper four-stage model, Stage I systems frequently fail all these criteria and almost never address future expenditures except in budgetary terms. Stage II systems are more reliable for past and present data but often fall short in accessibility and timeliness. Only in Stage III do CMS designs begin to fulfill all criteria. Obviously, if executives work with less than the full timeline (i.e., past, present, and future), their focus will most often be on historical data, while current and future cost conditions elude them.

2. Mirror the Organization's Cost Structure and Behaviors to Support Ongoing Improvement and Control. The CMS design must serve operations and management decision making first, and bookkeeping second. An effective cost system endeavors to clearly exhibit the sources, movement, use, and funding of organizational resources. The system must reflect how resources are actually used and how resource use aligns with or deviates from management intentions and plans. In the Kaplan/Cooper model, only Stages III and IV possess these attributes.

3. Support Realistic, Reliable Strategic Planning and Explicit Management Intention. In practice, profit generation has only two components: revenue/sales and expenditures (i.e., costs, expenses). Therefore, when planning for profitability (or breakeven) CMS information that fairly and accurately represents expenditure information promotes realistic planning and achievement targets. Again, only Stage III and IV cost management systems possess these attributes.

4. Influence Individual and Team Behaviors toward Goal Accomplishment. This attribute is among the most important for a CMS. If people do not find the cost system relevant to their daily activities and long-term responsibilities, they will not use it. Relevance includes accountability for predetermined performance standards, the prudent management of resources, and visibility of companywide cost structures and behaviors. A Stage III CMS provides opportunity for achieving this desired criterion; however, only Stage IV provides the level of integration needed to maximize this goal.

5. Monitor and Control Resource Use Against Mission and Strategic Intentions. This means that the cost management system assists in aligning and allocating resources where they will best serve management's strategic intentions. The managers of organizations in Stages I and II of the Kaplan/Cooper model overlook this characteristic when designing the CMS, if they give any thought to system design at all. When different managers perform budgeting and strategic planning processes at different times, the compartmentalization undermines strategic achievements that depend on appropriate resource alignment. Imagine an executive team energized from a strategic planning retreat returning to day-to-day operations, issuing mandates, directives, and a trainload of new projects, all without addressing resource allocation, budgets, or realignment of people, time, and facilities. This is a strategic plan scenario doomed to frustration and failure.

6. Provide Warning When Unhealthy Financial Thresholds Are Imminent. A thoughtfully designed CMS provides an early-warning system that identifies and averts overspending. It may also signal the need for additional resources due to volume and/or environmental changes. Often, CMS Stages I and II provide reactive reporting long after a decision opportunity for changing an operational process issue has passed. Imagine the frustration of a manufacturing manager who is held accountable for subpar performance in material and labor efficiencies, but who receives efficiency reports two to four weeks after the "damage" is done. Only Stage III and IV organizations rectify these demoralizing dynamics.

7. Facilitate the Repositioning of Resources. This CMS characteristic partners with number 6 by overseeing the movement and realignment of resources to adapt to strategic changes. In many companies, once an annual budget is set, woe to the manager who overspends it. If the strategic plan and the budget live separate lives, how can managers be expected to satisfy both?

8. Hold Specific Individuals and Groups Accountable for Standards of Performance. A recurring error in strategic planning is the failure to assign responsibility for action plans and performance targets. When set up properly, the CMS signals expectations for cost targets *and* identifies the individuals/groups responsible for meeting those targets. The CMS links cost targets with appropriate nonfinancial measures that discourage managers from working on cost and financial performance in isolation from other important indicators. (See Chapter 7 on performance measurement.)

9. Assist in Analyzing Discrete Points of Profitability: Customer, Process, Product, and Region. A financial accounting system provides an aggregate consolidated view of profitability. An effective CMS provides an analytical extension that searches for suspected areas of underperformance related to specific customers, product lines, market sectors, and other identifiable objects of analysis. Although a Stage II CMS may provide rudimentary historical data on these targets of analysis, only Stage III and IV systems provide decision-quality reporting through use of such techniques as activity-based costing (see Chapter 5).

10. Display a 360-Degree Unbiased View of the Organization's Cost Structure that is understood and actually used in decision-making by all executives and managers. A CMS that provides open-book views of companywide cost structures used concurrently by all managers to advance the organizational community's well-being as a whole encourages management creativity in resource use, as well as optimal use of available capacity. In most cases, only a Stage IV CMS can satisfy this attribute requirement.

To be an effective management decision-making guide, the cost management system has to be much more than a set of bookkeeping procedures, and it must not be the sole source of information for decision making. *Never use a cost management system in isolation for operational decision making.* Just as financial accounting delivers an important but narrow stream of results information, cost accounting also displays a critical but incomplete viewpoint. Nonfinancial, noncost information is part of any mature cost analysis. This is particularly true for making business development decisions. For example, a research and development (R&D) function usually shows continuous losses when subjected to a profit-and-loss, P&L (i.e., income statement), approach. However, the R&D function value remains invisible until seen in the context of potential future revenue and cost streams.

Control and Profitability

Every business professional wants to manage well by making the right decisions. Good decisions lead to profit. Effective management and profitability rely mutually on systems that control employee behavior. In turn, the control system receives accounting reports that detail

IN THE REAL WORLD

Primary Focus: Financial or Operational?

Quick! Which perspective is more important in your organization, financial or operational? This pop quiz has no right or wrong answer; however, if you can honestly answer "both" without stopping to think about it, your organization is fortunate. The blend of both financial and operational expertise creates synergy that supports better financial outcomes.

To determine your organization's perspective, take the following assessment. The question marks indicate the point in the query to insert "financial," "operations," or "both" choices. The more checks in the both column, the better. The more split or lopsided your answers, the more opportunity you have to create greater synergy between finance and operations expertise.

	Financial	Operations	Both
❶ Our ? executives conduct our strategic planning process.	___	___	___
❷ Our ? professionals manage our budget process.	___	___	___
❸ Our ? performance measurements are most important.	___	___	___
❹ Our ? executives select our critical performance measures.	___	___	___
❺ Primarily, ? concerns drive our organization.	___	___	___
❻ The ? managers usually win internal disagreements.	___	___	___

> **IN THE REAL WORLD CONTINUED**
>
> | | | False | True |
> |---|---|---|---|
> | ⑦ | We manage with one system that addresses both finance and operations. | ___ | ___ |
> | ⑧ | Our operations managers see the work our accountants do as value-added. | ___ | ___ |
> | ⑨ | Generally, our accountants are seen as good problem solvers. | ___ | ___ |
> | ⑩ | Our measurements are used for making improvements, as opposed to tracking and checking up on people. | ___ | ___ |

efficiency and profitability. Commonly, financial results are the "bottom line" of the control system of most organizations.

This is the time to distinguish cost accounting and cost management. Cost accounting can be thought of in terms of structured data elements; cost management can be thought of in terms of the information yielded by analyzing cost accounting data elements. As defined earlier, cost accounting includes cost systems and procedures, methods of determining costs, points of cost accountability, forecasts, cost comparisons (e.g., standard cost systems), and budgets (operational, project, and capital). Interestingly, in many companies, these and other functionalities exist but are not actively managed. Unless cost managers create meaning out of the cost accounting data and reports, a good portion of cost accounting effort is wasted, and critical information for decision making remains hidden. Significant resources can be applied to cost accounting work, but if executives view cost accounting simply as part of financial accounting, meaning and insight remain hidden within transaction data.

Cost Management: Control and Profitability

Only cost management can extract and create insight and meaning from raw cost data.

The cost accounting obligation is simple in concept: *Provide accurate cost information.* Implementing a cost accounting system that is accessible, aimed at the right targets of analysis, and supportive of management decision making is a more sophisticated task. The cost management responsibility is equally clear: *Promote improvement in cost structure.* Making good on this prospect is even more challenging.

Make no mistake, accounting is part of the organizational control system. The primary purpose of the control system is to *protect the organization's assets.* The important place that the accounting system occupies in the overall *control* system becomes more intriguing upon consideration of some basic accounting terminology. One common accounting definition of *assets* is "costs that have not yet been used." The accounting term for this is *unexpired costs.* These unexpired costs represent current or future value to the organization. *Controller* is the title of the head accountant in many organizations. Finally, consider that the two conventional financial statements that reflect this control and safeguarding of assets are (1) the balance sheet, and (2) the statement of cash flows. All this clearly speaks to the control focus in accounting activities.

The next most important function of the accounting system is to monitor *profitability* as recorded on the periodic income statement. Profitability results from effective control. All managers follow profit across the shortest available reporting interval; however, responsibility for calculating profitability lies with financial accountants, who in turn rely heavily on cost accountants. See Exhibit 1.4 for a recap of the fundamental differences between financial and cost accounting.

> **EXHIBIT 1.4**
>
> ## High-Level Comparison of Financial and Management Accounting
>
> | | Financial Accounting | Management Accounting |
> |---|---|---|
> | **Time Orientation** | Historical reporting | Future control |
> | **Information Perspective** | High-level aggregate | Operational detail |
> | **Rule Constraints** | Many; externally imposed | Few; internally decided |
> | **Primary Focus** | External | Internal |
> | **Discipline Dependence** | Finance and economics | Multidisciplinary |
> | **Reporting Formats** | Highly standardized | Highly customized |
> | **Typical Audiences** | Investors, creditors | Internal managers |

The Shifting Focus of Control in Accounting Systems

Traditionally, those charged with the maintenance of financial and cost accounting systems do not care what is happening in an organization as long as it is accurately recorded as a transaction and made available for reporting on the income statement and balance sheet. (Refer back to Exhibits 1.1 and 1.2 for schematic reminders of the general income statement and balance sheet components.) The focus of the mechanics of financial and cost accounting systems is distinctly different from the perspectives and priorities of internal control and audit systems, not to mention the concerns of executives and managers.

While all accounting systems have two primary concerns—control and profitability—managers and executives must be able to distinguish the specific aspects that financial and cost accounting systems each contribute to the understanding of control and profitability. Financial and management/cost accounting systems see business control and profitability from significantly different perspectives. Historically, the financial accounting focus has determined the organization's overriding control and profitability perspective: return on investment, which inherently includes profitability. The investor and the market in general focus on short-term financial results. Stock price performance reinforces the primacy of the financial accounting perspective. In contrast, cost accounting systems historically see business control and profitability from the operational perspective. Financial accounting sees the organization from an external perspective; managerial accounting sees the organization from an internal perspective.

Managers and executives who hope to steer their organizations toward continuous improvement have learned not to wait for the financials. They control and manage organizational performance based on continuous improvement and sustainable profit goals. This proactive approach is supported by cost and performance management methodology and technology innovations over the last 20 years that have helped elevate the status of internal operational information.

More recently, theoretical research and actual practice have shown that operational and nonfinancial elements are equally important in creating success and strategic achievement. The financial accounting system provides the motivation; the managerial cost accounting system information provides the means to improve processes and achieve profitability.

Where Financial and Cost Accounting Systems Connect

A return to the Kaplan/Cooper four-stage model helps to narrow the range of the many possible permutations of cost accounting system design. Using the context of the developmental stage of the organization's current cost accounting system, executives and managers can deliberately shepherd their cost accounting systems toward more integrated levels. The remainder of this chapter and Chapter 2 use a Stage II cost accounting system as a starting point: adequate and reliable for financial accounting requirements (e.g., audits) but limited in its cost management capabilities. Importantly, all cost accounting systems must first meet the Stage II baseline before aspiring to more advanced levels.

When business processes and accounting methods are in harmony, the aligned flow of a traditional, Stage II system would look like this:

Plan strategic objectives → then determine budget allocations → that create expenditures → that are assigned according to plan and budget. → Later, actual expenditures are compared to budget targets to show deviations → that lead to management intervention, as appropriate.

The accounting system tracks this overall process from financial and cost perspectives. Now consider three primary connection points that tie the cost and financial systems together as they each monitor the flow of value through business processes: inventories, capital spending, and period expenses (i.e., SG&A).

As each connection point is discussed below, consider how an accounting system might:

- Support understanding of the nature and behavior of cost—cost accounting.
- Promote, track, and give feedback on value creation—financial accounting.
- Assist management in wise use of resources—both.

Connection Point 1: Inventories. The first connection point, inventories valuation, flows as follows:

Material + labor + overhead → becomes inventory recorded on the balance sheet → becomes product cost → becomes cost of goods sold (COGS) reported on the income statement.

Material, labor, and overhead are cost information items that flow through the accounting system from the inventory assets on the balance sheet to COGS on the income statement—from the cost accounting system to the financial accounting system. Chapter 2 details the technical budget and standard cost system mechanisms behind this flow.

Connection Point 2: Capital Budgets. The second connection point, capital spending, has a flow that looks like this:

> Capital budget process selects investments. → Purchase is made and recorded as an asset, usually long-term. → Depreciation expense is recognized over the *estimated useful life* of the asset (tax methods aside). → Depreciation expense is recognized on the income statement.

In theory, traditional capital budgeting processes attempt to select long-term investments that will support strategic achievement over time. In practice, the process is often a cold-war battle between divisions, departments, or functions, wherein each attempts to garner as much investment money as possible for a parochial area. Once a capital investment is made—whether wisely or not—the expense of that investment is conventionally recognized over time by accounting formulas that most often do not reflect the actual use of the investment (e.g., machine, computer system).

Connection Point 3: Period Expenses. The third connection point, period expenses (i.e., SG&A), has a flow that looks like this:

> Administrative and selling costs are budgeted and then incurred → then assigned to the current time period → classified as SG&A → and reported on the income statement.

Many companies run into financial difficulties because they fail to manage expenditures "below the line," the SG&A expenses below the gross margin line on the income statement.

Cost Accounting and Operations

Now it is time to give due attention to support of operations as the primary responsibility of a cost accounting system. Consider the following questions, this time in light of cost accounting responsibilities to operations, compared to its obligations to financial reporting requirements. How might the accounting system:

- Support understanding of the nature and behavior of cost?
- Promote, track, and give feedback on value creation?
- Assist management in wise use of resources?

The answers lie in the design of the cost management system.

Deliberate and careful design of a cost management system promotes organizational control, as well as workforce focus. The managerial cost accounting system mandates specific control processes by means of the design of its cost management system. More and more organizations look to their CFOs, controllers, and accountants for vital decision-making information and participation in strategic and long-term planning. In contrast, operations-oriented firms often see accounting systems as a necessary evil, required by government and creditor agencies, but for the most part simply a nuisance to internal managers. The difference in viewpoint largely depends on the accounting system design. CMS designs that remain in Stage I and II may quickly become irrelevant to management's decision-making responsibilities.

The importance of CMS design extends throughout the entire organization. Dr. CJ McNair summarizes the situation eloquently. "What cost management chooses to make visible—the focus of its work—will inform and constrain the organizations of the future. In choosing a future for cost management, the future of business will be shaped."[5]

Cost management system design is a conscientious and deliberate process that avoids irrelevant detail and integrates seamlessly with the

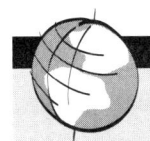

IN THE REAL WORLD

Test Your Cost System's Value

Wondering how your cost system measures up? The attributes listed in this checklist help to answer that question. On a scale of 1 to 5, rate your existing cost system:

1 = poor   2 = fair   3 = good   4 = very good   5 = excellent

Total your ratings and fit them into these profiles:

1–10: You might as well not have any cost system, as this one could cause more harm than good.

11–20: You have a conventional cost system, good for financial reporting purposes.

21–30: Your cost system can help answer some basic strategic and operational questions.

31–40: Your cost system is an important part of your management system, and helps to solve many business problems.

41–50: You have an excellent cost system that probably provides a competitive advantage.

❶ ____Our cost system makes available historical, current actual, and simulated future cost information.

❷ ____We use our cost system to support ongoing improvement in many areas.

❸ ____Our strategic planning process makes use of our cost information.

❹ ____Our cost system is realistic and reliable.

❺ ____Our executive team relies on our cost system to inform their decision making.

❻ ____We use our cost system to help realign resources when our business priorities change.

ESSENTIALS of Cost Management

> **IN THE REAL WORLD CONTINUED**
>
> ⑦ ____Our cost system regularly warns us when unhealthy financial thresholds are approaching.
>
> ⑧ ____Our cost system provides timely reporting, and its data is easy to access.
>
> ⑨ ____We use our cost system to hold individuals and groups accountable for reasonable performance standards.
>
> ⑩ ____We use our cost system to analyze discrete points of profitability such as customer, product, and region.

financial system. CMS design requires rigorous, periodic review to ascertain its continuing relevance. To reiterate:

- Cost accounting exists for a conceptually simple purpose: *Provide accurate cost information.*
- The purpose of cost management is equally clear: *Promote improvement in cost structure.*

This section will address the essential steps that executives and managers can take to achieve these elusive goals and thereby develop a CMS that is easy to use, aimed at the most important targets of analysis, and supportive of management decision making. In *Cost & Effect*, Kaplan and Cooper conclude their introductory chapter by describing the vision for such cost systems where, "cost and performance measurement systems are explicitly designed to produce the right information at the right time for essential managerial learning, decisions, and control."[6]

Historical Obstacles

Any executive with even a few years of experience knows the sharp difference between an accounting function that is pro-operations and one that is pro-finance. Likewise, any experienced accountant can tell when other functions (e.g., operations, marketing) see the finance function as a necessary burden and when the function is appreciated for the value it adds to the organization. As in most complex situations, the ideal practice is a blend of both perspectives. Until this becomes true in their own organizations, managers must come to understand and acknowledge the historical animosity and inherent conflicts between operations and accounting.

Passions would not run so high if the relationship between operations and accounting were not essential to business health. At the root of this friction is that, financial staff and operations people see their work from culturally different perspectives and business worldviews. These unspoken viewpoints generate misunderstandings and outright conflict. The different perspectives must be discovered, exposed, and reconciled before they can be blended. All too often, nothing happens. Both sides fear the loss of control, and each is reluctant to take on new roles.

Not long ago, a financial accounting professional might spend an entire career never setting foot on the factory floor or talking with a customer face-to-face. Huddled in back rooms with whirring pencils scratching numbers on green ledgers (and erasing them, too), accountants literally had no time for any activities other than tallying, ticking, and tying the numbers. Today, although computerized accounting systems have replaced the demanding drudgery of manual ledgers, some accountants still seldom set foot in the land of operations. Cost accountants who match this profile—then or now—cannot serve their organizations to the best of their abilities.

The connections and the conflicts within the accounting/operations dynamic are easiest to conceptualize in the manufacturing sector where the tangible nature of production makes conflict stand out. In his book, *Making the Numbers Count*, Brian Maskell cites five key shortcomings with management accounting: "(1) Lack of relevance, (2) cost distortion, (3) inflexibility, (4) incompatibility with world-class approaches, and (5) inappropriate links to financial accounts."[7] By inversely examining each of these shortcomings as attributes, the inherent connections between cost accounting and operations, whereby a CMS brings value to management, can be explored in terms of (1) relevance, (2) cost visibility, (3) flexibility, (4) support for advanced approaches, and (5) appropriate links to financial accounts. For reasons that will become obvious, the order is reversed.

Appropriate Links to Financial Accounts. Financial statements address the information needs of a range of constituents and government regulators. Since financial statements target external users and are governed by external standards and formats, at best they provide internal managers with a highly aggregated and shallow "report card" of business performance. Consequently, while the CMS should provide external managers the necessary and sufficient information to meet financial reporting requirements, the system should do so with all due dispatch in terms of the needs of internal managers for information focus and efficiency. Inventory valuation, COGS, expense classification, and absorption are among the few important connection points at issue between the financial accounting system and the CMS.

Support for Advanced Approaches. Because traditional accounting systems position cost accounting in the status of servant to the general ledger/financial statement system, the poorly designed CMS may consequently attempt to make vassals out of the other business functions. Practice the reverse. The most mature cost accountants have been given permission to support their executives to design a budgeting and cost reporting system that rapidly supports decision making, encourages efficiency throughout the organization, and requires value-added information from functional managers. In this context, all standard financial-accounting-related routines should be automated and transparent to nonfinancial staff.

Capital spending is another connection point between accounting and operations functions for CMS value creation. Typically, North American companies use discounted cash flow (DCF) or return-on-investment (ROI) measurements to choose between capital spending alternatives. These financially focused frameworks are based on tenuous estimates and forecasts that frequently prove grossly inaccurate. Additionally, these traditional, exclusively financial analysis tools look for rapid returns on invested capital. This is not always congruent with operations management or long-term strategic plans.

Flexibility. Protocols often become highly standardized when financial accounting perspectives control the cost accounting system. In contrast, when the CMS serves operations first and financial accounting second, its system and report designs adapt to changing operational environments.

Cost Visibility. As service organizations become a larger business sector and the business landscape loses its stability in terms of organizational structure (due to mergers, acquisitions, and virtual offices), traditional cost types become increasingly irrelevant. Cost types do not facilitate cost visibility—a transparency of the nature and behavior of costs and resource spending that sustains informed decision making. This understanding is one of the most essential messages of Chapters 1 and 2. More advanced cost management systems such as activity-based costing and resource consumption accounting, clarify cost dynamics and enable wise choices grounded on business interrelationships that more closely reflect business performance.

Relevance. Closing the circle, a CMS that serves operations, supports advanced cost management approaches, adapts flexibly, and clearly displays the nature and behavior of cost, de facto, becomes relevant. In a relevant CMS, cost work investments are generally viewed as value-added activities, and organizational management relies on them for essential decision-making information.

When a CMS exhibits these five attributes it becomes a valuable organizational asset. Inversely, for organizations missing some of these attributes, the executives and managers see one more reason for nonfinancial functions to pay less attention to CMS information.

Control and Performance Management Systems

At this point, it is worth making a final connection point. Since cost is such an integral element of the "profit imperative" and profit performance is a universal organizational requirement, it is natural and inevitable that cost and performance systems become intimately associated.

Organizations with CMS designs in Stages I and II use financial-only accounting systems. If it exists at all, nonfinancial performance measurement is typically fragmented and isolated within the functional domains of an organization. Everyone wants to "keep score," and without a formal measurement system, good managers will create their own scoreboard. For example, a competent production manager always has a control system in place based on the principles of quality, theory of constraints, or some homegrown paradigm.

> **TIPS & TECHNIQUES**
>
> ### Cost System Purposes
>
> The cost accounting obligation is simple in concept: *Provide accurate cost information.* Implementing a cost accounting system that is accessible, that is aimed at the right targets of analysis, and that reliably supports management decision making is a more sophisticated task. The cost management responsibility is equally clear: *Promote improvement in cost structure.*

Companies developing into a Stage III CMS almost always navigate the same important barrier: exclusive reliance on financial measures for management and accountability purposes. An intense struggle ensues between the financially based management system and the more mature emerging system that values nonfinancial measures as equally important. Consequently, this can result in *two* performance management systems within the same company—the original financial-based accountability framework and the more balanced performance information paradigm. The subsequent conflicts are all too familiar; but, eventually, they must be resolved so that the entire organization embraces a single performance measurement standard of accountability.

Once again, the primary responsibility of cost accounting activities is conceptually simple: Provide accurate cost information. The cost management responsibility is equally clear: Promote improvement in cost structure.

No Separation

Cost and organizational performance are inseparable. The link between cost and performance may seem obvious today, but not long ago financial results were the organizational report card of choice. From a capital market perspective, the financials still reign supreme. That said, studies reveal the same market analysts paying more and more attention to nonfinancial measurements and intangible asset valuation, as well as to short-term quarterly financial measures like *earnings per share* and *price/earnings ratio*. Other operational frameworks, like the Quality Movement, helped shift the emphasis to some degree. However, when, in the early 1990s, performance measurement and management systems began developing independently from financial systems, performance managers found a structured way to move beyond the information constraints of general ledger financial systems. Increasingly, powerful performance management methods and software applications support the development and reporting of nonfinancial information.

Summary and Lessons from the Field

Cost management systems can be powerful allies in organizational success, but only when deliberately designed and consistently utilized. Here are some key points in accomplishing this.

- An accounting system that meets financial reporting requirements is not necessarily adequate for management decision making.
- Cost accounting/management's first responsibility is to internal operations, and only secondarily to financial accounting.
- Traditional cost accounting systems do not always make good management systems. When a cost accounting system is constructed with a primary goal of servicing financial accounting systems, management decision-support information suffers.
- A cost management system serves its organization when it is relevant, makes costs visible, is flexible, is supportive of advanced approaches, and has appropriate links to financial accounts.
- Unlike general ledger systems, a CMS is more flexible and must be customized for each organization.
- A CMS should focus primarily on internal operations management.
- Finance and operations professionals must be vigilant in maintaining healthy relationships, where the contributions of each are recognized and appreciated.
- The behavioral implications of a CMS design have to be carefully anticipated and managed.
- Strategy, accountability, and performance concerns are central ingredients for CMS design to drive performance that is aligned with strategic intention.

Endnotes

1. The accounting instructor is one of the authors, Catherine Stenzel, who has taught undergraduate and MBA level courses in financial and management accounting since the mid-1980s.

2. *Kohler's Dictionary for Accountants*, 6th ed. (Englewood Cliffs, NJ: Prentice-Hall College Division, 1990), 528–529.

3. Robert S. Kaplan and Robin Cooper, *Cost & Effect: Using Integrated Cost Systems to Drive Profitability and Performance* (Boston: Harvard Business School Press, 1998), viii–ix.

4. Id., 24–27.

5. CJ McNair, "Defining and Shaping the Future of Cost Management," *Journal of Cost Management* 14, no. 5 (2000): 32.

6. Kaplan and Cooper, 10.

7. Brian Maskell, *Making the Numbers Count: The Accountant as Change Agent on the World-Class Team* (Portland: Productivity Press, 1996): 17.

CHAPTER 2

Traditional Cost Types, Terms, and Practices

After reading this chapter you will be able to

- Gain an understanding of the language and terminology of traditional cost accounting
- Begin to assess the organizational value of traditional cost accounting practices
- Begin to understand traditional cost accounting techniques and how cost accounting interfaces with financial accounting and operations systems

Whereas Chapter 1 explained the broad purposes and points of connection between the two primary accounting systems, financial and cost, this chapter explores how these connections are technically accomplished through a conventional cost accounting system. A method of cost classification called *cost types*, introduced in Chapter 1 (see page 4), is central to achieving these connections. This chapter provides an overview of conventional cost accounting's fundamental practices and principles, and continues developing common accounting terminology within the context of the language of cost accounting.

Compared to cost accounting, cost management is an advanced practice; yet the management of costs relies on a system that accounts for costs. Although cost accounting is subject to far fewer constraints than financial accounting, well-established concepts and frameworks also exist for cost/managerial accounting. These concepts and their related vocabulary are the subject of this chapter.

Any executive who expects to utilize advanced cost management methods to competitive advantage needs to (1) understand how traditional cost accounting affects reported financial results, and (2) acquire a general familiarity with conventional cost theory and principles. This also establishes a foundation for understanding the evolution of advanced cost management methods. Readers may refer to conventional cost accounting textbooks for more detailed representations. (See Suggested Readings at the end of this book.)

Just as a foreign visitor who does not know the language and customs of a country misses a great deal of information in day-to-day activities, managers who cannot confidently use at least rudimentary cost accounting terms will find themselves at a disadvantage in most business environments. This chapter aims to define and highlight essential cost terminology and practices as used in conventional accounting domains. In other words, the chapter focuses on cost accounting as it interfaces with financial accounting and operations systems. One reason this interface is important to all managers is because it is the conduit that organizations use to deliver information to the financial statements, particularly the income statement and the balance sheet.

As an example of a business transaction where a nonfinancial manager would need to understand how to speak the language of cost accounting, consider a sales manager who must quote a price for a customized product to a prospective customer, one that must be competitive with a rival supplier. The quotation process includes a standard cost-to-produce analysis from the cost accounting function. If the cost-to-produce analysis is formula-driven, as many are, and the cost accountant calculating the quote has no knowledge of the competitive situation, the sales manager could easily end up with a cost quote that will push pricing out of competitive range. Likewise, if the sales manager does not question the calculation, that manager is guilty of too much "reverence" for the accounting system.

The Language and Context of Cost Accounting

The entire cost accounting lexicon reflects the search for better ways to understand and describe the nature and behavior of cost as it impacts operations, profit, and the marketplace. The vocabulary of cost tells the history of this search. This chapter presents cost accounting terms in a context that seeks the raison d'être for their existence (i.e., why they feature so prominently in the language of business). Rather than merely listing terms and their definitions, this discussion logically connects the terms as they relate to the quest to understand and manage cost.

People of all ages learn languages more quickly when they study the new language in a context. The context for the study of cost accounting language has two primary components: *resource optimization* and *performance*. These two perspectives provide a context for the discussion of common cost accounting applications and for the cost accounting terminology that follows.

Resource Optimization

When learning any new language, it's important to avoid getting bogged down in memorizing particular words to the disadvantage of meaning and global understanding. As the terminology piles up, keep one thing in mind: The main purpose of the lexicon's specificity is to *support a clearer understanding of the nature and behavior of cost, and thereby facilitate the wise management of valuable assets through optimizing limited resources.* The foregoing sentence will be used as the mission statement for cost management practice in the remainder of this book.

The cost accounting drive to support resource optimization stems from the general accounting ethic of safeguarding assets. Thus, cost accounting is quite particular about its classifications and cost types in the interest of assisting managers in intelligent asset stewardship. Two of the major classifications, other than cost types, are (1) industry sector (e.g., service, government, manufacturing), and (2) operations profiles (e.g., a process profile such as petroleum, a job-order profile such as luxury yachts).

Performance

To continue its mission, every organization must perform well enough to at least break even. Recent history has shown that even Internet enterprise investors did not rely forever on prospective performance. A business idea concocted to generate heady amounts of revenue with little to no expenditures may look good, but it is another thing altogether to actually deliver on such a prospect. Ultimately, performance depends on resources, whether performance goals are framed in terms of financial capital or human capital.

Some organizations have truly grand missions: to heal the sick, to educate the young, to shelter the homeless, to feed the hungry, to raise the quality of life for the world. Hospitals, social services, universities, and some corporations work to deliver on the noble intentions expressed within their mission statements. Yet unless their performance attracts donations, sales dollars, tuition, grants, volunteer worker time, and other forms of resource inflow, they will not survive. Good ideas and good intentions are not enough. Therefore, executives and managers who heartily believe in their intentions and ideas need to understand the nature, behavior, and structure of cost. The language of cost is a good way to begin.

Conventional Cost Accounting Applications and Terms

Conventional cost accounting touches every functional area within any enterprise, but functional managers do not always know how cost accounting practices track and assess their areas of responsibility. Cost accountants do not necessarily consult functional managers or even executives when preparing cost analyses. Some costing practices are so embedded in the organization that for all practical purposes they have become invisible to everyone. Put another way, some cost practices are so old and so standard to the operation that no one questions the cost analyses or their underlying assumptions.

This is a very important point. Without broad training and exposure to functional operations, cost accountants can be guilty of mindlessly "cranking out formulas" or "crunching the numbers" with little or no understanding of how the numbers relate to other managers' most important decisions and problems.

Likewise, executives and managers too often accept financial and cost information as immutable, and they do not question the reports and analyses issued by the accounting department. Accounting professionals need to seek out experience and information pertaining to operational requirements and contexts. Nonfinancial executives and managers need to learn about their cost accounting system, and constructively question its structures for analyses and reporting. (See the Tips & Techniques in this chapter for suggested questions that readers can raise with the cost accountants in their own organizations to better understand existing cost management practices.)

Examples of Traditional Cost Accounting Applications

While reviewing the list of traditional cost accounting business applications below, you are encouraged to consider where underlying cost structures and assumptions need questioning or further exploration in the cost management system currently used in your organizations. Also, you should begin to assess the ability of the cost accounting system to deliver on its mission, as suggested earlier.

- Product/service quotations and pricing
- Make-or-buy supplier decisions (i.e., produce internally or outsource)
- Budget construction and monitoring
- Product cost setting through standard cost systems
- Financial variance analyses: material, labor, overhead
- Product mix decisions
- Job order and process costing
- Cost allocation design
- Capital investment analyses
- Inventory management
- Transfer pricing
- Valuation (e.g., in-process R&D, impaired asset)
- Leased assets (especially at end of lease)
- Insurance cost of replacement
- Liquidation and ceasing business

This list does not reflect developments in the field of cost management from the last 10-15 years. These are the subjects of upcoming chapters. The list provides a representative sample of cost accounting concerns for much of the twentieth century.

The "Story" as Told by Cost Accounting

Accounting is a noun defined as a narrative or record of events. In addition to providing a list of more essential cost accounting vocabulary, this

Traditional Cost Types, Terms, and Practices

section will convey the reason and logic of cost accounting language and the unique ways that it tells the story of business. If "strategy tells the story of the business,"[1] then traditional accounting provides the chapter that chronicles financial outcomes, the results of the strategic journey, in dollars and cents.

Cost accounting information puts a timeline to the strategic narrative: past, present, future. Cost accounting terminology introduces the temporal perspective with the terms *cost*, *expense*, and *expenditure*. When these terms interface with financial accounting terminology, even the best cost accountants have trouble keeping these three time-based cost perspectives separate. Imagine an articulate manager, who uses each term properly making the statement that follows:

> We are willing to incur this *cost* to improve our production process. After all, the *expense* we have already committed has laid the foundation for the improvements to come. All these *expenditures* should make us competitive in the marketplace.

Let's review the definition of these tems in light of that statement:

- *Cost.* The outflow of a resource, whether in cash, as a payable, as a rendered service, or as a trade or barter, that is consciously made with expectation of *future* benefit to the organization; goods, property, or services acquired for use in *current and/or future* operations. (Note, this is the same definition as provided in Chapter 1 but with the time perspective added.)

- *Expense.* Viewed by accountants as "expired cost." In other words, expense is cost viewed from the point of *past* events, and its value has already been used in generating revenues (hopefully). For example, an airline ticket expense will appear on the income statement as a deduction from revenue. In other words, expense is always associated with activities already done or commitments made beyond reasonable expectation of recovery.

- *Expenditure.* Accounting textbooks generally approach this term in one of two ways: (1) they carefully avoid it, because it is not part of the official cost accounting lexicon, or (2) they use the term as a convenient synonym for either or both, cost and expense. Regarding time frames, most accounting authors hedge their bets by placing "expenditure" in both the present and the future. For the remainder of this book, since both costs and expenses are expenditures, the word "expenditure" will be used to identify an organization's *total* outflow of assets in all forms.

With these three definitions in hand, nonfinancial managers may be able to correct some accountants! Why all the fuss? Behind the delicate interplay of terms is a very important question: How much spending was and how much spending will be necessary to generate expected revenue? The correct use of these three terms enables managers to chronologically match expenditures to the revenue they help generate. In fact, the matching determines profitability.

Cost Types

Cost accountants continue to use cost categories in an attempt to understand and even predict in the face of uncertainty. To predict is a strong urge in the human psyche, and foretelling the future has a long honored history in all civilizations. Be they investment portfolio fund managers or small business cost accountants doing forecasts, organizations value finance professionals who demonstrate talents in prediction.

In the context of the mission of cost management—to support a clear understanding of the nature and behavior of cost, and thereby facilitate the wise management of valuable assets through optimizing limited resources—accountants understandably want to be more capable of predicting how cost affects business dynamics. When accountants deal with "cost behavior," they actually attend to human spending

Traditional Cost Types, Terms, and Practices

behaviors as these manifest in any given organizational environment; however, accountants sometimes really do believe that it is the costs that are behaving, or misbehaving, not the humans. For the record, cost behavior denotes the way a cost changes over time in relation to changes in the level of an activity or in relation to the specific application of a resource/cost.

Fortunately, since accounting systems help control human spending behaviors, spending patterns usually change slowly. In an attempt to become more predictive, cost accountants leverage the slow patterns of change and create categories called cost types as components of the accounting control system to help them understand and communicate cost behaviors to management.

In short, cost type can be defined as a categorical set of characteristics and assumptions by which an accounting system structures and communicates the ways that the organization consumes its resources. Assumptions are critical to any understanding of cost types. An assumption is defined as a premise or statement often *accepted unconsciously*, or *without proof* as a *basis for a line of reasoning or course of action*, either because it seems applicable or self-evident or because its implications appear to justify further exploration.

Behavioral scientists must artificially integrate a rule-based structure and context into their studies because there are no laws or constants in the realm of human behavior. Cost assumptions work like Newtonian physical laws and give cost accountants the level of rule-based structure to follow cost behaviors over time. Quite naturally, different accountants in different organizations use different assumptions for the same cost type. Unfortunately, different accountants and managers within the same organization often do so as well.

Cost categories and assumptions must be chosen carefully to facilitate a consensual understanding and communication of cost behaviors. The following discussion of specific cost types focuses on the difficulties that conventional cost accountants have in reaching consensus on a common understanding of the characteristics and assumptions of each cost type.

Variably-Fixed or Fixedly-Variable?

Like so many categories of human behavior and consciousness, cost types often occur in pairs that naturally reflect the wide range of organizational activities and cost behaviors. The most familiar of these pairs is *fixed cost* and *variable cost*. Unlike many other terms and key words in this book, cost types cannot be meaningfully characterized in terms of standard definitions without some context regarding the way an organization uses cost types. For example, Kaplan and Cooper define fixed costs as, "Those costs, in total, that are constant within the relevant range as the level of the cost driver varies." [2]

Cost types can only be defined in terms of the assumptions they carry. In manufacturing, typical fixed cost examples include plant capacity and other previously incurred long-term assets or obligations that cannot easily be changed. As a fundamental working definition, fixed costs do not vary. In practical terms, a fixed cost will not vary within a reasonably expected range of business volume. In terms of capacity measurements, a cost fixed in respect to volume will vary as the size of the plant changes over time. Assumptions like these give cost type definitions a working context.

The same discussion defines *variable costs* as, "Those costs, in total, that vary as a cost driver (activity level) changes." Assumptions give such a general definition clearer context. Operationally, variable costs may vary directly or proportionally with sales, production volume, facility utilization, or other measures of activity. Particular business activities drive the use of resources: a computer is built to order or a customer calls for service to a product. These lead activities and events are called

Traditional Cost Types, Terms, and Practices

cost drivers. Remember this term and its fundamental meaning. It will take on increasing importance in future chapters. All cost types have two common characteristics: each is a measurement category; assumptions define how the measurement data is collected.

The debate over which costs are fixed and which are variable has a long history, and consensus remains elusive. The arguments run the gamut. Some schools teach that there are clear demarcation lines between cost types. Others believe that some costs are more fixed than others. The more stoic accountant believes that all costs are variable over the long term.

Truth be known, the fixed/variable debate is a waste of time. Only the exact context, growth rate, and operational specifics for any given organization can really determine the nature, behavior, and assumptions of a cost and, thereby, its type. Consequently, it is the business of every executive group to take an active interest in cost type categorization

TIPS & TECHNIQUES

Five Questions to Ask Your Accountant about Cost Types

1. Do we use cost types in our cost accounting structure? If so, what are they? If not, what is our method of categorizing costs?

2. How helpful do you think our method of categorizing costs is in helping us manage our costs better?

3. Specifically, what is your opinion of *fixed* and *variable* cost types, and their role in helping us make decisions about costs?

4. How much flexibility is there in the way we classify our costs?

5. When was the last time we reviewed our cost classification design?

since it directly affects profitability analysis. A profitability analysis can look quite different depending on how an organization classifies its costs across these two cost types.

The Evolution of Traditional Cost Types

Because each management team needs to design and communicate its own cost types and categories, a common baseline understanding of traditional terms will be helpful. Management teams who take cost types seriously and who choose to change them need to be prepared for resistance from the accounting side of the house—and with good reason.

Cost accounting language gives historical and comparability context to all financial and cost accounting measurement data. Financial accounting principles concerned with comparability argue against changing cost types. Changes in cost design mean that comparisons between products, services, and time periods lose validity. True enough. That may be one reason that a separate cost accounting system is a necessary phase in the Kaplan/Cooper four-stage journey of CMS design maturity. Some pioneers of cost management innovation barely mention the traditional terms discussed here because one of the goals behind advanced cost management systems is to provide nonfinancial decision makers with financial information that they can understand. The exploration of activities, capacity issues, and strategic applications of cost management consume their interests and energies.[3] Still, a discussion of the essential concepts governing cost types is important because so many cost systems continue to use these terms, and they comprise the history behind all advanced cost management theory and systems.

General disagreement within the accounting community about cost type definitions, as well as skepticism about the limitations of two categories, led some time ago to additional major classifications of fixed and variable cost types that utilize the prefixes "semi" and "step." In an attempt to characterize different forms of cost behavior variability, some cost accountants wanted to distinguish between costs that varied consistently (variable), inconsistently (semivariable), and incrementally (step-variable). To add to the nonfinancial manager's frustration, some cost accountants use the prefix "semi" interchangeably with the prefix "step." Some lexicons also apply these prefixes to fixed costs. Costs like electricity and phone lines contain some elements that are fixed and others that are variable. These costs typically follow the cost driver in neither a linear nor a proportional fashion. For instance, machine maintenance intuitively falls in the semivariable category when compared to the acquisition of more floor space for production, which intuitively falls in the semifixed category.

This third category of cost types generates many conceptual accounting fine points. Unfortunately, the debate over all three categories has proved a red herring for many managers. Few have stopped to ask, "Why categorize at all?" The short answer is that conventional financial accounting needs this categorization to maintain its integrity and comparability. The long answer is explored in later chapters of this book. Categories simplify and satisfy the financial side of the house, but more exacting methods (e.g., activity-based costing and resource consumption accounting, Chapter 5) translate the categories and create decision-making information for management purposes. Executive teams who wrestle with cost types long enough usually give up and abdicate, leaving the problem of cost type definition to the underground realm of conventional financial accounting.

Along the way, some thoughtful accountants theorized that if cost could be described more exactly, then the nature and behavior of cost would become more transparent. Consequently, a plethora of adjectives emerged over time to modify or add to the fundamental fixed and variable cost types. To get a feel for this adjective-adding approach, simply take the terms fixed cost and variable cost, and from the terms discussed next, attach any of the adjectives (e.g., direct, indirect) to either term. Then try to identify business costs that fit that category. Next, take the same business cost and map the movement of its flow through a business process. It will soon become apparent that without specified organizational context, the terms cause as much confusion as clarity.

Continuing to acknowledge the traditional pairing, this discussion defines and characterizes the use of the essential conventional cost types beyond fixed and variable.

- *Direct and Indirect Costs.* Direct and indirect costs define one another. A direct cost is the cost of any good or service that supports and can be attributed to the actual creation of product or service output. Any other attendant costs incurred in the output process are considered to be indirect. In manufacturing, direct costs of product manufacture include labor, material, and overhead costs that vary with the volume produced. Control-oriented cost management approaches use direct cost as the only cost type. In these systems, all costs can be attributed to some output or intermediate service.

- *Discretionary and Nondiscretionary.* Discretionary costs are those costs that can be varied at the option of a responsibility center or functional manager. All managers encounter activities where there is no clear relationship between the amount they spend and the benefits they expect to gain. Nondiscretionary cost is a no-choice cost type. Nondiscretionary costs must be spent; the manager has no choice—either in theory or in practice.

- *Budgeted and Actual.* These cost types can be understood only in the context of the budget as planning and control system. Budgeted costs are part of a larger blueprint for action. Budgets set fiscal boundaries; actual costs show real spending performance.

Traditional Cost Types, Terms, and Practices

- *Controllable and Noncontrollable.* Controllable costs have attributes in common with variable costs. Controllable costs vary with efficiency, volume, and management decision alternatives. Cost management systems use this cost type designation to measure and control the behavior of particular levels of management authority. Noncontrollable costs cannot be influenced at the local level of authority.
- *Standard and Current-Actual.* Standard costs are forecasts of probable actual costs under projected conditions that are fixed and frozen at the beginning of a fiscal year. As information about purchase price increases or decreases becomes obvious during the fiscal year, a cost category within a standard cost system (see Chapter 3) called *current-actual* costs is updated. In effect, the current-actual cost becomes the operational standard cost, although for comparability purposes, financial statements continue to use the standard costs, fixed at the beginning of the fiscal year.
- *Sunk.* Sunk costs are water under the bridge. They are historical costs that can neither be revised nor recovered. Consequently, they are not relevant to current decisions for increasing or decreasing profit levels except as they are wisely utilized.

Beyond keeping the financial statements honest, most cost types work to achieve two common ends.

1. Assign responsibility to specific managers (e.g., controllable/noncontrollable and discretionary/nondiscretionary).

2. Control costs. Cost types control costs in manufacturing environments by establishing how costs behave as human labor and machines convert raw material to saleable goods. Anyone who has worked in a manufacturing environment knows that cost type categories are of limited use in managing shop operations or making costs "behave." This point was validated repeatedly prior to the advanced costing methodologies. Prior to advanced approaches, whenever a cost didn't fall clearly into either "labor" or "material" it got thrown into the black hole of "overhead."

In a service firm such as a financial advisory company, costs incurred while entertaining clients, and nonbillable time spent with clients, can get lost in a type of cost called *expense accounts*. With more advanced methods, these expenses can easily be assigned to specific clients.

> **IN THE REAL WORLD**
>
> ## Cost Type Secrecy
>
> In the 1990s I* worked as the corporate operations controller for a multidivision manufacturing company. Seventy percent of the division controllers reported to me, and I coordinated their cost accounting and cost quotation systems. I hope you find no similarities between your experiences and mine in this story.
>
> Because the divisions all had different capacities but roughly similar process competencies, they often competed for orders generated by the corporate sales staff who handled all the large, national accounts. Corporate executives used production cost as the chief point of analysis for deciding which division would get the business booked at corporate. Each division was a profit center, and geographic location did not play a significant part in the plant booking decisions orders. Significantly, the industry as a whole frequently experienced excess capacity that exacerbated the competition for production orders across the company's divisions.
>
> Part of my job was to assure that the cost quotes (the "bids" for business) submitted by the divisions were valid and comparable. This proved difficult because of their competitive relationships. As a group, the controllers rarely shared any information with one another, and they never shared cost information. Thus the accounting

IN THE REAL WORLD CONTINUED

design of each division was unique because each controller was free to classify cost components and construct standard costs based on the wide range of assumptions across divisions. Even in basic material and labor categories, cost components varied greatly across the divisions.

I had to create a common cost structure for the competing divisions just to compare two or more cost quotes between them. This proved useless, however, because when monthly income statements were consolidated, costs were reported at standard, and these often bore little resemblance to the common comparative—or, more accurately—cost quotes I had produced. And it was the income statement by product line where all division performance was judged.

Some of the company's controllers constructed their standard costs "by the book." This typically meant that their cost types included the maximum number of cost components in cost of goods sold. Other controllers took liberties with cost type definitions and kept as many cost components as possible out of the standard to present a more favorable cost picture. The components they excluded usually ended up in the overhead of low-volume, low-profit products, or even below the gross margin line in SG&A expenses. None of the structures violated financial accounting principles, but they severely stressed good cost accounting practices. In the worst situations, one or two division general managers "persuaded" their controllers to low-ball the cost quotations in hopes of getting the corporate business to hit the quotation target, but once they acquired and produced the order, they typically came in with a "cost overrun."

I worked for over a year with the controllers I supervised. They learned the principles of standard cost practice, and I brainstormed with them for ways we might influence changes in the order-placement practices. Most importantly, they became convinced, through quantifiable proofs, that the value of knowing more accurate costs could only benefit everyone. However, unhealthy corporate and sales

> **IN THE REAL WORLD CONTINUED**
>
> dynamics thwarted us at every turn. We did not succeed in changing the order-placement process or the corporate sales staff incentive system—the root cause of difficulties.
>
> The danger signals in this story include:
>
> - Multiple production divisions of the same company competing for the same orders.
>
> - A centralized corporate salesforce, several of whom have been promoted from one of the divisions. This tends to bias their order-placement decisions.
>
> - Division general managers whose compensation is based largely on their own division profit, as opposed to total company profit.
>
> - Division controllers' freedom to designate cost types and standard cost components.
>
> And here are two insights:
>
> - Just because financial accounting principles are not violated doesn't mean the cost system is accurate and reliable for decision making.
>
> - Sometimes the root cause of accounting problems lies in a nonfinancial function, organizational design, or internal processes.
>
> * The "I" in this case is Catherine Stenzel.

When all is said and done, two additional important points limit the need for further discussion.

1. No matter how many adjectives describe cost behavior, a traditional CMS continues to require that *each* identifiable cost be put in a *single* cost type category. In reality, a single cost may behave as controllable variable in one part of the business and as uncontrollable fixed in another part of the business. This is especially true in larger organizations with a structure of divisions and business units. In these firms, the so-designated variable costs from a unit high in the organizational hierarchy are passed down to divisions using formula allocations where the costs become decidedly fixed. Once allocated, costs fall into the "out of sight, out of mind" zone for managers who could actually control them. Thus a slippery slope becomes more slippery.

2. All of this cost type terminology developed at a time when cost accounting was still done with pencils (and erasers!) on green ledger sheets. At that time, cost and financial accounting were inseparably tied together. They had to harmonize their categories, types, and definitions if they hoped to guarantee financial integrity while being able to "close the books" in less than a month. In contrast, the power of today's automated general ledger systems, databases, and other powerful IT applications enable both system harmony and decision-quality information. Therefore, accountants need not fuss so much over cost types. They can utilize a common database that employs a simple cost type design for financial statements, and a more advanced version for a CMS. In this way, valuable time is devoted to more complex designs for cost management that supports strategy.

Cost accounting and management practices in the manufacturing sector were the primary source of most conventional cost accounting terminology. Service sector applications sometimes require other cost-type characterization. For now, the important point is to have general familiarity with the history of the whole verbal catastrophe and with the vestigial terms still used within organizations operating with less mature accounting systems. Executives in these organizations will need this linguistic familiarity to intelligently simplify and mature their financial systems, to add rich layers of functional, operational information to the existing cost information, and to get the greatest value from accounting staff efforts.

Absorption and Overhead

Absorption accounting was designed to dispatch overhead. Once the lowest percentage of total cost, in the early part of the twentieth century, overhead grew rapidly to become the highest component of total cost in the majority of firms by the end of that century. Managers frequently forget that overhead is a formal cost type. However, overhead management is such a significant focus of concern for many managers that it seems more significant than a humble "cost type." The thinking process usually follows one of two lines: "We don't really know where this cost goes. Let's put it in overhead," or "We spent this amount, but we're not sure where it went." More advanced CMS approaches go a long way to solve this obvious shortcoming.

The Problem Children: Consumption Rates, Overhead, and Absorption

Traditional financial accounting has a vested interest in control, standardized formats, and comparability. Comparability is one of the foundation principles practiced by financial accountants as they prepare financial statements and reports. The comparability principle requires that the examination of data representing results over multiple periods be calculated using predetermined standard costs. All targets of analysis must be prepared under the same logic, formulas, and account groupings so that favorable or unfavorable results can be examined and corrected as appropriate.

IN THE REAL WORLD

Obsession with Absorption

This sidebar is based on thirty years of experience with absorption accounting pitfalls in dozens of organizations. Absorption caused less trouble and distortion (one hundred years ago) when labor costs were far greater than machine costs, and overhead cost was a much smaller percentage of total expenditures. Then, starting in the 1980s, as automation raced ahead of touch labor, overhead rates soared to 100 to 1200 percent of labor cost. Low-labor operations performance that was held accountable to absorption measures faced difficult trade-offs.

An operations manager who is measured by absorption must produce the right volume and mix of products to "absorb" overhead to look good in the absorption measure (whether or not the volume and mix match customer needs). Managers who miss absorption targets look like they didn't need all those overhead resources and/or were given too much capacity. Both or neither may be true or not; absorption measures simply don't reveal operational realities.

Mature firms have discovered the disadvantages of using absorption measures. Not everyone has. However, just in case, you know your firm has an "absorption obsession" if, in manufacturing:

1. Overhead rates steadily increase from year to year.

2. Customer on-time delivery is poor, and yet you have too much inventory in product that isn't selling. The excess inventory items do, however, have high absorption rates.

3. Financial accounting and business decisions utilize the overhead rates.

4. Obsolete or spoiled inventory is a chronic problem.

5. Investigation of delivery and inventory problems reveals that the build schedule is manipulated to favor high-absorption products.

> **IN THE REAL WORLD CONTINUED**
>
> In the service sector, overhead and pseudo-absorption mechanisms create issues as well. You know your service firm has an absorption/overhead problem if:
>
> 1. Hourly rates charged to customers and clients increase faster than the combination of salary/fringe benefit expenses plus general cost-of-living increases on nonsalary items.
>
> 2. Highly skilled professionals with high billing rates are doing chargeable work that could be done by lower-level, less expensive employees. In other words, the customer/client is overcharged so that the billing firm can recoup its expenses.
>
> 3. Your firm frequently loses business based on price, not on competency.

Resource consumption is hard to control or standardize by its nature, and the variety of business operations—from teaching a university class to building a large jetliner—defies a universally applicable comparison model. Indirect materials, support labor, and services are especially difficult to confine to accounting cost type paradigms. However, finance professionals long ago solved the messy business of the overhead "peanut butter jar" chock-full of hard-to-assign indirect manufacturing costs by using a concept called *absorption*. Overhead is defined simply as any cost of doing business other than a direct cost (i.e., component material and touch labor) of a product or service output. Absorption costing allocates all or a proportion of fixed and variable production costs into one of three categories: (1) work-in-process inventory, (2) finished-goods inventory, and (3) cost of goods sold. Think of three spongelike account classifications that absorb those fixed and variable costs that are difficult to assign. Although service organizations typically do not practice formal absorption accounting, most build cost allocations into their cost/pricing structures that accommodate indirect/overhead expenses.

Cost accountants use an absorption calculation called *consumption ratio* to approximate the indirect resources being consumed by product/service outputs. The consumption ratio is that proportion of overhead activity consumed by a product or service. Even though products, product lines, and services differ in the consumption of indirect resources, financial accounting sought an efficient way to *allocate* responsibility for these expenditures through the cost accounting system. The only way to do this was to use a *predetermined overhead rate* for each product/service, calculated prospectively as part of the budget cycle.

Accounting overhead rates were traditionally based on the direct labor hours used to create a product. This cost driver was the overhead costing method of choice for most manufacturers for much of the twentieth century, derived from late nineteenth- and early twentieth-century factories where low-cost, long-hour immigrant labor was a substantial portion of total cost. Today, this profile no longer holds for typical production facilities where labor, as a percent of total cost, has steadily decreased with technological advances.

In the final third of the last century, accountants sought more accurate cost drivers to calculate overhead rates. Although cost drivers like machine hours, material cost, and units of production provided greater levels of specificity, they did not satisfy managers' need for accuracy. In fact, managers came to realize that all predetermined rates based on financial concepts are prone to driving counterproductive behavior (cost and human) at one time or another.

Absorption costing provides the classic example of costing practices that drive ineffective behavior. Under absorption costing methods, each product/service has a predetermined (i.e., standard) overhead rate that, when combined with direct material and labor costs, equals total product/service cost. Some products/services have high rates, carrying the assumption that those products/services "absorb" more overhead cost, while other products/services have low rates, thus carrying the assumption that those products/services use up less overhead cost.

Since manufacturing-sector managers have traditionally been judged on their overhead performance and production variances, imagine the potential manipulations the managers are tempted to use to meet performance objectives. For example, a manufacturing manager might schedule the production of favorably rated units in order to appear in a positive light (i.e., spending less on indirect costs). If this same manager is not held accountable for specific performance in inventory mix targets and customer on-time delivery, the production process risks becoming dysfunctional. Inversely, the same manufacturing professional might be motivated to use high-rate units to show that capacity is fully used depending on the performance measures and incentives in place.

TIPS & TECHNIQUES

Five Questions to Ask Your Accountant about Cost Overhead

1. Which of our expenditures are considered "overhead"?
2. What are our exact, detailed formulas for assigning overhead expenditures?
3. How accurate do you think these formulas are in assigning resource charges where the resources are actually used?
4. Do managers ever complain about the overhead allocation costs? What is the nature of their complaints?
5. How much time does our accounting staff spend on calculating, charging, and analyzing overhead?

Summary and Lessons from the Field

Conventional accounting terminology is inadequate as a strategic business vocabulary. Conventional concepts hail from an era with high direct labor and relatively low capital investment costs as a portion of total cost, in contrast to current low levels and high investment in automation and technology. When used alone, conventional systems offer limited insight to underlying cost drivers, report only historically, and do not give due focus to nonfinancial performance aspects.

Advanced cost accounting methods design cost terminology and concepts that reflect the actual dynamics of an organization's activities, as opposed to simply providing inputs to financial accounting. Neither cost types or absorption costing inform decision making, nor do they support continuous improvement in cost and process structures. Clearly, more advanced frameworks are required to accomplish this. Automated financial systems, however, may continue to rely on simpler, aggregated cost accounting input. Points to remember include:

- Basic cost accounting terms and assumptions need to be commonly understood by all managers and executives so they can adequately assess cost analyses, and as appropriate change the analytical framework to more accurately reflect operational realities.

- Question the formats and assumptions of cost analyses to assure they reflect the actual particulars of business decisions.

- Never trust a cost accounting system with too many cost types.

- Make sure accountants are spending their time on decision-value analyses of indicated problems and not on debate over cost types and absorption constructs.

Endnotes

1. Robert S. Kaplan and David P. Norton, *The Balanced Scorecard: Translating Strategy into Action* (Boston: Harvard Business School Press, 1996). A basic premise of the BSC method is that "strategy tells the story of the business."

2. Robert S. Kaplan and Robin Cooper, *Cost & Effect: Using Integrated Cost Systems to Drive Profitability and Performance* (Boston: Harvard Business School Press, 1998).

3. Id., 13.

CHAPTER 3

Cost Accounting Structures: Standards, Budgets, and Controls

After reading this chapter you will be able to

- Understand the purposes and uses of budgets, standard costs, forecasts, and control
- Begin to assess organizational value offered by these traditional cost accounting practices

This chapter ties the macrocosms of the financial and managerial accounting systems to the microcosm of technical detail embedded in the logic and use of cost types. Budgets and standard costs (standard fees, in the service sector) are the concrete means by which conventional accounting systems enforce control and direct fiscal behavior.

Budgets remain a key control mechanism in the majority of organizations, and most executives consider doing business without a budget to be heresy. Therefore, business professionals can reasonably expect budgets to play an important role in their work lives, and often in their personal performance evaluations. A budget commits managers to volume and spending levels; if the budget is considered an immutable target, managers go to great lengths to achieve it. When budget surpluses are taken away from functional areas at year-end, functional managers do whatever it takes to spend every budget dollar. Budgets that lose their alignment with actual business conditions invariably lead to counterproductive behavior. Capital budgets are important because they focus on the acquisition of long-term assets that can affect a manager's performance for multiple years.

As an example of a business situation where a nonfinancial manager would need to understand how to negotiate budgets or how to interpret margin/volume analyses, consider an engineering firm that typically sets the budgets for all departments and functions using a simple inflation formula against predicted business volume. The accounting staff uses this simple method because executives decline to be involved in budget preparation; therefore, no better assumptions are available. However, the executives actually hold all departments and functions accountable for budget targets, and include this aspect in individual manager performance reviews.

Accounting Perspectives of Organization Structure

Accounting systems focus and assign control responsibilities for some combination of profitability, revenue, investment, or cost activities. In other words, accounting systems identify individuals or segments called *responsibility centers*. Therefore, organizations that hold the responsibility centers accountable for safeguarding assets and contributing to profitability, by definition, employ an accounting system structure called *responsibility accounting*. In organizations employing responsibility accounting, the accounting system sets standards, measures actual outcomes, and reports in terms of responsibility center performance. Responsibility accounting is not the only accounting paradigm for financial organization design, but it is arguably the most common. Responsibility accounting goes by other names such as *resource accounting*, or *profit-center accounting*.

Since financial measures remain the predominant coin of accountability for the stewardship of assets, it stands to reason that accounting systems exist to monitor cost management performance. Responsibility

Cost Accounting Structures: Standards, Budgets, and Controls

accounting uses the budget as the primary control leverage, supported and informed by financial measures such as net profit, return on investment, and economic value-added. Budgets and financial measures in turn rely heavily on standard costs.

Key terms to be aware of in this chapter are:

- *Budget.* A financial plan for the generation and allocation of financial resources or any estimate of forecast costs or revenues. The two main types of budgets are capital (usually high-dollar, long-term, and project-related), and operating (usually divided by function: manufacturing, sales, administration, and so forth).

- *Chart of accounts.* A system of classifying accounts in terms of asset, liability, equity, revenue, cost, and expense categories. The classification process assigns each account with an account number and name. General ledger systems and conventional budgets are organized according to a chart of accounts, an organized list of all accounts used to record financial transactions.

- *Opportunity cost.* When one investment alternative is chosen over another, the hypothetical calculation of potential benefit of and/or return on the foregone investment, usually expressed as estimated profit/income.

- *Responsibility accounting.* The method that seeks to manage costs at the points where they can be controlled by assigning revenues, costs, profit, and sometimes investment accountability to predefined organizational units called responsibility centers.

- *Responsibility center (RC).* A unit within an organization that is held accountable for revenues, costs, (or both) and sometimes for investments. Typically, a budget and limits of authority are set for the RC managers, who then report periodically to a higher authority.

  - *Cost center.* A responsibility center whose management is held accountable only for costs; also called responsibility costing.

- *Investment center.* A responsibility center whose management is held accountable for income (i.e., revenues and costs), as well as for investments.
- *Profit center.* A responsibility center whose management is held accountable only for profit.
- *Standard cost.* A cost *prediction* based on operational assumptions for material, labor, and related overhead expenditures for manufactured products and for identified fees for services. Predictions are generically understood as projected targets in this definition. Standard costs are usually revised annually. Actual costs are compared with the standard costs as a way of monitoring and controlling performance. Deviation from a standard is called a *variance*.
- *Variance.* A favorable or unfavorable difference between standard and actual costs, or any difference between a planned and actual amount in a financial system. Standard cost variances are concerned with fluctuations in material, labor, and overhead components.

Influencing Management Behavior

Management works to influence human performance behaviors by means of individual performance reviews, compensation/incentive plans, reprimands and sanctions, and many less formal practices. All managers want continuous improvement and cost reduction behaviors in their employees, but someone must quantitatively monitor and report actual performance before behavior can be influenced toward these ends.

Responsibility accounting traces many of its roots to three tenets of the Scientific Management world within its manufacturing context. The first tenet assumes that employees are uneducated; therefore, control must be centralized so workers need not make any decisions. The uneducated workforce assumption yields tenets two and three: individual

Cost Accounting Structures: Standards, Budgets, and Controls

performance must be modeled on a "best way" to perform each task; and rewards come to those individuals who perform well against the "best way."

Businesses now frequently operate in a decentralized manner. Highly educated and skilled workers are required to think, and often receive rewards based on group, rather than individual, performance. However, the accounting systems of many firms still reflect the almost one-hundred-year-old Scientific Management assumptions and exert control through accounting-based measures developed for a manufacturing environment.

These antiquated systems pit managers against one another in competition for resources and performance support. The same systems judge performance almost exclusively in terms of cost, profit, and budget adherence—all *results* measures with little or no formal accountability for *process* performance. This behavior control paradigm leads to an internally oriented, standards-focused management style. The focus can become so tightly inward over time that the internal predictive standard may not be accurate or competitive in terms of the industry standard. The outcome of this paradigm is a rigid hierarchy with a half-blind internal focus and a parochial competition for resources upon which many of today's organizations still manage their costs.

Originally, responsibility accounting developed as companies grew larger and more geographically dispersed. Corporate executives could not effectively manage beyond a certain scope and geographic range. Consequently, authority was delegated to division and business-unit level managers who typically were (and are) held accountable for cost, profit, and sometimes investments. In theory, responsibility centers like these also have the advantage of business unit autonomy with each division manager "running a separate business." In theory, this all seems logical; in practice, conflicts easily flare up between corporate and divisions, and between divisions as well.

The weakest link in the responsibility center management chain is usually the *implication* of autonomy, where in practice there are limited degrees of freedom. This comes about because corporate executives have their own expectations and are held accountable for certain performance levels. Naturally, they work to align the divisions under their control to achieve these ends. From that point on it is a short walk to the loss of autonomy for division managers.

The second link to snap in the responsibility chain is resource optimization among business units. Service and support departments—human resources, accounting, IT—can easily duplicate functions and waste resources that a centralized service would not. When the accounting system treats divisions, business units, or departments as cost or profit centers, however, they immediately become competitors that are uninterested in sharing resources. This is especially true in manufacturing companies with multiple divisions with similar capabilities. Because the divisions compete in the same marketplace, they see one another as part of the competition. Geographic dispersion is seldom a market barrier these days. Under responsibility center structures, where internal divisions or units compete for the same customers, they are loathe to share best-practice processes or information with each other. They keep their operations secret from one another even though they all report to one corporate entity. Where divisions do not have similar competencies or production capabilities, and where they do not compete for customers, such problems are less likely to occur.

Imagine the many forms of waste generated in these competitive internal environments when compared to those organizations that focus energies and resources on the external competition and customer/client satisfaction. Cost-savvy executives and managers examine their accounting systems for underlying assumptions and the role they play in influencing cost and employee behavior. Responsibility accounting metrics should be balanced with more strategically aligned accountabilities, at the very least. Fiscal control and financial performance frameworks should never engender the perils of internal competition. As a first step, executives and managers need a thorough understanding of budgets and standards to appreciate where the conventional accountability processes help and where they do harm.

Responsibility Accounting Principles

Accounting measures and reports are at the heart of the responsibility management framework. When structuring an organization under responsibility principles, the first step is to identify the centers and determine their scope of accountability in terms of cost, profit, and investment. Next, set performance expectations, including those within the budget process. Responsibility center managers almost always operate under an incentive system that is designed to motivate performance and that is determined by comparing plan/budget to actual. Superiors reward or sanction the RC managers based on performance at the level of the entire center. In summary, the chief attributes of a responsibility accounting system are:

- Hierarchical control
- Performance standards and evaluation, most often in terms of budget-to-actual analyses
- Behavior motivation consistent with organization goals, most often limited to profit

This framework creates a stage where managers act out a range of behaviors. More often than not, such systems determine executive/manager compensation and career advancement. When the organization sets clear goals and carefully aligns responsibility center objectives with them, the RC manager performance path is more obvious and more easily achieved.

Even when organizations establish initial goal clarity and alignment, leadership does not always allot the time to adjust and realign as business conditions change. Finally, the plan and budget must be administered from the top, consistently and logically. If center managers suspect favoritism or unfair treatment, behavior subversive to the greater good may ensue. Clearly, executives and managers who seek to participate in accounting system design and management must know their organizational design alternatives, as well as their budget and standard cost options, so thoroughly that they know what they are rejecting and what attributes they can expect.

Sector, Segment, and Production Perspectives

No narrative of the history of accounting perspectives on organizational structure would be complete without a discussion of sectors, segments, and the two major manufacturing cost accumulation methods: *job-order costing* and *process costing*. In commerce somewhere along the Silk Route, a traveling merchant wondered, "How much of my wealth do I spend on providing my goods to the City of Byzantium? How much to service the City of Kashgar?" This ancient trader was beginning to think in terms of sectors or segments of business. Perhaps the trader noticed that perfumes sold very well in Byzantium, but not in Kashgar where spices were in high demand. The trader may have then performed a basic analysis of the perfume versus the spice trade that yielded useful insights. Maybe the perfume trade was more profitable than spice. Such geography and product type questions were probably among the first points of profitability analysis.

Since those ancient times, sector and segment analysts have learned to slice and dice markets, customers, and organizations into innumerable categories. Technically, a *sector* refers to a specific area of organizational concern and activity: health care, manufacturing, not-for-profit, education, or service. The Standard Industrial Classification (SIC) coding system standardizes sectors for purposes of trade and commerce by grouping organizations with similar activity profiles.

A *segment* is some portion of a single organization of sufficient importance to merit performance reporting. A *segment analysis* dissects units within a single organization for purposes of gaining insight—usually to profitability—based on geography, product line, or, in very large companies, even sectors. In financial accounting, especially for publicly traded companies, *segment reporting* is considered so important that the Securities and Exchange Commission regulates it in the interest of providing investors with reliable information.

In contrast, the cost management focus of segment and sector analysis is typically internally motivated. Different sectors account for cost in entirely different ways. Governments focus on accountability to citizen-taxpayers. Not-for-profits hold themselves accountable to donors, members, and granting agencies. In both government and not-for-profit organizations, the sources and uses of funds are very important, and revenue streams are carefully mapped to related expenditures. After all, donors and citizens want to know how their money is spent. *Government and fund accounting* are distinct financial paradigms practiced in these sectors.

Similarly, cost accounting practices in the manufacturing sector differ from service sector practices. Merchandisers and retailers follow still other guidelines. Recall that service sector organizations typically have the majority of their expenditures in people-related categories, whereas manufacturing firms deal with cost of goods sold and SG&A. In fact, the manufacturing sector is supported by two additional types of cost accounting structure: *job-order costing* and *process costing*.

Job-order costing is a manufacturing cost accumulation method that gathers costs by specific project or production run, built either to demand or forecast. Expenditures are based on the production volume of a job order with boundaries such as a customer order (e.g., one luxury yacht) or forecast production run (e.g., 50,000 units for holiday production of a popular toy). Process costing is an accumulation method that accumulates cost by department or process. Manufacturers use process costing with product units that are not easily distinguishable (e.g., petroleum) and where the product is considered a commodity (e.g., safety pins, rubber bands). Distributors and merchandisers also use distinct accounting and reporting practices. Construction accounting operates under yet another paradigm.

The important point here is that, in contrast to financial accounting, cost accounting employs a wide variety of paradigms to reflect the expectations and environments of diverse organizations. Extending the ongoing comparison between financial and cost accounting systems, managers perform financial analysis comparisons across sectors and segments; cost accounting analyses are more focused within sectors and segments.

Budgets and Standard Costs

The armchair quarterback cost system has its roots in what accountants call "the audit trail." This means that every scrap of cost information can be traced to a financial transaction record and a book of account (i.e., general ledger system), all structured within a chart of accounts. Every number on any report must have a source document—a record of an actual economic event. Document signatures assure accountability. These "proof" requirements are vital to financial accounting with its externally focused reports.

Over time, the managerial/cost accounting discipline started to follow audit trail paths similar to those prescribed by financial accounting principles. This was unfortunate and need not have been so. By shadowing the highly aggregated, transaction-based reporting methods

Cost Accounting Structures: Standards, Budgets, and Controls

of financial accounting, cost accounting actually hid operational problems in variances (i.e., waste) rather than making these important, manageable cost insights visible.

More whimsically perhaps, cost accountants may have followed the example of their financial counterparts for more defensive reasons. Then and now, executives have been known to aggressively challenge accounting reports with statements and questions like, "That number isn't right!" and "I don't like the looks of that number!" and "Where did that number come from?" When accounting results do not meet executive expectations, accountants know they must be ready to guide the startled executive through the accounting entries one exasperating transaction at a time.

Likewise, the accountants who designed the first budgets were probably also put on the defensive upon hearing executive statements like, "I never said I wouldn't spend money to do the job!" and "I did what it took to make the sale!" and "You never told me there was a limit on spending!" The accountant usually walks the razor's edge when "the numbers" must be validated. In contrast, the battle-weary executive is as likely as not to dispatch the problem with an expeditious, "Off with the accountant's head!"

Budgets are those tools of control that everyone loves to hate, but an effective budgetary system of control has distinct advantages. For example, the intimidating questions change their tone: "Is that expenditure in budget?" and "Will you be able to stay below budget for the year?" At times, even, "Can you hurry up and spend these budget dollars so we won't get cut next year?" And let us not forget the ubiquitous, "Why is so-and-so's budget so much bigger than my department's allocation?" At least questions such as these provide a solid foundation for discussion. Still, the repartee is likely to remain heavy on the parochial slant of "more for me."

So goes the pitched battle for scarce resources, year after year. Although more enlightened organizations practice a "better way," too many firms continue to stage the annual War of the Resources. Some players actually seem to enjoy the sport of it, as if business were an intracompany athletic contest! Only one faction wins this battle: external competitors.

Control and Profitability—Again

Because budgets are a fundamental part of accounting systems, they share the two prime concerns of financial management: control and profitability. Budgets are plans primarily concerned with controlling *prospective* operational results. They exist in the context of the fourth dimension: time. Their adjunct focus on periodic comparisons of actual expenditures to budget predictions keeps responsible managers responsible. By convention, the focus of the traditional budget is strictly financial (i.e., results that can be measured over time in monetary terms).

All these concepts work fairly well in mature economies that remain stable over the long term. However, one might scan the economic timeline for quite a while to find such an environment in recent years. Lag time between budget construction and plan execution exacerbates the difficulty. Managers typically construct conventional budgets six to eighteen months prior to plan execution. Many government and public institutions plan as much as three years in advance, and even then in the context of changing administrations. Competitors, economic conditions, and executive players move and change faster than this. A static budget may easily become outdated in short order, or worse, may constrain management creativity and adaptability when accountabilities for budget targets remain fixed in the wrong time context or under significantly different business conditions.

Cost Accounting Structures: Standards, Budgets, and Controls

In summary, conventional budgets have three primary limitations:

1. They are financial only and do not consider related nonfinancial measures that may be the actual drivers of performance.

2. The excessive lag time between budget construction and plan execution risks budget irrelevancy.

3. The conventional annual budget is usually static and not amenable to adaptation when conditions change.

Regardless whether a company uses conventional or more advanced budget and standard cost systems, all need to be held to at least the following three attributes of the overall cost management system:

1. Support understanding of the nature and behavior of cost (and the humans doing the spending).

2. Promote, track, and give feedback on value creation and continuous improvement.

3. Assist management in wise use of resources.

A Brief History of Standard Costing in Managerial Accounting

The concept of cost is ancient, but it was only with the Industrial Revolution that cost accounting began to emerge as a stable, repeatable endeavor. These were times when processes were hopelessly inefficient, and there were no formalized production processes. Scientific Management changed this situation, and both product cost determination and cost control techniques were accepted.

Robin Cooper's observations on the Scientific Management movement and its influence on cost management practices, include the following:

> Before the scientific management movement, no effective mechanism existed whereby standard costing could emerge. Standard costing requires repetitive manufacturing processes that can be measured accurately each time they are performed.

Repetition is needed for the development of standards to be worthwhile.[1]

By the mid-1930s, things started to go downhill for managerial/cost accounting, as they did for everything else with the onset of the Great Depression. In the preface of *Relevance Lost: The Rise and Fall of Management Accounting*, H. Thomas Johnson and Robert S. Kaplan describe how management accounting started to lose its relevance because "the management accounting systems in Western companies were no longer providing relevant information for decision making and control."[2] Business professionals now widely acknowledge this premise.

The authors argue persuasively that the loss of relevance is a twentieth-century phenomenon. In a cogent summary, they state the following.

> Accounting systems for managerial decisions and control can be traced back to the origins of hierarchical enterprises in the early nineteenth century. Unencumbered by any demands for external reporting, management accounting practice developed and flourished in a wide variety of nineteenth- and early twentieth-century corporations. Only in the past sixty to seventy years have external auditing and financial reporting systems come to perform the original function of management accounting systems. The current inadequacy of corporate management accounting systems can therefore be recognized as a relatively recent decline in relevance, not as a lag in adapting older financial accounting systems to modern managerial needs.[3]

All this begs the question: What specifically are the relevant aspects that were lost? The best thinkers of the late 1990s concluded that management accounting systems needed the following improvements:[4]

- Alignment of cost information to strategic planning
- More meaningful methods to attach overhead to products, services, and customers

- Timely, decision-quality cost information and feedback (budget/plan and actual)
- Better ways to analyze capital investment options
- More measurement and reporting that makes nonfinancial performance visible and actionable
- Understanding of the real underlying cost drivers

These are some of the most pressing requirements. If present-day business thinkers and managers had universally established methodologies for these improvements in managerial accounting, the information that follows would be little more than an interesting historical anecdote. Instead, because many organizations continue with cost accounting systems based on conventional accounting practices that do not address these recommended attributes, the problem remains quite real. Therefore, managers must thoroughly understand conventional systems so that they can make relevant, timely steps toward the newer, more advanced cost management systems without demolishing the legacy system.

Standard Costs

If budgets are plans intended to control future operational results, what assumptions drive the predictions, and what information sources provide the inputs on which budgets are based? The easiest, but often most inappropriate, answer is that budgets are extrapolations based on cost/revenue history that take actual results and add/subtract 5 to 10 percent, based loosely on management guesses regarding prevailing variables, such as inflation and pricing. Conventional budget systems answer the same question in two words: standard costs. Therefore, managers in organizations that employ a conventional cost accounting system must thoroughly understand standard cost opportunities and limitations.

Standard costs for material, labor, and overhead of product components (i.e., planned product costs) are established during the traditional budget process and later compared to actual expenditures at regular intervals, usually monthly. The "standard" is also the cost used to calculate inventories on the balance sheet and COGS on the income statement. Deviations from standard are captured and reported in variance accounts. (Variances are discussed shortly.)

Referring to the definition of standard costs in this chapter, notice that for standard cost predictions to be relevant, economic conditions and major processes must be stable during the time period that the standards cover. If economic conditions are unstable, or significant operations processes change (e.g., automation of a manual process), then the logical approach seems to be to adjust the standard.

Logical, yes, but financial accounting principles do not make this easy. Recall that financial accounting honors the principle of comparability, and comparability is compromised if a product has one standard in the first quarter and another standard in the second quarter. Annual budgets lose some degree of their relative comparability, and variance analyses grow increasingly difficult. Accountants who oversee traditional standard cost systems eschew changing standards more than absolutely necessary (i.e., during the annual budget process).

Typically, conventional financial accounting holds standard costs steady for a long period—usually a year—captures actual differences in variance accounts for material, labor, and overhead, and reports the variances long after any manager could use the information to correct current operational performance. In manufacturing, there are two major variances for each COGS component, material, labor, and overhead, totaling six variances in all (see Exhibit 3.1). Manufacturing variances, particularly overhead, are complex calculations that have multiple cross-functional impacts. Although generally similar from firm to firm, every

EXHIBIT 3.1

The Six Traditional Manufacturing Variances

Variance	Areas Traditionally Responsible
Materials - Price	Purchasing
Materials - Usage	Manufacturing - labor and machines
Labor - Rate (or Price)	Human Resources Information (labor market, union contracts)
Labor - Efficiency	Manufacturing
Overhead - Spending	Functions controlling the resources
Overhead - Efficiency	Sales for volume Manufacturing for labor efficiency

organization will customize its variance formulas to some degree. (To learn the mathematical composition of common variance equations, refer to the management accounting textbooks listed as Suggested Reading at the end of this book.)

Behavioral Implications

Importantly, although traditional variances meet the needs of financial accounting, they can drive inappropriate behavior in practice. As well-intentioned managers and employees attempt to meet operational goals within a standard cost/variance control system, they frequently thwart the efforts of their cross-functional coworkers. A classic example is the purchasing manager, who is held accountable for the materials purchase-price variance (PPV). In all good faith, this manager negotiates the very best prices for material components, and thus creates a favorable PPV. However, if the purchasing manager is not also held accountable for material quality and lead times (nonfinancial performance measures), the production lines are more likely to suffer from defective components or from materials shortages. In the final analysis, an effective standard cost system must, at minimum:

- Contain enough account detail and stratification to be relevant.
- Provide for functional and cross-functional cost responsibility.
- Promote understanding of cross-functional impacts.
- Use standards as legitimate, achievable management targets.
- Collect actual costs to compare to the targets.
- Direct management action when unfavorable variances are detected.

Budget Reliance on Standard Costs

An organization's annual budget is a plan that estimates prospective revenue and expenses; that said, budgets fall into several other categories beyond the two main divisions, capital and operating, including:

- Functional budgets (e.g., manufacturing, sales, human resources, research and development)
- Cash budget
- Sales revenue (commonly called the "sales forecast")
- Production budget (material, labor, overhead)
- Inventory and COGS budgets
- SG&A budget
- Project budget (subordinate to, for example, the research/development budget or the capital budget)

Standard costing practices rely heavily on the sales forecast and on the manufacturing/production budget. Typically, the sales forecast displays predicted sales revenue in terms of the estimated number of unit sales for each product/service, times their respective estimated prices; in short, estimated unit sales times price. The manufacturing/production budget also tracks number of units but with minimal emphasis on *price*. The manufacturing/production budget controls the *cost* of the materials, labor, and overhead required to produce and deliver the product or service. In similar fashion, the support functions align their budgets to the volume levels predicted by sales through manufacturing. See Exhibit 3.2 for a depiction of this flow.

Interestingly, although managers take great pains to establish standard costs for products, there are no equivalent standard price or standard

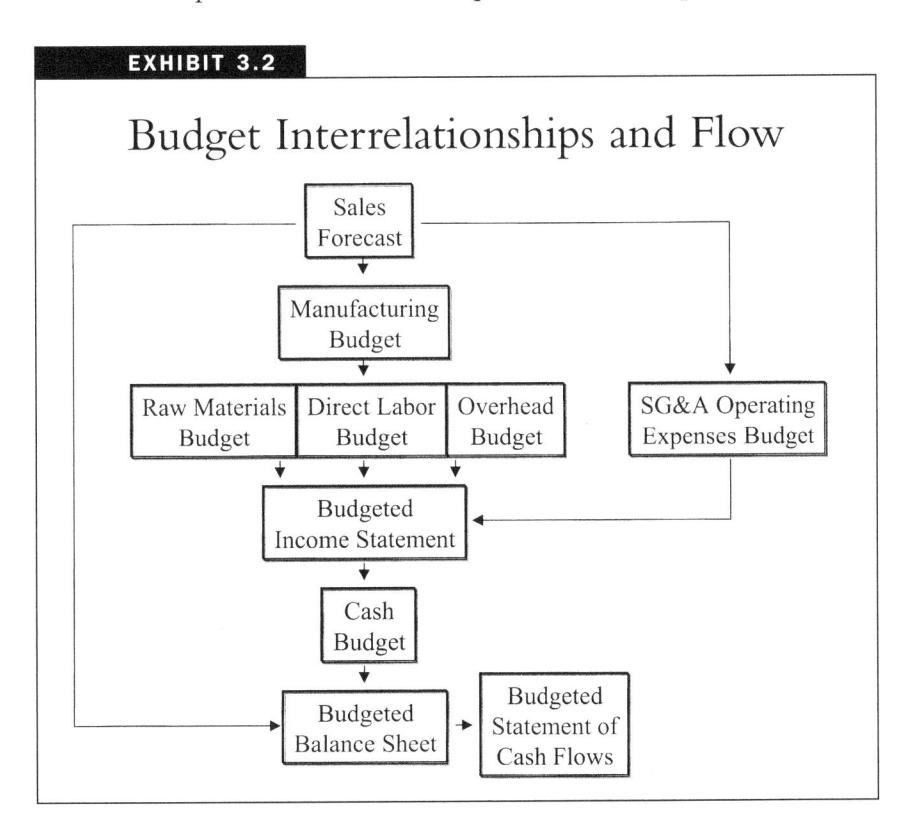

EXHIBIT 3.2

Budget Interrelationships and Flow

Sales Forecast → Manufacturing Budget → Raw Materials Budget, Direct Labor Budget, Overhead Budget → Budgeted Income Statement

Sales Forecast → SG&A Operating Expenses Budget → Budgeted Income Statement

Budgeted Income Statement → Cash Budget → Budgeted Balance Sheet → Budgeted Statement of Cash Flows sales volume concepts on the revenue side of the income statement. The different ways that the budget treats revenues and cost have some logical accounting practice consequences. First, when sales volume or price deviate from the budgeted amount, a budget revenue variance is recorded, plus or minus, in a simple, clean transaction. The consequences in the manufacturing sector are considerably more complicated. Based on sales predictions made many months in advance of actual production, management hires laborers, purchases machines, contracts for materials, and configures facilities. When competitive and economic conditions change, a company using conventional budgets and standard costs can be caught flat-footed, with either too many or too few resources.

Guiding Performance

Budgets aligned with targeted priorities that enable strategic achievement and adaptation to changing conditions more effectively guide human behavior and decision making. Budget design must map a clear course because all organizational systems interact with the budget. Some have no interaction except through the budget. An intuitive example is the relationship the budget creates between a sales staff commission structure and production incentive plans. The design of such systems requires close scrutiny for the effects that standard cost structures and incentives may have on spending behaviors.

The inherently financial focus of standard costing and budget systems is the biggest potential drawback to effective management practices. Financial information is a collection of important result measurements. Even nonfinancial budget elements such as number of units and labor hours are measured primarily to arrive at a financial result. If a budget is all about results, where is the information about the causes? Who is responsible for focusing on the processes that lead to the results? Erasers

IN THE REAL WORLD

The "Big One" of Aught–Nine

In the 1970s and 1980s, variances from standard were all the rage in accounting circles. Variance campfire stories were told and passed. These stories resembled the blizzard stories that Minnesotans tell, which usually begin something like, "I remember the big one of aught-nine that shut us down for weeks." When the "big one" came in the form of a variance, managers lost their jobs over a labor or material variance that couldn't be beaten into submission using the pre-total quality movement and financial methods of the time.

Behind such stories, other tales always lurked. For example, as controller for the electronics division of a multinational manufacturer, I assisted a production manager who was being "buried alive" by material usage (i.e., waste) variances. The production manager believed in the skills of his line workers, and suspected poor quality material components as the culprit. Together, we gathered data to show that, indeed, more than 90 percent of the root cause of the material usage variance was poor quality material, not incompetent workers. But why?

The answer wasn't far behind. We had noticed earlier the enormously positive purchase price variance (PPV), which halfway through the year had amounted to over $1 million, an amount equal to the division's profit. The data we gathered showed that, while the division's purchasing manager was receiving accolades for his PPV performance, he was also unwittingly supplying the production floor with substandard components. Once this was brought to everyone's attention, we all worked hard to assure cross-functional responsibility for variances, while most of us began a search for better performance measures.

Stories like this that spring from conventional cost accounting systems are becoming more and more rare. However, if your organization

> **IN THE REAL WORLD CONTINUED**
>
> continues to judge performance based on accounting variances—whether you are a manufacturing or service firm—investigate the following:
>
> 1. Do accounting reports consistently show one variance that is strongly favorable and another that runs strongly unfavorable? If so, see if there is a relationship between the two.
>
> 2. If many variances consistently report either very favorably or unfavorably, check the standard costs. They probably need updating.
>
> 3. Ensure cross-functional accountability for any measure that has multifunction impacts or multiple points of control.
>
> 4. Engage accounting staff in productive problem solving as opposed to "coming in after the blizzard to dig out the dead."

and delete keys change results; only managers armed with nonfinancial information change causes.

This is where the need for nonfinancial measurement and leading (or process) performance monitoring becomes more evident. Some interesting questions arise in the context of managing beyond the information contained within the conventional budget and standard costs. What decisions and activities cause the financial results that lag behind the standard costs? How can a budget be used wisely in the allocation of resources? Rather than constraining adaptation with rigid annual targets, how can a budget be flexible enough to guide the firm when conditions change rapidly?

A great deal of thought and effort has gone into answering these questions. A firm does not have to change all of its systems in order to have a better budgetary control system. The next segment discusses a few of the alternatives that have evolved in recent years.

Cost Accounting Structures: Standards, Budgets, and Controls

Alternative Budget Systems

Budgets can be one of the most visible, effective control mechanisms within organizations. However, some cost management pioneers have begun to ask the following questions:

- What value do we really get out of these systems?
- Should we eliminate them in favor of more effective methods?
- How can we assure fiscal responsibility and control, if we do away with or significantly modify these systems?

By the early 1990s, most mature organizations knew that budgets based on retrospective extrapolations did not provide effective control. Progressive executives dug deeper to discover and map relationships between costs and the forces that actually drive cost (i.e., cost drivers). As software applications gained strength and reliability, simulation techniques with carefully designed assumptions helped to create more accurate budgeting frameworks. The remainder of this section discusses six alternative budget frameworks in the approximate chronological order in which they were developed over the last thirty-forty years. The first three budget models were developed earliest and may be familiar. The fourth, fifth, and sixth budget models are more recent. Important budget developments are:

1. Responsibility-based budgets (RBB)
2. Continuous and flexible budgets
3. Zero-based budgets (ZBB)
4. Activity-based budgets (ABB)
5. Human capital budgets (HCB)
6. Innovation-based budgets (IB)

Budgeting Mistakes: The Flaccid Budget. Before exploring these six, the three most common budgeting mistakes need calling out. Any budget model becomes an increasingly impotent control system to the degree that it incorporates the three common mistakes of the flaccid budget.

The first mistake: *Failure to align resource allocation—functional and project budgets—to strategic objectives.* Unfortunately, strategic planning and budgeting remain two separate processes for many companies. The separation is illogical since budgets have the capacity to depict strategies in quantitative terms and translate strategy into actionable operations goals. Budget methodologies aside, budgets exist to assign funds, people, and time to identified priorities. If this definition of the purpose of budgets sounds surprising, recall in any past experience when: (1) strategic objectives were not achieved due to lack of resources, or (2) objectives were not met in projects and initiatives that management approved without adding staff, funding, or equipment. When goals or projects fail, look to the budget structure for causes.

A second more fundamental problem sometimes lurks as the root cause of the flaccid budget: *Failure to create an actionable strategic plan or other guiding vision.* Most organizations take time to develop mission, vision, and strategies. A smaller percentage takes the time to develop concrete business plans that set functional and business unit performance expectations. Even fewer regularly monitor these plans and take corrective action as necessary. Finally, an even smaller number of organizations measure progress toward strategic achievement.

One final flaw that can reduce budgeting relevance and lead to the flaccid budget centers on *parochial claims to resources.* The budget process will be undermined if it takes place in an atmosphere of competition for internal resources and justification of current staff and funding. Top executives must set the tone and firmly discourage such territorial behavior.

Cost Accounting Structures: Standards, Budgets, and Controls

Responsibility-Based Budgets (RBB). Responsibility-based budgets operate within a responsibility accounting mind-set. The structure of RBB mirrors the firm's chart of accounts, and therefore focuses on departments, functions, and expenditure categories. RBBs hold managers, departments, and business units accountable for fiscal prudence. Responsibility accounting does not usually focus on the interdependencies and synergies between divisions, departments, and functions. Therefore, these segments typically create budgets in isolation, which are aggregated and linked only at the corporate level. At the end of the budget cycle, corporate superiors compare the center's actual results and performance to the budget. An RC manager's compensation and prospects of continued employment are often based in part on these performance evaluations.

Continuous and Flexible Budgets. Organizations construct conventional budgets with a single volume-level prediction. Consequently, the budget loses relevance when sales/service demand significantly increases or decreases. Two alternative budget frameworks address these limitations: *continuous* and *flexible*.

Conventional budgeting typically occurs in the last three to four months of the fiscal year, creating obvious information lag issues. A continuous, or rolling, budget refreshes data periodically, either continuously (i.e., monthly) or when volume rises or falls significantly. Continuous budgets drop the oldest month and add one future month every accounting cycle (also one month). *Time* intervals become the basis for a process of continuous budget review and update.

Organizations use a flexible annual budget to accommodate a range of potential *volume* fluctuations within the budget time period. The focus of the flexible budget centers primarily on the variable costs related to volume, expressed typically as sales units in a manufacturing firm, billable hours in a service firm, or number of procedures in a medical setting. Both continuous and flexible budgets more closely mirror actual operations. They allow management to plan for a range of scenarios (flexible) or to adjust plan as changes occur (continuous). In addition, they eliminate the need for interim forecasts, and provide an improved control mechanism to track accountabilities under varying conditions.

Zero-Based Budgets (ZBB). Zero-based budgeting discourages budget shortcuts. Budget construction consumes a great deal of management time. So does running a business. Managers caught between daily urgencies and budget planning may be tempted to take budget construction shortcuts, especially in organizations where the budget is notoriously irrelevant—in other words, not used to actually manage.

Conventional budget reviews can too easily focus inordinate attention on comparative changes from current-year budgets to next-year budgets. For example, an executive reviewing a manager's incrementally higher budget may ask in-depth questions about an additional proposed project expenditure without questioning the baseline dollars carried forward from the manager's prior budget containing many expenditure line items. Thoughtless carry-forward was a driving force in ZBB development. In contrast to the budget model alternatives discussed so far, a ZBB process insists that managers assemble convincing rationale for every budget line item, every year. In other words, the budget process starts from zero, and preceding budgets are considered informative but not necessarily relevant.

In practice, a blind-eye to former budgets is impractical and impossible. However, the ZBB technique called *decision packages* significantly improves the chance of starting fresh. Decision packages are a ranked series of legitimate and fundable potential activities, usually for a responsibility center. ZBB enjoyed a surge of popularity in the 1970s. Unfortunately, ZBB created an information structure too complicated for the existing information technology. Within ten years, ZBB washed out as a "hot" management topic. Now with adequate technology applications, one targeted use for ZBB may be this: to configure those portions of a budget most difficult to control (e.g., indirect costs, discretionary expenses), while the rest of the budget stays under another model.

Activity-Based Budgets (ABB). Activity-based budgeting grew out of the activity-based costing (ABC) and activity-based management (ABC/M, and more recently, ABM) explosion that began in the late 1980s. (See Chapter 5 for details. This cross-reference may be necessary for readers with no background in activity-based management concepts.) Authors write more articles and books discussing ABC/M and ABB techniques than any other single accounting subject. ABC/M receives this attention because it is the first comprehensive accounting alternative to chart of accounts/general ledger systems as a way of viewing and controlling an organization's resource allocation to its activities.

Resource allocation is the primary function of all budget systems. ABB targets allocations differently from other budget models. In conventional budgeting, the funding allocation targets are chart of accounts/general ledger items. As its name implies, ABB uses *activities* as resource allocation targets. One of the most important implications of the activity-based focus is that cost types, especially fixed and variable, sink into irrelevancy. Conceptually, ABB is ABC backward.[5] ABB flow starts with the products and services a company wishes to market. ABB then extrapolates the activities and activity drivers needed to produce these products and services. Finally, ABB defines the resources and resource drivers required to carry out the specified activities.

The sequence of steps involved in configuring an ABB system begins with a sales forecast, just as in conventional budgeting. Next, instead of moving straight to resources, an ABB calls for a second forecast: the activities required to realize the sales forecast. The third step calculates resource requirements to fuel the activities. Finally, a reality check reconciles resource supplies to forecast resource demand, including decisions on the capacity levels that the organization is willing to fund in terms of employment base, floor space, and equipment.

ABB is among the most mature, decision-supportive budgeting systems available—but it's not for beginners. As Peter B.B. Turney, CEO of Cost Technologies, Inc., and an ABC pioneer, writes, ABB "is technically difficult to implement, requires that organizations be well along the activity-based learning curve, and requires advanced systems and tools. It also involves new thinking about the meaning of fixed cost, variable cost, and the role of capacity."[6]

Human Capital Budgets (HCB). Human resources are the perennial thorn in the side of dollar-focused budgets. Budgets easily quantify salaries and wages or the approximate number of person-hours needed to meet a specified demand level in production or service. Budgets struggle to quantify the cost of hiring and training a new person, the cost of losing a top sales manager, and the prospective lost revenue from future innovations when a premiere scientist takes a job with the competition. Financial accounting has half-heartedly wrestled with human-value issues for over fifty years, but balance sheets and income statements rarely reflect the value of humans as resources. The rise of the knowledge-worker and increased awareness of the value of intellectual capital disturb conventional financial statement assumptions. At this time, a standardized way of valuing human capital has not emerged. Perhaps, like cost management, each organization will create customized human capital reports.

Skills-Based Human Capital Budgeting[7] is one of many emerging paradigms in this new territory. This approach shares two things in common with most other models for human capital budgeting:

1. A strategic focus, with finance as an aligned secondary focus
2. A concern for capturing value not recorded on conventional financial statements

In an attempt to bridge from financial capital information to human capital understanding, this particular model of human resource budgeting borrows many terms that originate in finance and translates them into the human dimension. Concepts include human capital skills measurement, human capital inventory, and human capital capacity. Authors McKenzie and Melling emphasize that the "key issue in human capital planning budgeting is ensuring that the right people with the right skills are in the right jobs at the right time. This includes understanding the fungible nature of human skill and mobility, as well as the ability to measure and cost human capital capacity."[8] Though in their infancy, human capital budgeting and other recent budget methods cast the accounting function into a whole new realm of value creation.

Innovation-Based Budgets (IBB). Another example of budget system evolution is the innovation-based budget (IBB).[9] Notice that every model that has developed since the conventional budget uses the word "based" to show how it conceptually differs from predecessor forms. A message lurks here. In choosing a base, budget designers declare what is most critical to their management perspective—activities, human capital, and innovation. Motorola and 3M, both known for cultures based on innovation, have experimented in IBB. The IBB model recategorizes costs to meet the innovation focus. As a control system designed to influence behavior, an IBB design structure motivates employees to produce a continuous stream of new ideas. The most important cost categories in this paradigm are *strategic, elective,* and *obligatory*—a new set of cost types.

Beyond Budgeting[10]

Regardless of budget type, human behavior considerations are critical to a budget's effectiveness. The following attributes determine the ultimate effectiveness of any budget:

- Traces accountabilities for cost, profit, and investment decisions to the decision maker(s).
- Adapts to changing conditions.
- Creates incentives to align behavior with broader organizational goals.
- Provides regular—not just annual—performance feedback.
- Cultivates participation in realistic target setting.

Control and accountability are essential elements of profitability, and designing a budget framework to manifest these qualities is as much art as science. Some experts suggest more radical changes. Frustration with budget model limitations led, in 1998, to CAM-I's (Consortium for Advanced Manufacturing-International) formation of the Beyond Budgeting Round Table.

Upon deeper examination, the universality of the frustration-with-budget phenomenon suggests that the problem with budgets is not so much with the models as with: (1) a lack of a working connection to strategic planning, and (2) hierarchical organization structure that slows and muddies decision making. These disconnect and hierarchy concerns come full circle to the three errors of the flaccid budget discussed earlier in this chapter:

1. Failure to align resource allocation (i.e., functional and project budgets) to strategic objectives.
2. Failure to create an actionable strategic plan or other guiding vision.
3. Parochial claims to resources.

Cost Accounting Structures: Standards, Budgets, and Controls

Budget frustration arises not from the budget framework itself but from the failure to allocate resources according to strategic priorities. *Any* budget model must therefore be strategically aligned with the broader goals of the organization, not with parochial interests. Any budget model will disappoint employees at all levels if it does not support organizational priorities by assuring adequate resources for key objectives. Points 2 and 3 are logical consequences of point number 1. Managers and employees serve two masters in organizations with disconnected strategy and resource allocation—budget goals and strategic goals. Consequently, both sets of goals become flaccid.

Forecasts

As factory automation and robotics began to take hold in the 1980s, managers hoped that such computerized manufacturing would lead to a time when:

- Production processes could be accurately identified.
- Sales forecasts could be precisely met.
- The variance between sales units and production units would drop to near zero.

This has not occurred in any sector. In fact, destabilizing markets with diminishing entry barriers make forecasts less reliable than ever.

As integral components in conventional accounting systems, forecasts essentially create short-term budgets. In fact, organizations that control primarily through budgets and forecasts often create monthly income statements (and, less frequently, monthly balance sheets) with the following column headings:

Current Month			Year-to-Date		
Actual	Budget	Forecast	Actual	Budget	Forecast

Each of the significant financial statement line items is reported in these six categories. Naturally, a great deal of management time is wasted explaining the variances between the actual, budget, and forecast results. The analysis time is an even greater waste of human resources, considering that it is all used up on historical (over and done, can't change it) data.

Planning prudence demands that an organization seek some way to look down the road and estimate the:

- Kind and number of units of product/service that will be sold
- Costs associated with these sales
- Material, labor, and support components of the cost of sales
- And so on

How far into the future does an organization need these answers? Twenty years ago, when supply chains moved slowly and lead times for materials were long, materials forecasting was more important and more feasible. Since then, Total Quality techniques, Just-in-Time (JIT) materials management, and the newer supply chain management techniques have greatly compressed lead times.

Despite these changes, many companies continue to rely on legacy information systems such as material requirements planning (MRP). In a dismal, closed-loop process, MRPs rely on the best guesses from the salesforce, so that the accountants can create forecasts and provide sales estimates for future periods, so that the executives can analyze the forecast variances at the end of the month—over and over again. A desire for certainty, or at least information, about future results from an historical, results-based information system is a quest doomed to failure. Such searches steal time from current operations, the only place that future results can actually be managed.

Most of the advanced CMS models discussed later in this book completely omit forecasting discussions. Interestingly, although forecasts are all about sales and production—a major domain of cost management—the responsibility for forecasts has slipped over to financial accounting. Why is this so?

First, finance-driven organizations continue to hold executives and managers accountable for financial results; therefore, all employees become keenly interested in seeing "what my performance measures will be at the end of the month." Second and more importantly, the shareholder concern for future returns and attendant demands for predictions of those returns have kept forecasting alive and well. The *Wall Street Journal* reports earnings forecasts and adjustments to previously issued forecasts as part of its daily bread and butter. This whole market information complex is intended as part of fair and full disclosure to protect shareholder interests. However, some would say that such forecasting has become a game between large investors, analysts, and public companies. At any rate, these two drivers keep forecasting alive and squarely in the financial realm.

In August 2001, *CFO Magazine* reported that, "Yogi Berra got it wrong. For most companies, the future *is* what it used to be: a perpetually blurry hodge-podge of vague expectations, missed opportunities, and unpleasant surprises. Forecasting remains a blind alley."[11] The article describes software vendors who continue to try to invent the better-forecasting mousetrap. Some of the latest applications adjust for overly optimistic sales manager estimates, tap into stand-alone customer information databases, and generally attempt to tie together disparate points of data to better inform the forecast.

Just as in budgeting, there are many ways to construct a forecast; and just as in budgeting, forecasting produces as much frustration as help. Forecast expert, J. Scott Armstrong of the Wharton School of Business states, "There are 139 principles of forecasting... Businesses ignore most of them.... and little of what we've learned has been built into software."[12] The bottom line: Satisfaction with the art of forecasting remains elusive.

Perhaps the most important thing an executive can do regarding both budgets and forecasts is to challenge "the way we've always done it." Before spending more time on lengthy budget processes or backward-looking forecast analyses, ask those three familiar questions. How can budget, standards, and forecast systems:

- Support understanding of the nature and behavior of cost?
- Promote, track, and give feedback on value creation?
- Assist management in wise use of resources?

Whatever the budget and forecast frameworks in place, be sure they are creating value and not eroding valuable management time.

Capital Investment

Capital comes in many forms: cash, equipment, infrastructure, and people. With the exception of cash, capital investment decisions are almost always about long-term assets, be they machines, buildings, or, in newer paradigms, people. This section is limited to a discussion of financial capital. Recall that a long-term asset is one that has greater than one year useful service. A cost accounting expert will analyze and put into quantitative form the array of opportunities for long-term investment.

Capital budgeting is the process of making long-term investment decisions. Managers use capital budgeting as a plan for acquiring assets expected to serve the organization for longer than one year, usually, for a minimum of three. These capital budget outlays invest in the future because they lay a foundation of resources that employees require to execute strategic objectives. Therefore, large projects and major initiatives are often viewed as capital investments.

Cost Accounting Structures: Standards, Budgets, and Controls

IN THE REAL WORLD

Flash, Pre-Flash, and Pre-Flash Flash

Once upon a time, I worked with a national, brand-name company that was obsessed with its monthly income statement. Why? Simple: Income statement measurements framed virtually all performance management, compensation, and promotion activity. This firm was not just financially driven; it was financially myopic. The income statement obsession was particularly hard on the accounting staff's time.

Not satisfied with formal forecasts, updated monthly, nor with waiting for month-end actual results, the CEO required a "flash" income statement ten days before month-end. This became known simply as "the flash," although it was essentially a second forecast. Executives at divisions across the country spend significant time constructing and reviewing the flash before submitting it to headquarters. The idea behind the flash was to spot trouble before the month became history and to rectify emerging problems. Over time, the month-end continued to bring unwelcome "surprises." The executive team's response was to try income statement fortune-telling earlier in the month, so accountants were required to produce a "pre-flash" income statement at mid-month. Inevitably, this led to a "pre-flash flash" only one week into a new month. Eventually, three accountants at each division were occupied full-time on financial statement production, forecasts, and flashes. The actual results remained "unpredictable."

If your organization has its attention glued to the monthly income statement results, remember:

- Operations and processes can't be managed from the income statement; it is too highly aggregated.
- The month-end results are the after-the-fact report card. You have to "do your homework" to get an "A." No amount of "guessing the answers" will do.

> **IN THE REAL WORLD CONTINUED**
>
> - Forecast or flash versions of the income statement provide no decision-support value.
>
> - Your accounting professionals do more valuable work when they aren't kept busy refining their crystal ball predictions.
>
> - If your organization's forecasts are consistently far from the mark, so are the processes that deliver the actual results.
>
> - Compensation and incentive plans can cause forecast distortion; for example, if variable compensation is paid on sales revenue above forecast, salespeople are implicitly invited to low-ball their forecasts. If top executives receive bonuses on bottom-line profit, they can be tempted to compromise long-term viability for short-term personal interests.

By definition, capital investment commits substantial resources—monetary, time, and human. Capital investment decisions inherently involve risk because organizations have limited resources. Capital investment items that fall into the balance sheet categories of property, plant, and equipment are subject to *depreciation* based more on tax regulations and financial accounting principles than on operational realities.

Capital investment decisions are simply choices between good alternatives. Alternatives not chosen are opportunities not exercised; this in itself is a kind of cost: *opportunity cost*. Opportunity cost analyses are slippery slopes because the analysis contains potential investments that are foregone in favor of other options. The return on investment (ROI) and benefits of foregone opportunities cannot actually be calculated because the investment in the opportunity is not made.

When executives make capital investment decisions among competing alternatives, they have at least two financial objectives in mind:

1. The investment will earn back its initial cost (capital outlay) over time—the shorter the time period, the better.
2. Over time, the same investment will produce an ROI; in other words, cash in the door above the original cost of the capital item.

Conventionally, the investment decision analysis is entirely financial in the sense of maximizing shareholder wealth.

Analysis Methods

The following elements make up a capital investment analysis.

- Estimated cash flows of all types: purchase price, revenue generated by the investment, repairs and maintenance, sale price at the end of the asset's usefulness, or cost of disposing
- Estimated useful life in operational terms
- Time value of money (interest rates)
- Usually, criteria for accepting or rejecting an alternative; for example, a threshold ROI

The time value of money, commonly referred to as *discounted cash flow*, expresses future cash flows in present value terms. Accountants in the majority of firms use more than one method in their investment analyses; overall, the discounted cash flow techniques are favored in conventional circles because monetary flows across time are comparable. Cost accounting professionals employ four conventional approaches to analyze these capital investments.

1. *Payback period.* From the time the investment is made, the amount of time required for the organization to recover its original investment (e.g., purchase price) in terms of cash flows generated.
2. *Accounting rate of return.* This is a percentage calculation based on income, not cash flows. The annual average of the sum of all

income over the life of the investment is the numerator. The original cost of the investment is the denominator.

3. *Internal rate of return.* A more complex calculation, this method seeks the interest rate that will result in the investment's net present value equaling zero. This interest rate is compared to the organization's preestablished required rate of return, which serves as a selection threshold.

4. *Net present value method.* An investment's present value cash inflows netted against its present value outflows are compared for an adequate rate of return. The choice of a discount (interest) rate(s) is a key part of this method.

Observations

These conventional methods of capital investment analysis, by necessity, make many assumptions; cash flows and interest rates are two of the most volatile sources of assumption error, and cause enough uncertainty on their own. A subtler and seldom-named factor poses even greater risks: internal competition for resources. In a financially driven company, where everyone's performance measures are primarily financial, resource competition is inevitable. The cure is a familiar one: strategic alignment of capital investments. This assumes, of course, a viable strategy.

Executives and managers must recognize the impact of financial accounting practices on capital investment decisions. Accounting principles require a focus on a discrete period of time, usually one year, with interim monthly and/or quarterly reporting. Assets that are in service for more than one year pose a challenging situation for financial accounting with its reporting period of one fiscal year. Financial accounting uses capitalization and depreciation frameworks to apportion capital investment expenses over multiple years. Put simply, this financial accounting practice means that the cost of the original investment is recognized on the balance sheet at the time the asset is put into service. Then, over a set number of years, the value of the investment is depreciated (i.e., a portion of the cost is recognized as an expense for each year the asset is in service).

These are matters that concern cost and financial accountants; however, the relatively rigid depreciation constraints on the financial accounting side often distort cost analyses. Importantly, significant financial influences characterize capital budgeting practices, but accountants take a fair amount of latitude in applying the financial principles. This is true right down to basic distinctions, such as whether a purchase is viewed as a capital asset (expense recognized over multiple years) or as a current expense (recognized on the income statement in one accounting period).

It should be noted that advanced cost management system frameworks are much less concerned with the many permutations of conventional capital investment analysis, viewing them as based on unreliable assumptions.

More recently, capital investment analysis methods include:

- Regression analysis
- Decision trees to manage investment risk
- Post-investment analysis, with comparison to original projections
- Capital asset pricing models that calculate the cost of capital (e.g., interest rates), considering industry sectors, and other risk elements

No matter the method, no matter the tool, large investment decisions remain among the most important, and most difficult, decisions executives make.

Summary and Lessons from the Field

Organizations need more than a conventional accounting system as the sole paradigm and information resource supporting strategic planning, management decision making, and performance evaluation. Conventional systems hail from an era when direct labor costs were a significant portion of total cost (versus current low levels) and had relatively low capital investment costs (versus current high levels in automation and technology). When used as the only control paradigm and decision-support information system, conventional approaches offer limited insight to underlying cost drivers. They overreport on historical information, and underreport current, future, and nonfinancial performance aspects.

Today's cost management systems and structures need to be designed to reflect the actual dynamics of organizational activities rather than simply providing inputs to financial accounting reports. Cost types, budgets, and all other cost management tools must inform decision making and support continuous improvement in cost and process structures.

Cost accountants and cost managers must balance financial considerations with a more encompassing focus—*value management.* Value management starts with customers and clients, and value-conscious cost managers create customer and client information profiles. As organizations work to engage and retain customers/clients, cost management systems must move away from transaction analysis and offer executive-level insights that suggest timely course corrections. Instead of just "keeping the books," cost accounting and management systems in mature organizations help chart clear strategic journeys.

Endnotes

1. Robin Cooper, "Cost Management: From Frederick Taylor to the Present," *Journal of Cost Management* 14, no. 5 (2000): 4–5.

2. H. Thomas Johnson and Robert S. Kaplan, *Relevance Lost: The Rise and Fall of Management Accounting* (Boston: Harvard Business School Press, 1991), xii. Chapter 6 of this book is particularly recommended as a foundation for understanding the history behind the emphasis on financial accounting.

3. Id., xx.

4. This list was compiled by Catherine and Joseph Stezel. It is a synthesis of eleven opinion essays by members of the advisory board for the *Journal of Cost Management* 14, no. 5 (2000).

5. Robert S. Kaplan and Robin Cooper, *Cost & Effect: Using Integrated Cost Systems to Drive Profitability and Performance* (Boston: Harvard Business School Press, 1998): 303. Kaplan and Cooper take this view. Another leading expert insists that ABB is not ABC in reverse. Ron Bleeker, Cost Management Systems Director for CAM-I (Consortium for Advanced Manufacturing – International), sees ABB as significantly more complex, involving work method analyses, process improvement efforts, and many other facets. See Ron Bleeker, "Key Features of Activity-Based Budgeting," *Journal of Cost Management* 15, no. 4 (2001):5–20.

6. Peter B. B. Turney, "The State of 21st Century Cost Management," *Journal of Cost Management* 14, no. 5 (2000): 46–47.

7. J. Lehr McKenzie and Gary L. Melling, "Skills-Based Human Capital Budgeting: A Strategic Initiative, Not a Financial Exercise," *Journal of Cost Management* 15, no. 3 (2001): 30-36.

8. Id., 30.

9. This description of innovation budgeting is excerpted and paraphrased from an article by Michael F. Latimer, "Linking Strategy-Based Costing and Innovation-Based Budgeting," *Strategic Finance* (March 2001): 39–42.

10. The authors devised this heading, "Beyond Budgeting," based on associations with CAM-I. Later during research, they discovered that the same words were the title for an excellent article on the subject. Jeremy Hope and Robin Fraser,

"Beyond Budgeting," *Emerging Practices in Cost Management: 2001-2 Edition*, Chapter D1, James B. Edwards, ed. (Valhalla, NY: WG&L/RIA, 2001).

11. Scott Leibs, "Techwatch," *CFO Magazine* (August 2001): 19.
12. Ibid.

CHAPTER 4

Operational Resource Accounting

After reading this chapter you will be able to

- Contrast operational and financial cost management models
- Appreciate an integrated perspective of organizational resource management
- Understand inventory and capacity management, and product/service rationalization
- View from a wider perspective expense item management and employee headcount control
- View pricing from an enhanced perspective
- Create a conceptual bridge between conventional and advanced cost management practices
- Evaluate and select resource management projects that fit your organization

From this chapter forward, the term *resource* will be used interchangeably with *cost*, but the value-conscious connotations of the former will be emphasized as the discussion expands to include more mature cost management methodologies. Cost has developed negative connotations due to the legacies of conventional systems still struggling without operational and strategic guidance. In the static, conventional systems, costs are bad; costs are a necessary evil. In the world of the purely financial mind-set, revenue without cost is the ideal. Sound naïve? Consider the recent dot-com saga. Wasn't "revenue without cost" the theme? A healthier, more realistic perspective sees expenditures as resources to fuel revenue. Thus the word "resource" on its own can clear a cost-muddled head and provide a fresh perspective. Just feel the difference between "operational resource accounting" and "financial cost accounting." Sometimes a rose by another name does smell sweeter.

Operational resource accounting provides a conceptual bridge to advanced cost management practices, as it extends the perspectives of financial cost management information with two fundamental principles:

1. *Resources* fuel the profit imperative; therefore, the primary responsibility of the cost accounting function is to make resource utilization information visible to cross-functional managers within an organizational context and purpose.

2. Guided by strategy, organizational design, operations, and activities *execute the processes* that generate profit and market success.

The information generated with an operational resource accounting perspective:

- Places operational processes in the context of a cross-functional model of wealth creation.
- Uses operational processes as the primary management focus rather than financial results.

Initially, the *financial-cost* perspective is an important viewpoint, but its information perspective is limited. Next, the *operations-process* dimension increases management's depth of insight, thereby promoting decisions based on more complete information. Increased insight and information generate more options and choices that enhance the decision-making process. Later chapters add a third perspective—*tactics and strategy*—that complete management's range of vision. Together, these three perspectives make resources visible, manageable, and purposeful.

In spite of the impressive array of technology and management tools currently available to executives, most organizations continue to report failures in large, expensive change initiatives, mergers and acquisitions, and strategic execution. Cost management systems are neither the culprit nor the cure. However, a myopic focus on financial/cost measures, without attention to what drives these measures, is a root cause of failure to execute stated objectives. Functional protectionism and internal competition for resources are more explicit causes of failure, although these behaviors are often masked in cost-based control systems that force functions to meet misaligned performance standards in isolation. Operational resource accounting provides a more integrated, cross-functional perspective on organizational resources that corrects these common experiences.

The operational-process perspective is a way of *seeing* an organization as an interdependent unit, without artificial functional boundaries, but with functional expertise contributions. This perspective encourages optimization of limited organizational resources and targets them toward applications for the common good. By viewing familiar business activities through the more panoramic operational/process lens, a critical foundation is laid for the more mature cost accounting methods described in upcoming chapters.

Accounting for resources is not just about cost. Resource accounting creates decision-support information for activity visibility, process timing, and continuous feedback for diverse management interests—strategic, operational, fiduciary.

Examples of situations where the operational/process perspective is required for good cost management include product customization that requires high inventory levels, and the demands of seasonal production requirements on capacity. Terminology associated with such concerns are explained next.

- *Backflush Accounting.* A manufacturing inventory accounting method that records product labor, material, and overhead costs at the time that the product is shipped to the customer, thereby effectively eliminating conventional inventory accounts. This method can only be used in an advanced manufacturing environment where inventory levels are near zero, and from an accounting perspective, immaterial.
- *Break-Even Analysis.* A particular form of cost-volume-profit (CVP) calculation where total revenue equals total expenditures; that is, net income equals zero. Put simply, no loss, but no profit either.
- *Capacity.* Performance ability given specified conditions and constraints of equipment, space, personnel, and techniques.
    - *Theoretical capacity.* Maximum possible output (i.e., 100 percent)
    - *Practical capacity.* Theoretical capacity adjusted for expected conditions: training of new hires, equipment downtime, vacations, and sick leave, and so on (i.e., usually calculated at about 80 to 85 percent of theoretical)
    - *Actual capacity.* Real output achieved (i.e., productive time realized as a portion of theoretical)
- *Just-in-Time Production.* A set of lean manufacturing practices used primarily in repetitive manufacturing processes that work to minimize waste by (1) creating efficient flow processes through linked work centers, and (2) eliminating any activity that adds cost without adding value. As materials move through the assembly process across a work cell, the right part can be found in the right place at the right time. See the Lean Manufacturing section in Chapter 6 for a detailed discussion.
- *Kanban.* Japanese word meaning card or visible record; popular pull-system method in Just-in-Time manufacturing systems

where one or two cards attached to small batches provide a visible signal across different work teams authorizing sub-assembly movement and production activities coordinated by a Materials Requirements Planning (MRP) or other schedule-based production system.

- *Operations—Organizational Activities.* From *opus*-work; often thought of as the counterparts of financial transactions in that "operations" activities lead to financial transactions (e.g., the purchase of material, billing for services).

- *Price.* A relative concept dependent on time, market, cost, competition, government regulations, and type of customer (e.g. trade, wholesale, cash). In essence, price is the monetary value asked for a product or service. Typically, in accounting, price is the amount received for a sale or the amount paid for materials and services. *Transfer pricing* is a method of recording sales within an organizational entity, usually from one responsibility center to another. Such prices should be set to benefit the entire organization, but profit center motivations often make this difficult.

  Price variance is the monetary difference between the standard (i.e. list, expected) price and the actual price paid. On the revenue side, the variance is booked as customer credit, allowance, or discount. On the accounts payable side, the price variance is typically a discount based on quantity, condition of goods, or other factors. The *purchase price variance,* is a conventional calculation in standard costing. (See Chapter 3 for more on variances.)

- *Quality at the Source.* A method of quality management used in lean manufacturing environments where quality inspection and product rework occur at any point during production, rather than sampling at receipt of goods and after final assembly as in traditional manufacturing environments.

Contrasting Operational and Financial Methods

Finance and operations were not always strangers; nor were they always at odds with each other. In *Relevance Lost: The Rise and Fall of Management Accounting*, H. Thomas Johnson and Robert S. Kaplan argue that the "fall of management accounting" is a twentieth-century phenomenon:

> After 1925 a subtle change occurred in the information used by managers to direct the affairs of complex hierarchies. Until the 1920s, managers invariably relied on information about the underlying processes, transactions, and events that produce financial numbers. By the 1960s and 1970s, however, managers commonly relied on the financial numbers alone.[1]

Johnson and Kaplan go on to explore probable causes for this shift to a financial view of the business. Their exploration includes the high cost of information gathering prior to the computer age, the influence of academic financial theory, the emergence of audit practices, and the 1913 United States Constitutional Amendment that established federal income tax.[2] The shift of primary focus away from operations toward financial management models left a serious operations information gap for more than fifty years. Operational information became even more inadequate as multinational organizations became more complex and as economic markets became more volatile.

Today, one of the most dangerous factors of all is that many executives believe that they are making decisions with advanced information and accounting models, when in fact, they are not. The growing popularity of Enterprise Resource Planning (ERP) systems contributes to this belief. Too frequently, ERP installations merely automate conventional paradigms. Recently, Kaplan stated, "I suspect that many more companies believe that they are in Stage IV than are actually in Stage IV. A good number of those may actually still be in Stage II, running essentially volume-based costing systems on advanced enterprise software."[3]

Operational Resource Accounting

While most business publishers suggest that many organizations are actively experimenting with new, mature cost accounting systems, most organizations continue to make decisions based on management information from 1980's-style systems. Read the following excerpt from *Relevance Lost* and decide from personal experience how much of the description pertains to the current management landscape, keeping in mind that this passage was written nearly fifteen years ago.

> Typical 1980s cost accounting systems are helpful neither for product costing nor for operational cost control; they do not provide information useful for cost management. The rationalization for their production and existence seems only for the periodic, usually monthly, financial reports prepared for senior management.... the preparation of periodic profit and loss statements for senior management has its roots in the decentralization movement earlier in the twentieth century. The periodic return on investment (ROI) measure was developed and used by innovative organizations such as the Du Pont Corporation and General Motors. In order to produce a monthly profit and loss (P&L) statement and ROI measure, the accounting group needed to be able to close the books each month to estimate and record all accruals and to make a reasonable allocation of the period's production expenses between inventory and cost of goods sold. There is no doubt that ROI control and the profit center form of organization were not only greatly useful but likely necessary for the growth and prosperity of large, hierarchical organizations during the past sixty years. Nevertheless, despite the successes, problems associated with short-term performance measures such as ROI have become painfully evident in recent years.[4]

All this begs the question, "If financial models are not the best source of good management information, what is?" The answer: A holistic blend of financial, operational, and strategic perspectives that encourages functional integration, clarity of organizational purpose, and predictable strategic execution.

The critical management insight from the operations/process information perspective is *seeing the advantages of integration* and managing functions for the production of *common wealth*. The logic of this perspective can be extrapolated to the detail of all organization functions.

Accounting for Resources Is Customized and Iterative

Managers creating or using an operational/process information perspective as the basis for cost management decision making quickly learn that their cost accounting information systems must be adaptable to changing conditions. They acknowledge impermanence as a part of doing business and understand that information management is an iterative process. Resource management is customized to some degree in every organization. When a firm takes the first steps in its evolution from traditional cost accounting to more advanced systems, several fundamental components need immediate, serious attention. These include inventory valuation comparability, consistency of formulas and calculations, expense item management, and, for manufacturing firms, a migration from a variance focus to more controllable, real-time measures. Traditional concepts such as inventory and expense items may sound immutable. They are not. Fortunately a variety of readily available mature resource management methods and tactics simultaneously provide decision-quality information *and* the required financial data. To meet changing conditions, a healthy organization may redesign its resource management approaches many times during its lifetime.

Companies that monitor their resource management systems to assure that they keep pace with evolutions in operations constantly cycle through the following exploratory questions:

- What advanced resource management approaches are available, and which ones apply to the most pressing needs within our organization?
- What are our current information system capabilities, and what would it take to migrate to preferred resource management methods?
- Considering our most important needs and available resources, how shall we redesign our resource management system?

The ability to focus attention on resources (not just cost) is the critical distinction between conventional cost accounting and mature cost/resource management information. Conventional theory is driven by accounting measures that depict the *effects of production volume*. Advanced systems relentlessly pursue the *elements that truly drive cost* (i.e., cost drivers) as well as the causes of complex cost structures.

Mature organizations that have broadened the scope of their decision-support information beyond the financial perspective have learned that managing strategic course corrections depends upon reliable, current measurements and indicators. If financial information represents organizational performance, what time period does this performance information summarize? The past; and the past is hard to change. Organizations that manage by financial information alone make decisions with a significant time lag. They focus too heavily on lagging indicators and lose the chance to react before problems make their way to the bottom line.

Exhibit 4.1 shows an example of an operations/resource-focused organization with a balanced set of leading and lagging indicators in their performance measurement set. Leading indicators measure the success of operations, processes, and activities as they occur. What can we do to improve the bottom line—now? The organization that balances leading and lagging indicators has many choices and can correlate

EXHIBIT 4.1

Leading Indicators and Process Management

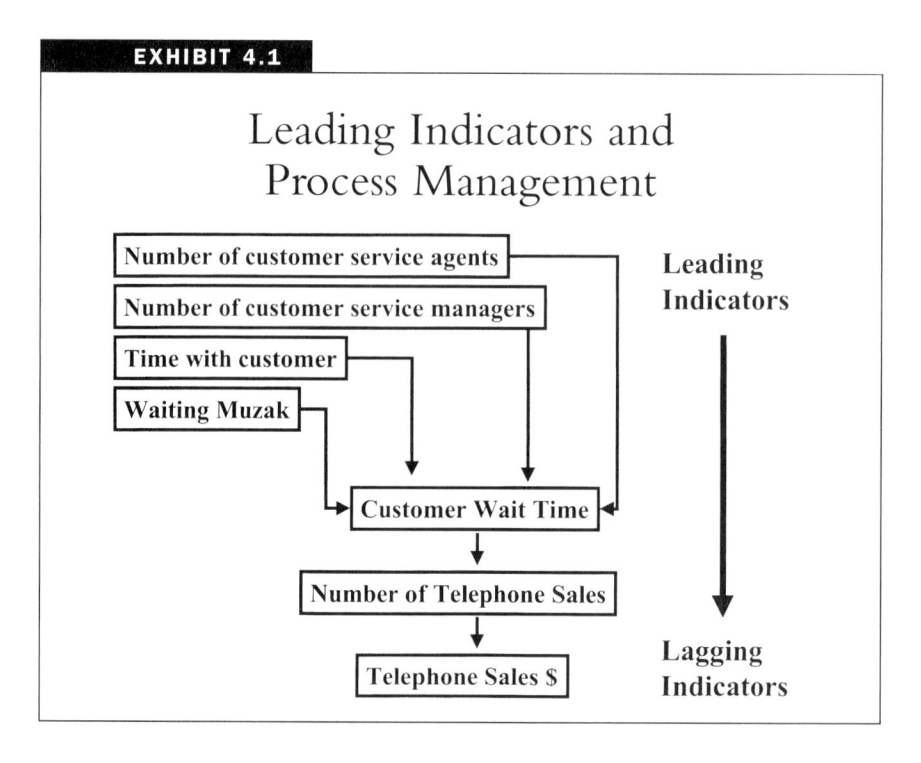

```
Number of customer service agents  ─┐
Number of customer service managers ─┤      Leading
Time with customer ─┐                │      Indicators
Waiting Muzak ─┐    │                │
               ↓    ↓                │
          Customer Wait Time ←───────┘
                   ↓
          Number of Telephone Sales
                   ↓
          Telephone Sales $            Lagging
                                       Indicators
```

different choices with different financial outcomes. In this example, the company can experiment with the cost of more service agents, managers, customer interface process reengineering, or the kind of music the customer listens to while on hold. Balanced measurement sets help identify those elements that truly utilize resources and drive cost.

No matter how resources are viewed, a resource management system must not lose the essential capabilities of a more conventional system, usually found in Stage II cost management systems:

- Determine the costs of products and product lines
- Cost planning and development for purposes of quotation, pricing, and business opportunity analysis
- Cost reduction activities (i.e., control and eliminate cost of scrap, waste, rework)
- Transfer pricing (i.e., intracompany)

- Production (and capacity) cost reporting and management
- Inventories control from component procurement through sales
- Deliver reasonably accurate estimates to the books of account using consistent principles

Control and Profit

Control and profit remain central priorities in systems that emphasize operations and resources as essential perspectives of cost management practice. Cost and resource structures organize competencies and capacities to yield maximum profit. However, while structures require oversight and control, human beings behave differently in positions of authority. No matter how small or large the sphere of influence, local "turf" becomes part of one's identity. Inevitably, the need to control overshadows the need to maximize the common wealth in many cultures.

Attempts to control, even in good faith, lead to organizational infrastructures that are better at tight surveillance than they are at generating profit. Those who are invested in the control structure believe at some level that the organization is better off under *their* control—that it will yield more profit than if they give up their control. In the absence of a commonly accepted control structure, or if the formal control structure is not clear, employees create local informal control frameworks.

What is the optimal organization control structure to yield the most profit? An examination of core operations through the lens of operational resource accounting will point any organization in the right direction when it attempts to answer this question.

Financially, nothing changes unless routine processes and activities change, thereby altering underlying cost structures. Processes do not change unless there is a strategic reason for doing so. This means that organizations maturing beyond the financial control systems of conventional cost accounting must begin to work with organizational design and strategy at the front end to produce gradual and steady changes in cost structure as the result of improved processes and clear strategic intentions. Unfortunately, executives schooled in conventional methods continue to go for the cost throat first. So, to make the distinction absolutely clear, each of the following sections in this chapter contrasts the "conventional view" with the operations-resource information perspective.

Analysis with a Purpose

Every analysis needs a decision-support *purpose*. Each analysis takes resources away from other activities, and usually more time than the requestor expects. So, curiosity and random exploration are not good enough reasons to spend those resources. Analysts need to be absolutely clear what they are expected to deliver. Therefore, two questions need asking:

1. What is the purpose of this analysis? The answer to this question comes through the synthesis of answers to four more fundamental questions:
    - How will the analysis be used?
    - What decisions will be made with the analysis results?
    - What problem is the analysis trying to shed light on, or solve?
    - Is the purpose of the investigation worth using valuable resources?

2. What are the best tools to perform the analysis based on its purpose?
    - Which disciplines are likely to understand this situation best?
    - Are financial factors most important?

- How can cross-functional views and multiple variables be included?
- Where has this question been asked before that we might find data?
- When was the last time our analytics were reviewed for currency?

Conventional cost accounting frameworks do not typically ask such questions. Accountants want to be known for their timely and accurate reporting capabilities. Therefore, because conventional analytics are readily available for all the concerns in Chapters 1 through 4, a time-constrained accountant within a conventional system may fall quickly to work using a traditional analytical method before fully understanding how the analysis will be used.

For example, a manufacturing executive may ask a cost accountant for a product mix analysis (i.e., how many of which products should we build to optimize resources)? The traditional operations/cost accounting tool for this analysis is linear programming (LP); however, if the accountant does not know the executive's analysis objectives, linear programming may be exactly the wrong tool to use. If the executive actually wants to promote the elimination of one or two products that are difficult to build and cause unfavorable manufacturing variances, the accountant using the LP without proper context to analyze a profitable production mix will look like a bonehead. The executive's true agenda (valid or not) is cloaked in a "product mix" analysis, for which a product profitability analysis is more appropriate—an analysis where the negative variances are disaggregated and charged to products directly and not just reported in lump sum on the income statement.

Like information technology specialists, experienced accountants often find that executives are not sure what they really want, even when they behave otherwise. Wanting to appear "in control" and knowledgeable, this kind of executive asks for a type of accounting analysis that *seems* like the right one based on academic coursework, current reading, or even on personal experience. For their part, endeavoring to supply good service and avoid the discomfort of questioning superiors, accountants may be tempted to perform the work as requested without exploring the context and purpose. After all, accounting is a support function and accountants are trained to comply with information requests. Both the executive and the accountant would be better served by engaging in an open dialogue.

Inventory Management

A flavor for the contrast between conventional and operations-resource perspectives on inventory is presented in Exhibit 4.2, where resources, listed in the far left column, are contrasted in terms of conventional and advanced management methods. Mature manufacturers with highly repetitive production processes have developed Just-in-Time (JIT) methods to streamline the flow of production and minimize waste. JIT manufacturers define waste as any activity that adds cost without adding value. Therefore, they design process methodologies to minimize the costs of moving and storing inventory before, during, and after production.

Exhibit 4.2 contrasts more advanced operational resource management perspectives to conventional cost management systems at the same stages in the manufacturing process. For example, kanban methods create more efficient production flow by organizing subassembly components efficiently through the chain of work cells during production. Quality at the Source is another cost-saving methodology.

Note that the more mature method frequently presents the option of reducing or eliminating the activity and associated costs in question. In contrast, numerous complex, often redundant, activities characterize the conventional, financially based system that attempts to compensate

EXHIBIT 4.2

Manufacturing Inventory Management: Conventional Steps and Advanced Alternatives

Inventory Resources	Operations Functions	Accounting Functions	Remedies
Material/Components Receiving dock labor	Receiving function processes purchased material items	Record Inventory Asset and A/P Liability	Kaban, JIT: materials received directly to production
Quality assurance labor	Inspection for fitness/rejects	Record returns to supplier	Quality at the source, supplier certification: limits rejects
Warehouse/stockroom space Materials management labor	Material recorded and stored	Record inventory adjustments	Eliminated by Kaban, JIT, and backflush accounting
Production planning labor Materials management labor	Job process orders released Components kitted and issued to production	Record work in process (WIP) Inventory -- material	Eliminated by backflush accounting
Production labor Manufacturing supplies	Production routing Fabrication Machining Component assembly	Record WIP inventory -- labor and overhead	Replaced by lean/agile, cellular methods and cycle time management
Production labor Labor support materials	Final assembly	Record WIP inventory -- labor and overhead Record scrap	Eliminated by backflush accounting Quality-at-the-source
Quality assurance labor	Inspect for fitness/rejects	Record waste, rework labor, and material	Quality methods reduce inspection labor
Test labor Test equipment and materials	Examine product against fitness specifications	Record rejects, rework, scrap	Quality methods reduce inspection labor
Materials management labor	Store product in Finished Goods	Record Finished Goods Inventory	Eliminated by backflush accounting
Shipping labor and materials Transportation costs	Ship custom orders	Record Revenue, COGS	Cycle time and logistics management
Accounting and materials management labor	Periodic inventory counts	Record adjustments, obsolete excess inventory	Value-added inventory management

for control ineffectiveness by increasing the *number* of activities and control systems. In a detailed account of the many agencies responsible for the Enron bankruptcy, Jim Brimson's summary of conventional accounting professional tendencies hits the nail right on the head:

> How did this situation evolve? Where were the guardians of the accounting profession? The AICPA and the FASB spent time on the finer points of specific issues that are of minimal importance to a limited number of organizations. Such efforts misdirect management attention. Organizations have to expend vast resources to navigate complex GAAP regulations. This effort wastes an organization's valuable accounting time and resources that should be spent helping the organization create value through operational excellence.[5]

Brimson's theme runs throughout the rest of this chapter and Chapter 5. As described in the operations-resource information perspective, more mature methods strive to eliminate nonvalue-adding activities, where "value-added" is defined as "something the customer will pay for."

Conventional Accounting Inventory Perspectives

From a conventional accounting information perspective, inventory is an asset on the balance sheet—a class or group of materials not yet expensed or capitalized. Similarly, the interactive natures of processes affecting inventory also make it notoriously difficult to manage in a traditional framework. Since no single owner is responsible for inventory control, blame and abdication of responsibility are endemic to the traditional inventory management environment.

Manufacturers cannot afford to ignore inventory because it is usually one of their largest assets, and capacity to generate it one of their biggest concerns. Service organizations also carry a substantial part of their wealth in their inventory of human skills; however, these human assets are not reported on conventional statements.

In the first part of the twentieth century, inventory valuations first emerged from the external audits of financial statements. Today, inventory valuation continues to make up a healthy portion of many management accounting classroom textbooks, and inventory control still consumes significant internal and external employee hours in conventionally managed organizations. On top of this, many managers working within the constraints of conventional systems and, lacking better alternatives, continue to rely on inventory valuations calculated using standard costs.

As estimates, standard costs are useful conventions for budgets and financial statements, but they are almost never accurate representations of current product cost. (See ABC/M discussions in Chapters 3 and 5.)

Therefore, using standard cost information for real-time pricing, process management, and other cost-dependent decisions involves risk. The way a company is organized and managed, and the efficiency of its inventory management processes determine the value of the inventory asset. So it is the value of inventory, not its valuation, that should occupy the most vigilance.

A common inventory management mistake falls into the "software as solution" category. Only the truly naïve think that controlling inventory through sophisticated software applications (i.e., ERP) will eliminate inventory problems. Material Requirements Planning (MRP) preceded ERP. MRP systems attempt to determine optimum inventory quantities and then back into component orders from suppliers based on expected delivery lead times. The trouble with MRP systems is that they typically rely on unreliable sales forecasts. ERP inventory systems simply perpetuate this situation unless the underlying operational processes are changed first.

Operational Resource Accounting Inventory Perspectives

Interestingly, the operational resource accounting inventory perspective reflects the management thought of one hundred years ago, prior to the rise of external audits. As Johnson and Kaplan report, managers originally "developed cost accounts for two purposes: (1) to evaluate internal opportunities for gain from their resources, and (2) to control the internal processes and activities that generated those higher returns."[6]

This sounds remarkably similar to the operational resource accounting point of view—optimize operational resource utilization to maximize profit. Managing inventories "by the numbers" cannot meet this goal. On the other hand, operationally focused inventory managers can use the balance sheet to their advantage if they learn to see it in terms of the resources that it represents. Both inventory and cash accounts reside in the Current Assets section of the balance sheet. An operationally focused inventory manager with a cross-functional resource perspective thinks of inventory *as* cash, for cash is what it takes to translate resources into inventory, and cash is what inventory is expected to generate when it is sold. This encourages proactive inventory management as opposed to passive valuation and reporting.

Specifically, if conventional accounting cannot adequately manage inventory, what can? Some alternative ideas about inventory management arose during the operationally oriented Quality Movement of the 1980s and 1990s (see Chapter 5 section on TQM). Courageous manufacturers even dared to experiment with "zero inventory." Less aggressive approaches include JIT and kanban. These techniques attempt to reduce inventory levels by locating component materials at the point of use and placing inventory decisions in the hands of those making the product.

The point is that operationally focused inventory management cannot be performed by the accounting function alone. The web of cross-functional inventory-related impacts is complex and, therefore, needs to be treated in a holistic fashion.

Capacity Management

Capacity is determined for the organization as a whole with many assets working in an integrated fashion. Because capacity is irrelevant to the focus of financial reporting on recording and accumulating individual, isolated transactions, conventional accounting lacks the perspective required to manage capacity. To be blunt, it is not possible to manage capacity because the conventional methods do not measure capacity.

Conventional Accounting Capacity Perspectives

In contrast to inventory, capacity is easier to observe in a service organization than in a manufacturing firm. A service company has x human beings, multiplied by y working hours, supported by z equipment and other resources (e.g., computers, service vehicles). In a manufacturing company, capacity relies on the interaction of multiple functions and resources operating with cross-functional understanding: floor space, machine efficiency, raw material availability, and human effectiveness, to name a few. In both sectors, capacity determines an organization's ability to meet its customers/clients demands. Sports equipment manufacturers commonly experience seasonal changes in capacity requirements, as do tax preparation services. No company has complete control over the timing and level of demand for products/services. Thus, capacity oversight is often viewed as an ad hoc management activity, commonly called "firefighting."

To emphasize an earlier point, conventional accounting does not calculate any category of capacity—utilization, excess/idle, or misused. Traditional management accounting may attempt to track capacity, but for the most part leaves capacity management concerns to operations employees. Traditional accounting indirectly records the *results* of capacity utilization; however, it is of no help in learning how to make improvements based on this history.

Operational Resource Accounting Capacity Perspectives

From an operations resource accounting viewpoint, it is important to know if valuable resources are being utilized to generate profit, whether they are sitting idle, and of course, whether resources in use could be applied elsewhere to make greater profit—all concerns congruent with the profit imperative. Advanced cost management approaches such as activity-based and resource-based accounting (see Chapter 5) provide methods to calculate unused capacity and report it in hard numbers on financial statements. More mature methods are inherently operational because they work across the interconnected functions and processes that comprise available capacity.

The essence of capacity management from the operational resource accounting perspective is *quality availability*. Availability use state of labor, materials, machine time, and logi channels. If any of these are subquality—untrained labo "eat" parts, a consultant with a hangover—the resource cost more than it earns. Capacity management requires b to supply material and human resources, the quantity resources can perform, and the rapid connection to deliv

A more accurate "cost to produce" underlies the entire capacity management effort. When accounting systems fail to differentiate idle resources from those that consistently perform, profits decline while the reasons for unused capacity remain hidden. Once again, activity-based and resource-based accounting techniques can disclose a more accurate set of relationships between available resources and units or work produced.

It is unrealistic to believe that an organization can continuously hold the exact amount of resources it needs to meet changes in demand levels. It is inevitable that resources (including people) will either become idle but be retained for expected future demand, or run out on occasion. This ties into the earlier discussion of fixed and variable costs that depend on an operational context for their meaning. In other words, when capacity cannot be used for an unforeseeable period, management must translate this excess/idle capacity into either increased sales from new markets or reduced spending in some combination of product discontinuation, process outsourcing, equipment or plant sales, and employee termination.

Operational Resource Accounting

CJ McNair, practitioner and academic expert in the cost management field has an approach to capacity management that might be paraphrased as "find it—measure it—fix it." She discusses this tactic in "The Hidden Costs of Capacity."[7] First, she characterizes capacity issues in terms of waste. Next she identifies types of "hidden waste," including waste produced by management, technical sources, accounting requirements, and infrastructure. From a process improvement perspective, the consequent capacity management focus becomes idle capacity and the creation of ways to improve processes to eliminate or utilize the unused resources. Operationally oriented resource managers are more and more often "abandoning engineered standards" (i.e., traditional standard costing methods) and developing process measurements around a continuous improvement model that encourages sustainable change. It is worth noting that part of Dr. McNair's rationale for abandoning engineered standards is because they actually "build in acceptable levels of waste...."[8]

Perhaps the most difficult characteristic of capacity management is that it requires a long-term perspective. Making capacity management decisions based only on *this* month's earnings and *this* quarter's shareholder meeting does little to encourage the long view. However, managing capacity as a long-term operational resource creates sustainable value generation and profit.

Expense Item Management

Expense item reporting, tracking, and containment consumes resources. The question at hand is "What *value* is created in these activities?" Some of the more common categories of expense are listed in Exhibit 4.3. Many companies go to a great deal of trouble to enforce expense controls and verify expense validity. Tax laws require a certain level of vigilance here, but an intelligent balance must be sought between expense item accountability and wasted resources.

> **EXHIBIT 4.3**
>
> # Common Expense Categories
>
> **Function/Department**
> Selling
> Marketing
> Research (Product, Market)
> Strategic Planning
> Human Resources
> Customer Service
> Finance & Accounting
> Information Technology Services
>
> **Types (nonemployee)**
> **Travel:** meals, lodging, transportation
>
> **Rentals/Leases:** copiers, computers, projectors
>
> **Supplies:** paper, forms, promotional pieces
>
> **Phone Lines:** long distance
>
> **Advertising space and time**
>
> **Professional services, legal, tax, contractors**
>
> **Training:** instructors, materials, participant time

Conventional Accounting Expense Item Perspectives

In terms of conventional accounting systems and their tight focus on the generation of financial reports, expense items are to the income statement SG&A section what COGS is to the statement's Gross Margin section. The focus of conventional accounting system analyses continues to be the relationship between expenses and profit, and analyses targets typically examine things like copying costs, computer equipment, and travel and entertainment (the winner and still champion for most "disturbing" conventional expense item analyses).

Functional expense areas such as advertising and IT are often subjected to scrutiny. The search is active and ongoing for performance metrics related to advertising dollars and IT investments.[9] These areas are treated more like capital investments than expense categories.

Information technology investments are an analytical thorn in the side for financial professionals working in conventional accounting systems: "We know we need the stuff, but we can't say exactly what it's doing for us." The wave of ERP implementations in the last decade has made this problem especially urgent.[10] Conventional financial analysis tools are simply incapable of depicting complex assessments like IT system value, the impact of advertising on sales volume, or influence of brand on stock price. These examinations require far more sophisticated approaches, such as multiple regression analyses and other advanced statistical methods set in operational or strategic contexts. Clearly, conventional analytic tools designed to monitor pencils and paper clips cannot capture the value of integrated investments.

Expense items are the favorite targets during cost-cutting efforts. Cut advertising by 30 percent. Easy. Delay those three R&D projects we haven't started. Easy. Nobody travels until further notice. Easy. Now predict the impact of lost sales, outdated products, missed customer contacts, and their subsequent effect on profitability. Cost cutting is easy. Managing resources takes skill and a broader perspective.

Operational Resource Accounting Expense Item Perspectives

Operational resource accounting systems see every resource (i.e., cost, expense, revenue, assets) at work within the context of a value-generation process. Departments, teams, and individuals work cross-functionally to create the "big picture." Consequently, the specimen slide of microscopic expense item control transforms to the telescopic panorama of resources working together to create value and common wealth.

Recall that, by definition, an expense is an expired cost. This means that the resource value is history: it can be reported, but it cannot be changed. Operational resource managers spend little time on such analyses. What's the point?

The success or failure of most business initiatives depends on many variables, not just a single technology investment or an advertising campaign. For example, a complex mix of variables affects the lagging indicators, brand equity, and average share price. Consider a typical mix of variables that directly or indirectly impact average share price: advertising, profit, brand equity, pricing, promotions, and earnings. Care to make a predictive model out of these? Advertising agencies are usually more than willing to help prove their case. Executives spending resources on advertising need to put some blood, sweat, and tears into justifying advertising expenditures. What value do they really create? Business professionals who continue to believe that advertising cannot be linked to financial results need to bone up on recent work on models that do indeed make such relationships visible. It is expected that within a few years these hard-to-get-at connections will become not only visible, but predictable.[11]

As an inherently operational function, information technology serves as a model for operational resource expense item valuation and management. Operationally oriented IT teams pay close attention to company strategy, making sure that applications development has a clear strategic purpose. They also develop performance metrics that clearly communicate IT contributions and adherence to service-level agreements. A few IT functions have actually managed to transform themselves into revenue centers by providing valued services to external customers.

Finally, getting back down to the compliance side of expense item management, how do operational resource accounting systems work with those travel and expense (T & E) reports? Automation was helped, and several software companies have stepped up to the plate. A few companies have stopped T & E reporting altogether, except for retaining the required receipts for the IRS. Expense items are not tracked to enforce compliance. Expense items become part of an interrelated set of operational performance measures. In these companies, managers and executives are given a T & E budget that must not be exceeded but

Operational Resource Accounting

that can be used at the professional's discretion. "Oh, you didn't make your sales quota, but you've maxed your expense account? Hmmm...we need to talk."

All of these operational resource accounting examples have some common advantages over the less mature conventional methods. They:

- View expense items as part of a cross-functional process leading to profitability.
- Seek to identify and understand multiple influential variables, as opposed to containing costs in isolation.
- Connect expense items to expected value creation (i.e., profit).
- Promote understanding of and alignment with customer/client needs.
- Reduce compliance work, including authorizations and audits.
- Automate transactions (e.g., a flight charged on a credit card is automatically posted to an "airfare expense account").
- Manage by exception, requiring management action only when dollar limits are exceeded or a policy is breached.
- First and foremost, honor the strategic and process goals of the activity.

Employee Headcount Control

The operational-resource information framework differs most markedly from conventional systems in its perspective on the value of human beings. For who or what, if not human beings, is the ultimate overseer of wealth creation—not just executives, but every employee. But, most of today's top managers were trained in a competitive paradigm where financial capital serves as the key resource and foundation for making decisions. Two problems with this view became obvious in the 1990s. First, the value of knowledge and intellectual capital clearly proved that

IN THE REAL WORLD

The "Little Person" on the Line

This is a true story about one manufacturing employee, but truly, it is also the story of many. Dana works on the factory floor of a window manufacturer that employs thousands of people. Dana's job focuses on the fitting and sealing of glass to wood and metal. If the work is done poorly, the windows leak—a fact that becomes apparent long after the window has left her workstation. Dana knows why some windows fail quality standards, and she has definite ideas about ways the problems can be corrected. She has even tried to share these ideas with her supervisor, but nothing has changed. "I'm just the little person on the line!" she sneers angrily to a coworker over a lunch break one day. The coworker shares Dana's frustration and commiserates, "Yeah, what could *we* possibly know about the way things work? We only *make* the things every day!"

Traditional, hierarchical organizations often lack the communication channels to make improvements. Executives, managers, and supervisors make all the decisions and figure out all the solutions to problems. Line employees who transform raw materials into finished products are not encouraged to share improvement ideas. When they suggest "a better way," supervisors are often too busy to test the idea, and so keep following standard processes. Yet, insights lie in the hands and minds of line workers—solutions to defect, rework, and cost management problems. The line worker makes or breaks value as much as any employee. Four operational resource principles help align every employee's energy and intelligence:

1. Clearly communicate what is important to the company as a whole. Everyone knows that making money is essential, but knowing how each job contributes to that end requires specific, repetitive communication.

Operational Resource Accounting

> **IN THE REAL WORLD CONTINUED**
>
> **②** Line workers in manufacturing convert valuable raw material resources into saleable products that are the chief means of revenue generation. To produce this revenue, they need to know why "doing a good job" is important. In addition, they can often help make job performance more efficient and effective.
>
> **③** In a service organization, the line worker is much closer to the customer. Knowing how and why to "do a good job" is immediately visible to customers and clients.
>
> **④** Strategic execution occurs only in operations processes and activities; therefore, this is where value creation needs to be understood most thoroughly.

some resources could be virtually infinite. Second, crafting and implementing a strategic market position or developing an excellent core competency takes time, and the pace of change in the last two decades argues against taking too much time. Critical factors shift in the time it takes to put a strategy or competence in place.

What's an executive to do? Some pioneering leaders are turning to their most flexible, adaptable, trainable, and unlimited resource—the energy and creativity of people who drive the process excellence and create the market image. Viewing people as the chief financial resource is a long, long way from the conventional financial view of human resources. Technology, especially wireless communications, has devalued bricks and mortar and enhanced the value of people. Simply put, people matter now more than ever. Many executives, however, are babes in the woods when it comes to understanding what workers want, how to recruit the best talent, and how to retain unique human resources.

Conventional Accounting Employee Headcount Control Perspectives

Conventional cost accounting breaks employees into roughly three categories—(1) direct labor, (2) manufacturing support labor, and (3) staff (i.e., SG&A)—because these categories fit nicely into income statement categories and standard cost structures. This works well as long as labor is a significant component of total cost. Times have changed since the inception of conventional accounting headcount methods. Throughout the twentieth century, direct labor steadily became a less significant cost component until at the turn of the century it accounted for less than 10 percent of total cost for the majority of manufacturers, and as low as 1 to 2 percent of the total costs for some highly automated plants. More and more, employees shift from being workers with knowledge to being knowledge workers. Increasingly, the organization's capital resides in people's heads. How does conventional accounting manage and control this new capital? It doesn't. There is no place for the value of human resources on the conventional balance sheet and no line item for *gain or loss from talent expense* on the income statement.

Operational Resource Accounting Employee Headcount Control Perspectives

Organizations that use operational resource accounting principles accept the simple relationship between people and operational processes: people run the processes that create value and profit. People cannot be appropriated as can financial and market capital. Employees need to be viewed as living, breathing value creators, who *choose* to exchange their time and energy for the value an organization can provide them, extrinsically and intrinsically. Machines, suppliers, materials, services, marketing, and advertising can all be easily interchanged. In contrast, once a human being matures into a strategic resource, that person cannot easily be

TIPS & TECHNIQUES

Questions to Ask Your Accountant about People

The answers to the queries below indicate how "people as resources" are viewed. Usually, financial reports reflect the entire organization culture's viewpoint.

1. What is our cost of labor as a percent of total cost?
2. Is any of our overhead allocated using direct labor hours/dollars?
3. What are the root causes of our employee turnover?
4. How much time does accounting staff spend analyzing labor variances?
5. How much time does it take and what does it cost us to train a (1) line worker, (2) supervisor, (3) IT professional?
6. What does it cost us when an employee walks out the door?

Notes:

- Look for advanced alternatives if questions 1 and 2 reveal that percent of labor is less than 12 percent and drives a significant part of overhead.
- If answers are hard to come by for questions 3, 5, and 6, human resources have yet to take their appropriate priority in the organization.

copied. An employee who has developed an enjoyable and productive life in the organization is hard to buy. Even if the employee can be "bought" by a competitor, the intellectual capital is difficult to translate into another company culture; thus, while gifted employees have become more expensive, their intellectual capital is not as transferable as financial capital.

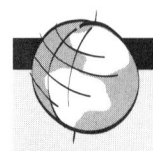

IN THE REAL WORLD

Focus on People— and Mean It!

People know whether or not their employers consider them valuable. Even though organizational mission statements and strategic objectives may contain high-sounding phrases about the importance of employees, very few firms make good on stated intentions. In such environments, public statements about the importance of people can backfire. If a mission statement speaks about "quality products" and quality standards fall short, the units of product won't complain about a faulty mission statement. Conversely, if the value of human beings is preached but not practiced, people observe the omission and ridicule the mission's hypocrisy. So executives are well advised to refrain from human-related pronouncements in their public statements unless they are prepared to put their money where their mouths are.

Within the software industry, where grueling hours are the norm, SAS Institute makes good on its commitment to employees, and is guided by four principles:

1. Treat everyone equally and fairly.
2. Trust people to do a good job.
3. Think long term.
4. Practice bottom-up decision making.

Laudable principles are good only if lived day to day. Some of the uncommon ways SAS stays true to its commitments are:

1. A 35-hour workweek—it's company policy.
2. Free on-site:
    a. medical facility for employees and their families
    b. day care
    c. gymnasium

> **IN THE REAL WORLD CONTINUED**
>
> ❸ Subsidized restaurants and cafes.
>
> ❹ A culture that recognizes the unique contributions each employee brings to the SAS Institute community.
>
> Source: Christopher A. Bartlett and Sumantra Ghosahl, "Building Competitive Advantage Through People," *MIT Sloan Management Review*, Winter 2002, volume 43, number 2, pp. 34–41. (The SAS story is on p. 40.)

Pricing

Pricing is another term that carries many connotations. At its most basic, pricing means the amount of currency charged for a product or service. A price may be prospective, as in a price quotation. More commonly, price is concurrent with product/service order (e.g., deposit, prepay), or postdelivery (e.g., invoice, fee statement). A price can be related to an external customer (a sale) or an internal customer (*transfer pricing* for intracompany sales).

Conventional Accounting Pricing Perspectives

Traditionally, all manufacturing pricing relies on standard costs, and in service firms, on standard billing rates. Conventional pricing in both these sectors is based on a *cost-plus* approach, where the "plus" refers to the profit margin the firm predicts it can add to cost based on the market's sensitivity to prices.

For much of the twentieth century, this cost-plus pricing model prevailed. Prior to the last quarter of the twentieth century, a combination of factors made it possible for suppliers to use their standard costs (assumed to be very close to actual) as the basis for price calculation. The factors included slow inflation rates, relatively low market competition, unavailability of relevant data (e.g., competitor prices, internal activity costs), and lack of alternative pricing approaches.

Breakeven and other *cost-volume-profit* (CVP) analyses are two additional conventional models sometimes used in pricing. They also typically rely on standard costs. All these pricing calculation methods have rapidly fallen from favor in the last ten to fifteen years due to the rate of change in business conditions, data availability, and price volatility.

Intracompany transfer pricing also relies on standard costs in a conventional cost system. Transfer pricing practices exist along a continuum. At one end, the seller calculates the transfer price, including costs of direct material and labor, plus predetermined overhead. Then, if the seller is a profit center, it adds a margin of profit. Often, the corporate entity sets a standard rate for this marginal profit. At the other end of the continuum, the transfer price transaction is calculated using only the variable costs related to the specific number of product units, and excludes overhead. This method is typically used when the seller is a cost center. Although theoretically transfer prices are supposed to mimic market prices, they rarely do.

When product/service requests are new to the organization, conventional companies seeking a better pricing model may base all prices on a current-actual or forecast cost. Many conventional accounting systems, especially those based on Material Requirements Planning (MRP), employ three cost fields—standard, current, actual—to provide richer information for developing price quotations. In this paradigm, every new customer request for a quotation can mean long, intensive analysis. Often the effort culminates in a best guess and usually does not capture organizationwide costs (e.g., customer service, field service response, relationship efforts). Organizations that use these conventional systems frequently employ full-time staff members whose sole responsibility is quotation and pricing.

Operational Resource Accounting Pricing Perspectives

Managers in an organization that uses operational resource accounting methodologies see pricing as a natural outcome of process efficiency and healthy partnerships with customers and clients. They recognize the customer as a critical and active partner in cost/price decisions. The organizations that use operational resource accounting methods *want* their customers and clients to know about internal, relevant costs—costs often driven by customers/clients themselves. These firms share cost information with customers as a way to determine the customers' true needs, examine what fulfilling those needs will cost, and then *with* the customer determine priority services/charges. In this kind of relationship, pricing decisions are impaired when either party works with incomplete or secretive cost information.

This open-book style of customer relations is foreign to the competitive worldview of the 1970s and 1980s—a view many executives in less mature, conventionally managed organizations still embrace. First things first: The managers of any organization must be able to see and understand its cost structure before they can contemplate moving to more open, mature approaches to accounting; conventional accounting systems fail to show them what they need to see. Activity-based and resource-based systems are particularly helpful in this regard, and are often used to analyze customer cost and profitability.[12] Target costing (also discussed in Chapter 6) is another mature method that supports strategic pricing.

Customers rarely turn down free services, but quickly prioritize their needs when services carry a charge. For example, a brand-name sporting goods manufacturer greatly valued its largest customer—another brand-name company; but underneath the millions in revenue from this customer, the accounting system booked many of the activity costs that clearly belonged to the large customer in general overhead accounts and SG&A, thereby burdening all the manufacturer's products instead of only the ones actually causing the costs. These activities included extra services required by the customer. For example, although the customer placed large orders, the orders contained hundreds of different drop-ship instructions that resulted in increased packaging, freight, and logistics expenditures for the manufacturer. An activity-based costing analysis focused on customer profitability revealed that this largest customer was also the most unprofitable!

Transfer pricing can also be readily adapted to the operational-resource information perspective. If internal managers in diverse organization units see a clear, consistent, and understandable flow of economic/cost information, they can much more easily find win-win solutions in this difficult, conflict-laden practice. Price quotations are facilitated by the information made available by the operational resource perspective.

Product/Service Development and Abandonment

Product/service development and abandonment (i.e., termination, discontinuance) are really two ends of the same process called *life cycle management* (see Chapter 6). Fifteen years ago, when product/service life cycles were still relatively long, and maturity rates slow, the long time intervals and the paucity of available methods made life cycle management a theoretical pipe dream. Since then, drastically shortened development timelines and the increasing rates of innovation have converged to make life cycle management a business necessity.

No other time in the life cycle of a product/service has more potential for cost management than the design and development phase. Design engineers can do many things to control costs, which include limiting the number of new components and, conversely, incorporating components that the firm already uses. Service providers can design highly efficient processes. In addition, providers of components, supplies, and services can be leveraged during the start-up phase.

Conventional Accounting Product/Service Development and Abandonment Perspectives

Development is usually a long, slow process in traditionally managed organizations. Make no mistake: An organization that continues to use conventional cost systems for decision making also manages conventionally in other important areas. In other words, if an organization's executives are satisfied with cost management information generated by a financial-only reporting system, it by default manages with limited information at the operational level. In addition, traditional cost management cultures do not typically foster risk-taking, nor do they practice rewarding creativity. Even though their executives may expect these qualities, they do not consciously cultivate them.

As a result, organizational control systems subject new initiatives to lengthy and rigid review and approval procedures in most conventional cost accounting atmospheres. For reasons all too familiar, the odds are against the fresh idea seeing the light of day. First, the new idea is conceived in a relatively sterile, risk-averse environment. Second, "the boss" must acknowledge parenthood of the new concept. Then procedure happens. Studies and competitive analyses may follow. Reviews and approvals take their pace. Product managers compete for development resources in a scarcity mind-set, ever narrowing the chances that the new idea might be embraced long enough to "grow up." If the idea navigates this far, some brave somebody has to find a budget and assign human resources. Frequently, by the time all this has happened, the idea has already withered or become an orphan, and a nimbler competitor has not only begun production, but also entered the marketplace.

Conventional companies use these process hierarchies because new product launches are, at best, educated guesses. Highly aggregated financial reporting and standard cost structures cannot begin to inform new endeavors. With limited support information, management becomes culturally conditioned to be uncomfortable with risk. Risk is part of every new product/service launch; however, conventional accounting systems magnify risk because they attempt to make decisions using conservative financial approaches (i.e., payback rates, ROI hurdle rates, and discounted cash flow methods).

Similarly, at the slightest suggestion that a product/service needs to be abandoned because its life cycle has ended, the lack of appropriate information throws the decision into political territory. Sales personnel argue for a "full product line." Production staff members negotiate for a more reasonable product mix. Conventional cost accountants become frustrated because they cannot provide reliable information on product and customer profitability. In making abandonment decisions, executives must rely on experience and intuition rather than clear performance data.

Operational Resource Accounting
Product/Service Development and Abandonment
Perspectives

Flexible. Agile. Lean. Innovative. These are words frequently used to describe organizations that have learned to add a new layer of operational resource information to the financial substrate. Organizations that emphasize the importance of operational information are lean, but they "waste" time prodigiously on creative endeavors. They are agile, but in contrast to their financially limited traditional counterparts, they live by rigorous development procedures that can be executed rapidly to match market speed. They manage innovation with equally ruthless withdrawal from markets when advantage wanes.

Organizations that add operational metrics information to complement the financials are flexible, but they carefully shepherd human resource skills, regularly upgrade skill profiles, and deliberately manage recruiting and retention. In short, these operationally focused organizations take the time to learn how to measure and manage flexibility, agility, fitness, and innovation for human and financial capital.

At the end of the natural life cycle, operational resource accounting methods for measuring and gathering financial and operational information, such as activity-based and resource-based analyses, clearly point out when it is "time to get out of the pool."

Project and Initiative Evaluation

New product and service development is but one important area for innovation management. Healthy organizations continually renew their own internal processes and the people who drive them. Strategic planning, total quality efforts, performance measurement initiatives, and many more "tools in the toolbox" are all aimed at continually getting better. Like products and services, projects and initiatives also have a life cycle that is a continuous process from emergence through concept development, prototype launch, implementation, maintenance, and renewal or abandonment.

Change efforts generate more uncertainty than any other organizational activity. The efforts are usually engaged because something seems wrong or needs improvement, or someone has an idea how it might be fixed, but no one really knows if the energy and resources devoted to the change initiative will pay off. Even so, executives continue to authorize significant, costly organizational change projects based on imperfect information.

Conventional Accounting Project and Initiative Evaluation Perspectives

The conventional mind-set just wishes everything would just settle down. A thoughtful strategic plan is crafted, and then the business condition assumptions that formed the basis of its logic change overnight. Dealing with a range of uncertainties is a reasonably simple definition for management practice. As a system of management, conventional accounting was built a long time ago for stable, slow-changing organizations and a limited business information environment.

Traditional firms take on projects and initiatives with high hopes and low budgets and virtually no decision-support information. People are frequently asked to take on the extra work of the change initiative or technical project in addition to their full-time-plus regular jobs. Busy executives raise their hands, bless the project, and then disappear. They reappear for monthly or quarterly reviews, and usually hear that the project has come up against "obstacles." Lack of top management commitment and failure to assign appropriate project resources are both near the top of the list of reasons for project dissatisfaction and abandonment.

Conventional accounting systems support change initiative decision making and management from a purely financial, "I told you so" information perspective. In monitoring change, financial numbers are the first to abdicate. Whereas conventional cost accounting assigns and tracks R&D project expenditures by an account number, improvement projects frequently receive no charge numbers, and expenditures are not tracked. Naturally, without operationally oriented performance measurements, initiative objectives, milestones, and achievements remain hazy.

The conventional cost accounting view of change management can be summed up in ten simple words: The best way to manage risk is to avoid it. The conventional approach tries to leave little to chance but is continually "surprised." Formulas drive results. Accountants report variances. Deviations from performance standards remain mysteries.

Operational Resource Accounting Project and Initiative Evaluation Perspectives

There is always work to be done. With the benefit of a complementary layer of operational metrics information, managers recognize that, like life, the process of "doing business" is dynamic, not static. When work is performed without expectation of permanent solutions, and so-called creative failure is celebrated for its lessons, activities regularly adjust from day to day, and continuous change becomes part of daily work life, not a periodic spectacle. Specifically, when included in the decision-support database with the financials, operational information explores the very nature and actual behavior of resources/cost; and through the exploration, managers build professional experience and useful knowledge incrementally.

Since operational information enhances the understanding of costs in terms of resource value, executives understand that major change initiatives cannot be accomplished with existing staff and resources in current configurations. Operationally informed executives do their homework, commit resources with confidence, and more often than not, lead initiatives themselves. Committed resources mean peoples' time (additional staff or release time of existing staff), space (project headquarters), and appropriate equipment. It does not always mean lavish budgets; it does mean reasonable budgets with periodic accountability. Along with financial accountability, executives put in place operational project milestone reporting and, later, expectation for improvements to financial and nonfinancial metrics. Tracking numbers and performance measures (i.e., expectations for milestones, deliverables, budget adherence) are designed as part of the initiative.

Perhaps most important, because the organizations that manage by operational and resource information are by definition culturally more holistic and cross-functional, executives keep an eye on (and a hand in) the multiple projects around the organizations. By doing so, they avert duplication of effort, cross-pollinate insights between projects, and oversee project management as an integrated activity across all initiatives.

Summary and Lessons from the Field

The best way to sum up this chapter is with a riddle. "What is only two decades old, bigger than Microsoft, and the best-performing stock of the 1990s?" Most business people guess right with just a little thought. The answer, of course, is Dell Corporation, "the world's largest PC company."[13] There is a good reason why people like Michael Dell and their enterprises become legends: They change everything. They blow the socks off complacent competitors; they have a passion for giving customers value for money; they know their operations inside out; they are forever focused on "the next big thing"; and they see "doing business" as one huge process, end to end. Whatever they call their perspective, it fits snugly into an operations/resource view of value creation that depends upon current, readily available, continuously renewed operational information that supports the lagging financial information.

A quote from Michael Dell states it well, "People look at Dell and they see the customer-facing aspects of the direct-business model, the one-to-one relationships. What is not really understood is that behind these relationships lies the entire value chain: invention, development, design, manufacturing, logistics, service, delivery, sales. The value created for our customer is a function of integrating all those things."[14] Michael Dell knows his operations and the resources they run on.

This chapter creates a bridge between conventional and more operationally mature perspectives by covering some important essentials of how different information perspectives determine management work life from both conventional and mature viewpoints. The most important takeaway is not a technique or a method, but a point of view:

accounting for and managing the resources that fuel operations. This perspective recognizes cost as the raw stuff of value, the resources upon which value is built and revenue generated. Costs—resources—value: these three cannot be separated.

In short, cost management *is* value management; and value management occurs only within organizational processes. Within these operational processes, only robust, deliberately designed business methods generate value. The path to value is the *process* road through the organization; the financial *results* simply reflect value created through process execution. In the simplest terms, profit is the accumulated outcome of the activities and processes performed by a firm's people.

All the various organization structures and management methods are created with control in mind—control of resources to yield maximum profit and/or to continue the life of the organizational entity. However, those who are invested in the control systems may stay with those systems for the wrong reasons: familiarity, locus of power, historical precedent, and, not least, comfort. The central question is not "How to continue current control mechanisms?", but rather, "What are the best systems of control for yielding maximum value?"

Persons who currently have control consciously or unconsciously believe that the organization is better off with their modes than with alternative means of carrying on business. But what are the characteristics of the organization structure that will yield maximum profit? More control? Less control? What kind of control? Where does control (i.e., decision making) reside? Obviously, answers vary across organizations and their cultures. The answer is created over and over until a solution, however temporary, is found or the entity ceases to operate. So although the "right" answers may not be clear, some of the wrong ones are beginning to surface. This iterative process is captured in the following points:

- Costs—resources—value are inseparable within *real* operations and activities.
- The primary purpose of inventory is to generate value, not to *be* valued.
- Capacity can't be managed if it can't be seen.
- Expense items are only worth the value they produce.
- People are the most important process, product, and purpose.
- Pricing is a partnership, not a competition.
- Products/services have natural life cycles, just like people.
- Internal projects and initiatives are all about renewal of people and processes.
- An operational-resource perspective is created with the operational information unique to each organization, not copied from others.

Endnotes

1. H. Thomas Johnson and Robert S. Kaplan, *Relevance Lost: The Rise and Fall of Management Accounting* (Boston: Harvard Business School Press, 1987 and 1991), 125–126.
2. Id., 126–135.
3. November 2001, personal communiqué from Dr. Kaplan to the authors.
4. Johnson and Kaplan, 195.
5. James Brimson, "Accounting Charlatanism or Information Fog?" *Journal of Cost Management* 16, no. 4 (2002): 37.
6. Johnson and Kaplan, 131.
7. CJ McNair, "The Hidden Costs of Capacity," *Handbook of Cost Management* (New York: Warren, Gorham & Lamont/RIA Group): Section E5.
8. Id., E5–26.

9. For example, see Kris Frieswick, "Performance Metrics: New Brand Day," *CFO Magazine* (November 2001): 97–99.

10. For an accessible discussion of this dilemma as it relates to ERP systems, see Eliyahu M. Goldratt, *Necessary But Not Sufficient* (Great Barrington, MA: North River Press, 2000).

11. Frieswick, 97–98.

12. For a cogent exposition of the power of customer profitability analysis, see Robert S. Kaplan and V.G. Narayanan, "Measuring and Managing Customer Profitability," *Journal of Cost Management* 15, no. 5 (2001): 5–15.

13. This information and what follows on Dell Corporation is from "Direct from Dell," *Technology Review* (Jul-Aug 2001): 79–83.

14. Id., 80.

CHAPTER 5

Process and Resource-Based Cost Management

After reading this chapter you will be able to

- Understand the conceptual workings of Total Quality Management (TQM), Theory of Constraints (TOC), Activity-Based Costing and Management (ABC/M), and Resource Consumption Accounting (RCA)
- Recognize how each method is designed to assist the understanding of cost and provide opportunities for cost structure improvement
- Gain a better understanding of which methodologies are the right fit for your organization

Once managers become aware that the structure of an organization is made up of processes, operational activities, and the resources that fuel them, they begin to see the need for enhanced decision-support information. Mapping existing internal processes is a good place to start, but this takes considerable time. The profit imperative relentlessly pressures executives (and what executive isn't pressured?) to seek rapid, effective solutions. Unfortunately, process mapping, insight, and improvement all take time, and time is a resource in short supply. This and the next two chapters develop management "selection sense" to more rapidly identify the best-fit framework for dealing with current conditions.

Method availability is not the issue. Business professionals can select from an array of approaches for understanding and improving processes. Most often, the chief exigencies are (1) funding and resources and (2) certainty about the effectiveness of the method. Project failure rates are high, and investing in improvement initiatives carries measurable risk.[1] Moreover, the process-oriented methodologies are only one category of business tools among several options that managers can choose as their organizations mature beyond conventional, financially myopic management. Chapter 6 discusses *tactics*, a set of tools targeted for specialized situations. Chapter 7 addresses the broad scope of strategic systems. Taken as a unit, Chapters 5, 6, and 7 provide a walking tour of available initiatives that enhance cost management decision making, as well as insights for choosing them.

Once an organization sets foot upon the path of continuous process improvement, life will never be the same. Though unsatisfactory initiative results and incomplete information are inevitable, setbacks encourage learning and refine the search for more appropriate approaches in healthy organizations. Eventually, with persistence and enough time in the marketplace, the informed management of a healthy firm develops a knack for learning from its missteps. They also gain experience in risk mitigation.

For example, consider the situation of a firearms manufacturer where cost *and* quality management had to be taken into account. At one point, the manufacturer's costs of rework, returned goods, and warranty fulfillment had increased dramatically. Executives realized that they were also at risk for liability suits over faulty products. They knew both cost and quality needed addressing, but they were unsure how to keep them in balance. Only a series of ever-improving trials stabilized the situation.

IN THE REAL WORLD

Cross-Functional Design of ABC Models Is a Critical Success Factor

During ABC's rise in popularity from 1980 to 1990, one of the authors implemented an activity-based costing system at a $40 million electronics division of Cummins Engine. Cummins was already an experienced TQM practitioner and encouraged experimentation with continuous improvement methods. In contrast, no other division had implemented ABC within the larger parent group that contained the electronics division. At the time, ABC software was both new and expensive; therefore, the division chose to house ABC data in the "current cost" function of its standard cost system, run on an IBM System 36 mainframe. ABC reporting was produced on spreadsheets on an ad hoc basis, usually for use in preparing price quotations for new business. The ABCM analyses proved supportive to more accurate and competitive quotation work, and the executive managers of the division considered it a significant improvement over the standard cost system that had previously been used for all costing functions. The comparative decision quality of the ABC information was due in large part to the work of a cross-functional ABC design and oversight team.

The manufacturing VP of the parent group became aware of the division's ABC work at a quarterly operations review. He charged his own financial group to make themselves familiar with the division's work and then develop their own ABC model. They did so. Although the group parent's model was technically equal to or better than the division's, ABCM languished at the parent. The primary reason: In spite of the division's strong recommendation for cross-functional design and oversight, the parent chose to develop the ABC model using only its financial professionals. They wanted to "get the design right" and then "roll it out to manufacturing." In spite of the fact that the model was sound, the manufacturing function did not

> **IN THE REAL WORLD CONTINUED**
>
> accept it because they had not participated in the design phase and did not trust the finance staff to understand operations. A second design phase, including nonfinancial function representatives, was engaged to move the ABC model toward organizational acceptance.
>
> Lesson learned: Always use a cross-functional team in ABC design. No matter how good financial professionals are, they cannot get the ABC design right without input from operations.

Total Quality Management

Although neither Total Quality Management (TQM) nor Theory of Constraints (TOC) was designed to be a cost management system, each has had undeniable impacts on the understanding and practical management of cost. In some of its earlier versions TQM did not explicitly include cost considerations. The earliest TQM mantra was, "Do the right things for quality improvement and the money will follow." Naturally, this incomplete view did not last very long, and within short order, the profit imperative motivated executives to establish concrete links between quality efforts and bottom-line results. In the late 1980s and the first half of the 1990s, statistical research from companies practicing TQM for over five years showed the clear relationship between TQM and financial results. However, the lag time between TQM-related process improvement *causes* and significant financial *effects* is measured in years, not months or quarters.[2] Quality control and TQM methods were each first implemented in the manufacturing sector; service sector quality efforts came later.

Core TQM Principles and Management Objectives

An important Quality Management insight, stated in the Pareto principle, states that 80 percent of all problems are generated by 20 percent of all causes; thus, management must discover and attend to the 20-percent causes. Quality efforts relentlessly probe processes for these causes, understanding that a process is a series of defined, reproducible steps within which resources are transformed to achieve a particular result that is valued by those the process is designed to serve. Statistical process control (SPC) tracks and helps remedy the chief causes of waste and error. SPC views process outcome variation within predefined tolerance levels, working from the core assumption that variation exists in processes and activities that are designed for repetition. Some important TQM tenets that bear directly on cost management include:

- *Higher quality at lower costs.* This is the heart of TQM. The remaining four principles expand on this central tenet.
- *Fitness for use.* This means a finished product/service meets requirements for intended use, thereby reducing after-sales costs: warranty fulfillment, field repairs, and product returns.
- *Design.* The engineered construction protocols and procedures for creating a product/service that facilitate efficiency and effectiveness. Research clearly shows that significant (~80 percent) of product cost is determined during the design phase.
- *Conformance to intended-use requirements.* Conformance depends on how well quality design and efficient production yield a product/ service that is "fit for use." A more aggressive definition understands conformance as a *deficiency-free* product or service. Conformance cost impacts include reduced scrap and waste.
- *Customer satisfaction.* This refers to meeting or exceeding customer expectations.

Six additional TQM principles have become standard management practice in many businesses. The first four are attributed to Joseph Juran, and the last two to Philip Crosby.

1. Training in quality principles throughout the organization.
2. Applying project management to continuous improvement methods.
3. Top executive commitment and involvement in all TQM activities.
4. Focusing attention on quality management with the Pareto principle.[3]
5. Do it right the first time.
6. Zero defects.

TQM provided the impetus for *customer-focused* approaches of many kinds, including the Customer Relationship Management (CRM) and Partner Relationship Management (PRM) methods currently in vogue. *Waste elimination* in its many guises grew out of the TQM focus on continuous improvement. Thus, even though TQM is not designed to be a cost management system, its implementation impacts most aspects of revenue (customer), and cost (COGS, operating expenses).

TQM and Operations

TQM and operations maintain a directly interdependent relationship. As a quality management precursor to TQM, quality control methods include test protocols, inspection for errors (i.e., quality inspection), rejection of failed units, and a great deal of rework, scrap, and wasted resources. The costly and inefficient control/inspection era of quality management stands in sharp contrast to performance results and cost savings of the TQM "do it right the first time" and "zero defects" methods. TQM identifies and tracks product/service/process defects and variation within predetermined ranges called *tolerance thresholds*.

The ongoing development of fresh new TQM practices continues to be supported by quality achievement recognition in the form of prizes, such as the Baldrige National Quality Award, and in certifications, such as the ISO 9000 series. In addition, several organizations actively support TQM, including the Conference Board, American Society for Quality, and American Supplier Institute. These efforts to refine and enhance a variety of quality management practices have particularly helped businesses identify high-performing suppliers. For many corporate customers, supplier quality certification is a prerequisite for doing business.

TQM Advantages and Shortcomings for Cost Management Applications

TQM identifies resources that slip through the cracks of process as waste expenditures—a never-ending cost management improvement opportunity. As a mature management methodology proven in research and practice, managers may easily become complacent or bored with continuous TQM. Since everyone practices TQM, ongoing efforts do not appear to deliver any exciting competitive advantages. TQM may have evolved into a market-entry business practice, but how many times can a tainted bottle of over-the-counter medicine go to market? In addition, TQM continues to evolve, reinvent itself, and expand its applications to less tangible areas like information quality, the interface between human beings and technology, and even quality of life. For example, the City of Jacksonville, Florida, manages its operational processes with quality-of-life measurements.

TQM and Conventional Cost Accounting. A conventional accounting system is hard-pressed to directly justify TQM and improvement activities. Generally Accepted Accounting Principles (GAAP) are not designed to guide product and service quality management, and general ledger systems typically do not make it easy to track costs of quality. Obstacles to success arise from the very inception of TQM proposals within a conventionally managed cost accounting system. The cost-benefit analysis of TQM proposals must be timely, and proposal costs must be correlated with benefits over several accounting periods. Feedback reports on active TQM initiatives must reach managers while adjustments can still be made. Conventional cost accounting systems (Stage I and II) usually fall far short of these capabilities. Conventional systems have a well-earned reputation among TQM practitioners: These systems deliver reports too late and fail to capture the appropriate cost-benefit relationships.

Even with the inherent incompatibility of conventional systems with TQM requirements, financial professionals attempted to adjust accounting systems to integrate TQM requirements as it emerged as a management standard during the 1980s. Cost of quality (COQ) methods were the first of these attempts to develop in parallel with TQM. COQ modestly supports waste reduction related to poor quality, and reports on the resources expended on TQM efforts.

Executives intuitively understand the direct relationship between quality failures and bottom-line impact. However, failures in processes can remain hidden within conventional financial reporting. Finding the specific locations of process failures and then designing process remedies requires operations knowledge. Some of the initial COQ attempts to trace the improvement path include data reported in four COQ categories:

1. Prevention

2. Appraisal (later termed, detection)

3. Internal failure

4. External failure

Different COQ practices vary in their specific application, but all COQ approaches strive to calculate the resources to achieve performance improvement through practices in these four TQM categories and compare these expenditures to benefits that result from TQM efforts—

that is, TQM expenditures versus TQM savings. At heart, this is a classic cost-benefit analysis, but in practice, quite challenging for conventional accounting systems not designed with TQM in mind.

When examining some of the specific items that must be tracked under the first three COQ categories, it is easy to see why conventional accounting has a hard time. Consider the following: costs of supplier certification, TQM planning and training, and product engineering design changes.

TQM and Advanced Resource Management Methodologies. In the early days of TQM, there was so much opportunity to reduce waste that companies enjoyed considerable expenditure reduction in their initial efforts. As the easier initiatives were completed, it became harder to attain the same level of savings in the same amount of time with the same level of effort. Advanced methods have been developed to reach relatively inaccessible quality levels. Six Sigma, for example, is a statistical, data-driven, systematic approach to continuous improvement that seeks to achieve a 99.99966 percent level of quality. Motorola's Six Sigma quality efforts focus on process performance expressed in terms of statistical results. For any selected quality criterion, a six-sigma performance target is plus or minus six standard deviations. Another, more accessible improvement measure popularized by Motorola is defective parts per million (PPM). These measures help move organizations toward the zero defects TQM goal. Some process experts, such as Michael Hammer find fault with the relentless Six Sigma push for process perfection. If the process design is substandard, people can work as hard as they are able and achieve only insignificant improvement and savings.[4]

The intuitive links between quality management, cost reduction, and increased profitability encourage organizations to move toward advanced accounting and performance systems that can track and report process management progress and the cost savings achieved. Improvement intentions and targets need to be absolutely clear for even the advanced accounting systems. "Better quality" is an ambiguous goal. Defining the parameters of implementing "better" can mean the difference between a COQ of $1,000 and a COQ of $1,000,000. *Context* and specificity of requirements determine appropriate resource expenditure levels. Context relates to intended use. A heart pacemaker quality level generally has to be more reliable than a $50 pair of walkie-talkies.

So far, this discussion has covered the established rudiments of TQM that focus on relatively obvious, visible quality issues. More recent evolutions of TQM target subtler costs. CJ McNair in *The Profit Potential* identifies these "hidden costs of quality," including:

- Expediting
- Customer *dis*satisfaction
- Lost orders
- Stress
- Back-office waste[5]

Discovering and eliminating waste (i.e., expenditures) in these areas is much harder than finding the causes and solutions to defective materials and untrained employees. Quality-cost-profit linkages seem obvious, but try to monitor and manage them with conventional accounting information systems and hierarchy perspectives. Cultivating and influencing behavior is one of the most important characteristics of TQM and one of the most fruitful grounds for a close partnership between TQM and cost management.

Theory of Constraints

Dr. Eliyahu (Eli) Goldratt, the creator of Theory of Constraints (TOC), has also presented public lectures under the title, "Cost Accounting—Public Enemy Number One of Productivity."[6] So fifteen years ago,

Dr. Goldratt may very well have been annoyed and/or amused to find his approaches included in books about cost management. Rather rapidly, however, financial and operations professionals both recognized the value of TOC. TOC does not fit into any of the larger business categories such as "process," or "targeted tactic." Handbooks and method surveys usually tuck TOC carefully inside sections called something like "management trends." TOC really doesn't fit any conventional business or accounting category because it is one of the first of a growing number of science-based approaches called "systems thinking," a category that has yet to truly form and take root in organizational management. Thus the typical financial treatment of TOC frequently tries to blend TOC with financially based methods like ABC/M, instead of fitting the financial pieces into a larger, more comprehensive perspective on the management of the organization as a system. TOC is a *system* for thinking differently about organizational management.

Core TOC Principles and Management Objectives

As with many systems of thought, TOC must be understood in terms of the mind and intentions of its designer. The systems thinking approach inherent in TOC contrasts with conventional cost management in key organizational perspectives. Dr. Goldratt was trained first as a physicist. This training gave him a practical and rigorously scientific mind-set uncommon in business circles. TOC treats the organization as a dynamic physical system, and considers the chief management responsibility "to control and predict the behavior of the system."[7] This contrasts sharply with the fragmented departmental, functional, and center-oriented perspectives on most organization charts commonly taught in business curricula.

The physicist assesses management complexity by answering a fundamental question: "Observe the system and ask yourself, What is the minimum number of points you have to touch in order to impact the entire system? The more points you have to touch, the more complex the system.... I [Dr. Goldratt] think[s] that physics is based on a fundamental belief regarding the concept of 'complexity.' My impression is that physicists, in their search for more knowledge, are guided by the assumption that there are no complex systems in reality."[8]

An additional difference addresses the way employees manage organizational problems. In contrast to the scientific method, as a behavioral science, business management approaches (and sometimes solves) problems as if they occur in isolation rather than as a manifestation of the operations of the larger system in which they emerge. Lacking a holistic view, the common business approach usually addresses each problem separately.

The terms *bottleneck* and *throughput* are key to understanding the global organizational perspective possible with TOC. A bottleneck is a system constraint that hinders throughput optimization, which in turn impacts profit. Put another way, a constraint limits a system. If no constraint exists, the system theoretically has unlimited potential output. Bottlenecks and constraints are related to capacity; and, typically, lower capacity means greater risk of constraint. Later refinements in TOC addressed the scenario where market demand is the constraint (i.e., where market demand is less than supplier capacity).

The profit imperative remains a core TOC assumption. Throughput, a key TOC profitability measure is calculated as sales minus raw materials (alternatively, revenue minus totally variable costs). Constraints and throughput both assume that the goal of the majority of organizations is profit. Relative to profit, TOC poses two essential, systematic relationships between operations and financial results:

$$\text{Net Profit} = \text{Throughput} - \text{Operating Expense}; (NP = T - OE)$$

$$\text{Return on Investment} = (\text{Throughput} - \text{Operating Expense})/\text{Inventory};$$
$$(ROI = (T - OE)/I)$$

Process and Resource-Based Cost Management

According to TOC, operations management creates profit through ongoing process improvement. TOC claims that cost accounting has no answer to the question, "What is the process?" TOC process management does have an answer, which can be summarized in five activities:

1. Identify the system's constraint(s).
2. Decide how to exploit the system's constraint(s).
3. Subordinate everything else to the previous decision.
4. Elevate the system's constraint(s).
5. If, in a previous step, a constraint has been broken, go back to step 1, but do not allow inertia to become the system's constraint.

These five points comprise the rudiments of TOC.[9] Simply put, TOC elevates the management of process above the management of cost.

TOC and Operations

Manufacturing firms were the first to embrace TOC and implement it deep within their operations. TOC organizations can become fanatically devoted to Dr. Goldratt's approaches. The original TOC work concentrated strictly on manufacturing operations, but quickly spread to areas such as strategic planning, marketing, and human resources, and later to nonmanufacturing sectors. Since TOC was first embraced in the manufacturing sector, it developed strengths in logistics, distribution, production, and project management. One of Dr. Goldratt's most recent TOC novels, *Necessary But Not Sufficient*, explores the reasons that ERP implementations commonly fail to improve operations.[10] While TQM explicitly gives managers new, nonfinancial perspectives on the organization, TOC does so with a passion.

TOC Advantages and Shortcomings for Cost Management Applications

TOC and Conventional Cost Accounting. The TOC systems/process management focus contrasts sharply with traditional cost management perspectives. Conventional cost accounting managers see incremental and isolated improvements as productive and supportive of organizational goals. In TOC language, conventional cost accounting posits that "global improvement equals the sum of local improvements." In the TOC, or Throughput, perspective, a linked chain analogy depicts the fallacy of this equation because improvements in isolated links of the chain do not necessarily improve the strength of the chain.

Since a conventional cost accounting system relies on transaction data—each transaction a separate event—it is incapable of a global or system perspective except in "closing the books." Thus a conventional approach can only track and report on focused, separate improvement efforts and sum their cost savings, regardless of system interactions and impacts.

TOC and Advanced Resource Management Methodologies. Financial professionals working in firms that have adopted TOC usually practice so-called throughput accounting to reflect changes in operations. They frequently use a management accounting system separate from the general ledger system. The three chief elements of this accounting method are (1) throughput, (2) operating expenses, and (3) assets, especially inventory.

Except for inventory, throughput accountants view the balance sheet in the same way as conventional accountants. Throughput inventories resemble conventional direct costing inventories in that they contain only variable costs. Throughput accounting classifies all expenses not included in calculating throughput as operating expenses (OE). The profit or loss on a conventional income statement does not differ from a throughput income statement. The throughput line (i.e., sales minus raw materials) is conceptually similar to a conventional contribution margin, except that throughput does not deduct labor and overhead. Likewise, throughput accounting does not capitalize labor and overhead in inventory.

Inventory is a key management focus in TOC. Under the throughput paradigm, operating expenses and other assets influence inventory management. Unlike conventional accounting practices such as absorption accounting, which may actually encourage organizations to build unnecessary inventory, throughput accounting principles directly seek to prevent excess and obsolete inventories. Throughput is defined as "the rate at which the system generates money (i.e., incremental cash flows) through sales. Assets are defined as all the money the system invests in purchasing things the system intends to sell. Operating expenses are defined as all the money the system spends in turning inventory into throughput."[11]

In practice, the specific applications of throughput accounting particulars vary; however, two of this method's strengths are its relative simplicity and its ability to generate weekly or even daily reports. Since throughput accounting is not GAAP, and must be performed separately from official financial statements, the specifics of the TOC accounting design are less important than how throughput reporting supports the most important TOC goal: making money. More recently, Dr. Goldratt has expanded his systems thinking inherent in the TOC approach to include business problem solving, in general.

Activity-Based Costing, Budgeting, and Management

Activity-based costing (ABC) caused a great deal of excitement in accounting circles in the late 1980s. Unlike TQM and TOC, ABC was designed to present financial data. In fact, classic ABC theory provides a kind of safety net for conservative accountants: The classic ABC version of reality reconciles with the general ledger. In other words, total ABC costs must equal total general ledger costs. This feature reassures management at all levels when a firm first adopts ABC; ABC analyses do not abandon preexisting costs. The translation of the entire general ledger into ABC activity accounts/categories is a significant effort, and not always necessary if the targets of analysis do not include the entire organization. As executives come to trust ABC data and to mature in their use of it, they may choose to translate a limited group of general ledger accounts into an ABC format. For example, a single division, function, or product can be the analysis target. However, in a partial analysis there is a risk of overlooking some relevant costs in accounts not analyzed.

The consistency between ABC reconciliation features and the G/L encourages accounting professionals, also in transition, to engage proactive analysis and to offer their insights and recommendations to management. Their confidence is reinforced by the experience that, at last, the accountants do not have to sit on the sidelines, calling out results of plays already run. Instead, they get off the bench and into the game by proactively creating cost structure visibility. The financial roots of ABC may very well explain why it proliferated at a rapid rate (i.e., simply, accountants understand ABC better than nonfinancial models, hence more ably communicate its insights to executives). In turn, executive teams usually welcome ABC information as more relevant to decision support than inscrutable financial statements.

ABC was developed to address the inadequacy of general ledger information for decision making, and as it rapidly gained popularity, many seasoned accounting elders wryly observed that ABC was "just good cost accounting for operations." Conceptually, they were correct. ABC does indeed return to the operational roots of management science; however, it also furnishes an adaptable design and disciplined analyses within a language that can be shared among professionals. Prior to ABC, "good cost accounting" was created from the ground up in every organization.

Core ABC/M Principles and Management Objectives

Activity-based costing practitioners seek better understanding of the nature and behavior of cost through *resource*, *activity* and *cost object* analysis. The responsibility center management structure of the so-called financial era grew out of the need to assure control of ever-larger organizations (global) while allowing units and divisions to manage the day-to-day (local). Financial accounting systems brought a needed measure of consistency and comparability by requiring use of standard charts of

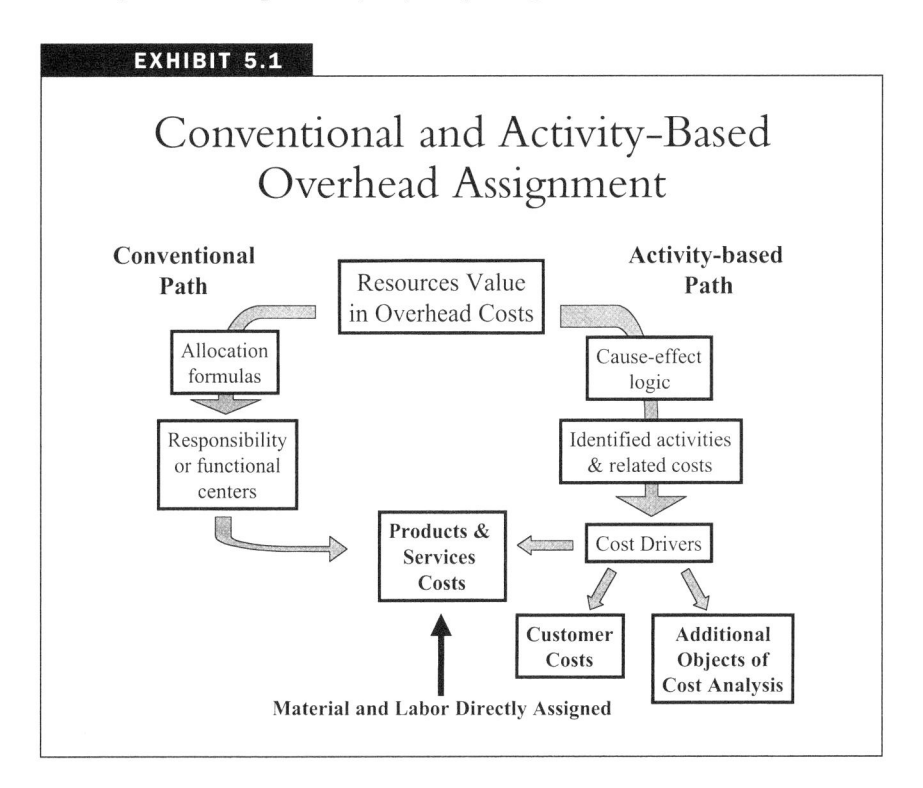

EXHIBIT 5.1

Conventional and Activity-Based Overhead Assignment

Conventional Path → Resources Value in Overhead Costs → Allocation formulas → Responsibility or functional centers → Products & Services Costs

Activity-based Path → Resources Value in Overhead Costs → Cause-effect logic → Identified activities & related costs → Cost Drivers → Products & Services Costs / Customer Costs / Additional Objects of Cost Analysis

Material and Labor Directly Assigned

accounts, standard cost systems, and financial report formats. Exhibit 5.1 parallels the conventional and ABC/M cost management focuses.

This conventional structure is well and good for efficient aggregation of financial results. However, it constrains the development of useful management information. Insight and the ability to manage suffer in two particular areas: (1) input-side resources and (2) overhead cost structures. ABC aims to address both shortcomings by clarifying how activities consume resources and by disaggregating overhead into its components and directly assigning costs to activities, whenever possible. By doing so, resources, mediated and structured through meaningful operational activities, are more accurately (i.e., in cause-effect fashion) assigned to cost objects, the targets of ABC analysis.

Activity-Based Costing. The ABC Glossary[12] defines activity-based costing as "a methodology that measures the cost and performance of cost objects, activities, and resources. Resource costs are assigned to activities based on their use of those resources, and activity costs are assigned to cost objects based on the cost objects' proportional use of those activities. Activity-based costing incorporates causal relationships between cost objects and activities and between activities and resources."[13] Resources fuel activities, and activities enable cost objects. Viewed from output back to input, cost objects consume activities and activities consume resources.

Two people in particular are generally credited with developing ABC theory and practice: Robin Cooper and Robert Kaplan.[14] Their initial work together focused on product costing in manufacturing environments. Cooper and Kaplan were also among the first to place a resource perspective prominently in their model and methods. The classic expenditure flow from the G/L to ABC reports clearly displays this prominence and looks like this:

specified in more detail by using activity *attribute* labels that further characterize each activity for cost structure analyses purposes. "Value-added" and "nonvalue-added" (i.e., waste) were among the first distinguishing attributes. Attributes can be related to time, performance, location, and variability, as well as any other objective or subjective descriptor that aids in cost structure insights and improvements.

Activity-Based Management. In its original applications, ABC simply gave better *visibility* to product and customer costs. Interesting as these may be, insights alone do not change cost structure; improvement actions do. Consequently, ABC quickly evolved into ABC/M, activity-based costing and management, where ABC is the technical cost reporting model, and ABM focuses on the specific management actions and initiatives undertaken to alter cost structure.

In the 1980s, TQM, TOC, and ABC developed side by side, with proponents from each camp often disparaging the others. By the time activity-based methods matured to include ABC/M, advanced practitioners actually began blending operationally focused improvement methods (e.g., TOC, TQM), with ABC insights to manage resources, processes, and costs simultaneously. ABC versions to assist in capacity management also arose. These developments amounted to a quantum leap in linking accounting and operational data.

Activity-Based Budgeting. Activity-based budgeting (ABB) evolved next. (See Chapter 3 for additional discussion of ABB.) Since cost pools of resources and activities are the first transformation point in translating expenditures from the G/L to the ABC model, the question of budget allocations naturally arises. As managers at all levels become more comfortable with the advantages of the ABC/M perspective, they also become more frustrated with the allocation of organizational resources through a conventional budget model (e.g., based on a fragile sales forecast, and/or on a plus or minus x percent change over last budget

Process and Resource-Based Cost Management

G/L Accounts → Resources → *Resource Cost Pools* → Activities → *Activity Cost Pools* → Cost Objects → ABC Reports

Resources, usually represented in dollars, move through the dynamics of the ABC model based on a cause-effect logic. *Cost pools* are essential components in moving costs from resources, the starting point of the ABC accounting method, to activities and on to cost objects. Cost object analysis is one of the primary reporting outputs of ABC work. As illustrated in Exhibit 5.1, cost objects, most typically products and customers, are the targets of ABC analysis, the reasons for ABC implementation, and the subjects of ABC management. Recall the twentieth-century manufacturing shift from a high to low labor dependency as a percent of COGS, and the inverse trend in overhead. This shift made overhead an increasingly significant portion of total cost, and thus an important analysis target.

Primarily, ABC aims to deconstruct the "peanut butter jar" of manufacturing overhead by reconfiguring expenditures in terms of available resources. These resources, in turn, are assigned to operations activities and subsequently linked to cost objects. As ABC practice evolved its customer and product profitability analyses, SG&A expenditures, in addition to overhead costs, were more frequently added to the "resource pools."

Resource drivers move resources from resource pools to activities. Resource drivers are the most reliable and accurate measure of how often and how much a demand is made on a resource by activities or other resources. A resource driver is used to assign resource costs to activities, and cost objects, or to other resources. Viewed from a traditional perspective, resource drivers create visible cause-effect links between G/L accounts and operational activities. In the same manner, *activity drivers* link resources to activity cost objects. Activity descriptions may be cycle). ABB logic is easy to see and very hard to implement. The obvious activity-based logic is that budgets are made up of resources designated to specified managers and their functional areas. It stands to reason that when activities change, budgets need to change.

From the beginning, activity-based models were heavily dependent on computerized models. An ABC model is nearly impossible to develop on green ledger paper, and spreadsheets lack the power to support even moderately complex models. Seeing a valid opportunity, software providers quickly stepped up to the plate in the last half of the 1980s.

ABC Software. Today, organizations can choose from a number of freestanding ABC/M software applications, and most ERP designs contain an option for an ABC module. Prices have decreased as the software competition escalated, and now there is no financial reason why a firm investing in ABC/M should not use a software package to ease implementation and encourage the use of ABC data. Recently speaking of customer profitability analysis, Robert S. Kaplan stated, "Activity-based costing (ABC) and associated software provide the conceptual framework for linking customer transactional data from ERP and CRM systems with financial information. With ABC, calculating individual customer profitability data becomes a straightforward exercise."[15]

ABC/M and Operations

Since ABC focuses on the management of resources, activities, and cost objects, it becomes an "economic map of the organization's expenses and profitability based on organizational activities," according to Cooper and Kaplan. They suggest calling an ABC model "an activity-based economic map," to more precisely express its purpose. [16]

A Stage III cost management system must contain an accounting model that partners with continuous improvement methods. Activity-based models endeavor to make operational activity costs visible, provide insights on cost structures, and monitor the results of cost structure improvement activities (i.e., continuous improvement). Improving cost structure means eliminating waste; therefore, by producing cost structure insights, ABC supports operations enhancements through improved financial/cost reporting. From an operational/resource perspective, all this improves the chances of wise resource management.

Specifically, an ABC model reveals expenditure flow and the activity structure of what goes on in day-to-day operations. ABC explores:

- The organization's set of current activities and the resources they consume
- The cost of performing current activities based on the cost of the resources consumed
- The difference between activities that need to be performed and those that can be changed or eliminated to improve the cost structure; in other words, the cost of activities consumed by customers, products, and other "cost objects"

Today, many early adopters of ABC/M have institutionalized their activity-based models (Stage III), and integrated them into ERPs (Stage IV). A number of these pioneers have moved on to organizationwide performance measurement and management (see Chapter 7), in which they use ABC information for the financial perspective of their performance reporting systems.

ABC/M Advantages and Shortcomings for Cost Management Applications

In its early days, ABC was hailed as the "miracle cure" for what ails the general ledger. Though not a cure-all, ABC definitely improves the decision-support quality of management information when appropriately applied. ABC arose just as nonfinancial managers had all but given up hope of extracting relevant information from G/L systems. On its own, ABC provides a level of insight not possible with conventional systems; however, "insights" do not automatically generate cost savings. To get the most out of ABC, management needs to follow a sequence:

1. Acquire reliable ABC information for selected cost objects based on widely accepted, field-tested model designs. (Cost object examples: service profitability, process waste, customer profitability.)

2. Acquire complementary current process information using TQM, TOC, or another continuous improvement method.

3. Identify and rank improvement opportunities in terms of estimated cost savings.

4. Test highest-ranked improvement opportunities from a global perspective.
    - Determine the interactive effects that the proposed changes may have on other processes.
    - Set up monitoring for important cost management improvement milestones or delay/eliminate the ABC opportunity.

5. Select the organization's best improvement opportunities and assign resources to them.

6. Implement improvements and track actual cost savings against estimates.

7. Watch for unexpected interactions between processes and functions, as well as customer reactions.

ABC/M and Conventional Cost Accounting. Conventional accounting systems focus on departmental cost control, standard costs, variances, and budget management. The chart of accounts and general ledger structure shepherd all financial transactions. In essence, these characteristics support a Stage II CMS, assuming that the accounting functions are reliable and contain accurate data. Stage II competence is required as a beginning platform for ABC endeavors.

For readers in organizations that do not yet use ABC or some operational costing equivalent, the following "ask your accountant" questions can help determine management accounting report reliability:

- *What is the focus of our cost accountants' background and what training do our cost accountants have?* (Bad news: Only financial. Good news: Financial plus operations and/or spends a lot of time working directly with operations personnel.)

- *When accountants perform cost analyses, what sources of information do they use?* (Bad news: Only the G/L accounts and standard costs. Good news: Specialized cost data, operations reports, most current costs.)

- *Do our accountants work with operations staff to verify assumptions?* (Bad news: No. Good news: Yes, they do so prior to doing the analysis *and* in postanalysis review/revision by operations staff.)

- *Are the analysis methods suited to the exploration objective?* (Bad news: No, we usually use the same basic format, such as variable cost analysis or standard quotation forms. Good news: Yes, we design the analysis to suit the purpose, but we also use consistent, up-to-date cost rates for consistency and comparability.)

This is a good time to put in a word about revenue. The astute reader will have noticed that, so far, ABC profitability analyses refer to costs, but revenues have yet to be mentioned. Naturally, any profit analysis requires both. In this case, conventional accounting methods can provide revenue information. Revenue accounts are usually available in a G/L system due to information generated for:

- Product/service mix decisions
- Sales commission calculations
- Customer discount calculations
- Other revenue source analyses

So, with rare exceptions, the challenge of the ABC technical implementation is in parsing expenditure data, not revenue.

ABC/M and Advanced Resource Management: Product/Service Profitability. At their best, conventional accounting reports segment profitability and product/service line profitability as subsidiary reports of the income statement. The revenue line of these reports is usually reliable; however, the costs in these reports are subject to overhead allocations, standard cost consistencies, and fairly arbitrary variance cost assignment. In addition, conventional reports often contain SG&A expenditures that are spread across lines by simplistic "percent of revenue" allocations, hiding many important cost relationships.

TIPS & TECHNIQUES

ABC Applications Examples

- Product mix and pricing
- Distribution channel options
- Product and customer profitability management
- Shared services cost assignment
- Product/service design and development
- Budgeting (ABB)
- Transfer pricing
- New business opportunity analysis
- Expansion/contraction of product/service; impacts on revenue
- Production and capacity decisions
- Make-buy and outsourcing decisions
- Cost driver analysis and improvement

In contrast, ABC profitability analysis presents more accurate relationships of product/service resource consumption by (1) demonstrating a logical, cause–effect assignment (versus allocation) of overhead components, and (2) linking SG&A costs to revenue-line items. As standard features of conventional accounting systems, raw material components and direct labor can often be transplanted directly into the ABC model unchanged. Because overhead is such a large cost component for most organizations, ABC methods significantly change the product-level profitability picture compared to conventional overhead absorption methods that use direct labor or material as an allocation base. Total profitability remains equal between ABC and the G/L.

Errors can creep into the application of the ABC technique. Continuous improvement and waste elimination are the real objectives of ABC work. If an ABC model data is based only on current activity performance, without regard for potential better practices, then the ABC reports simply trace a picture of what is and fail to provide insight into what may be. A second potential failure in ABC work is to report only on the ABC-design costs (usually based on estimates) interviews, or even budgets. In essence, this amounts to a forecast or an historical view without a reference pointing to actual results. Targets, benchmarks, and/or actual comparisons are essential to performance visibility. Not to make such comparisons in a conventional system would be akin to paying attention only to standard costs and never reporting variances!

ABC/M and Advanced Resource Management: Customer Profitability. ABC analyses of customer profitability evolved almost as quickly as ABC product analysis, and today both are considered equally important. The recent emergence of customer relationship management (CRM) has increased the value of ABC customer analyses more than ever. In addition to direct product cost, organizations invest significant and diverse organizational resources into a customer relationship:

order processing, logistics, packaging, distribution, inventories, sales and customer service attention. Conventional accounting barely recognizes these costs as customer-driven, and typically aggregates these expenditures in balance sheet and SG&A accounts. However, a clear customer-profitability picture arises only when all the costs of all the resources used to serve a customer are accumulated. It is imperative to remember that:

> Some of the largest customers often turn out to be the most unprofitable. A company cannot lose significant amounts of money with small customers. It does not do enough business with a small customer to incur large (i.e., absolute) losses. Only a large customer can be a large-loss customer. Large customers tend to be either the most profitable or the least profitable in the entire customer base. It is unusual for a large customer to be in the middle of the total profitability rankings.[17]

One particular problem crops up frequently in ABC customer work: cost/resource design disputes. Wherever possible, management must build all ABC models on explicit cause-effect assumptions about the relationships between resources, activities, and cost objects, and validate the assumptions with those performing or managing the activities. Developing design assumptions for customer expenditures is not as straightforward as for products and services. Executives involved in customer applications need to be especially rigorous in determining the customer-related resource, activity, and cost object cause-effect relationships in the design stage.

A second problem related to customer analyses is the "profit-only" approach. Management may make a simplistic profitability decision and automatically "fire" unprofitable customers. This is a classic ABC error, called the "death spiral" in the literature. In contrast, strategic use of ABC will reveal opportunities to improve the cost structure of a customer relationship and save the relationship by turning the unprofitable customer into a profitable one. Still, firing the customer remains an option.

Another overall issue that arises in ABC design and implementation is the tendency of financial professionals to concentrate on local detail and lose sight of the big picture and cross-functional impacts. Accountants who have been schooled to reconcile to the penny, find it hard to swallow "approximately correct" standards as adequate performance for ABC accounting. "Precisely correct" reporting standards are never possible in a dynamic environment, and the effort to achieve perfection can erode the cost-benefit ratio for an ABC implementation.

Resource Consumption Accounting

Resources: the beginning of all processes; the means to all profit. All of the methods discussed in this chapter deal with *resources*. However, Resource Consumption Accounting (RCA), one of the most recently developed cost management methods to be explored by both the practitioner and academic management communities, puts resources front and center, just as activities function as the centerpiece of ABC/M, and quality as the driving force in TQM. RCA complements the activity focus of ABC with its methods for detailed analysis of the nature and behavior of resources and by introducing ways to measure and manage capacity, including the many aspects of inactivity inherent in capacity management.

Core Principles and Management Objectives

In the first iterations of RCA, proponents focused the discussion on features that distinguished it from ABC/M, but soon realized the importance of blending the strengths of the two approaches. In a natural evolution, RCA practitioners concentrate on the resources/operations perspective that launched ABC logic. A related word of caution to long-time ABC practitioners: If an existing ABC/M system design has not changed significantly in the last three to five years, this may be a good time to revisit it in light of recent developments, like RCA.

Process and Resource-Based Cost Management

RCA seeks more precise understanding of resource elements, leading to better management of limited assets. It employs the discipline of a mapping method to more accurately identify and delineate resources utilized by processes and activities. RCA works with eight specific ABC shortcomings concerning resource management:

1. As a system that recognizes activities, ABC is incapable of measuring or managing inactivity, therefore a homogeneous measure of *capacity* is not possible.

2. While ABC took an important first step in better resource management by creating resource pools, its methods primarily analyzed activities and cost objects, not resources; therefore, ABC insufficiently addresses the interrelationships among resource elements (e.g., output quantities, utilization statistics).

3. ABC fails to characterize specific relationships between resource pools and the customers who use them. Because ABC model designs often use estimates, as opposed to actual data, costs, and quantities for each cost pool, the initial inherent *nature of resource cost* is not reflected (i.e., the fixed and proportional characteristics of the costs, given the capacity, skill, technology, operating characteristics of the resources deployed).

4. Excess and idle *capacity* is not properly accounted for.

5. *Interrelationships* between resource pools (i.e., the grouping of related resource elements into a pool) are only indirectly expressed.

6. The changing *nature of cost* as it relates to the cost model is not reflected.

7. Fully burdened resource costs are not provided.

8. Inferior information is supplied for effective resource management and certain strategic decisions.[18]

The RCA list highlights three important complementary threads to the evolution of ABC/M methods: capacity, interrelationships, and the nature of cost. ABC/M practitioners developed methods for managing capacity, but the methods matured some time after the first major phase of activity-based implementations; therefore, a hefty percentage of active ABC models do not address capacity management. RCA creates an intuitive answer to capacity management by formally attending to comparable measures of capacity and by measuring resource pool outputs.

In a second complementary thread, RCA reveals the interrelationships within a group of resource elements and between resource pools. A change in a process changes the resources that are intimate with the process. The relationship between resources and the people who use them exist in ever-changing dynamics. RCA more deliberately defines resource pools so that pools contain similar technologies, machinery, or human capabilities. The pooling of interrelated resource elements contributes to more homogeneous cost pools with more accurate output measures. This is important to capacity management and to continuous improvement, as well as to planning and budgeting. Finally, financial and nonfinancial cost managers have been looking for better ways to understand the nature of cost since the beginning of business itself. Better capacity management and more transparent views of resource pool interrelationships create more insight and, therefore, more management options. However, potential RCA practitioners must be patient in order to reap the rewards RCA has to offer. Understanding the nature and behavior of resource costs in a dynamic system requires considerable time investment. But once understood, management decision making is simplified.

RCA and Operations

RCA methods work from a perspective that is embedded in operational detail looking outward toward strategic execution and improved cost structures. The methods focus on the wise management of limited resources, where resource utilization is predominantly determined and managed at the input end of processes.

RCA resembles the input-output logic of process analysis in many ways that naturally align with process improvement initiatives. With the important role that consumption rates play in its methodology, RCA is a natural partner for organizational cultures that regularly monitor process improvement.

RCA Advantages and Shortcomings for Cost Management Applications

RCA is best used in partnership with ABC/M because it effectively extends the logic of the ABC resource viewpoint, but lacks some intuitive ABC strengths in terms of activity management and cost object analysis. An organization should have significant grounding in ABC/M before attempting to understand or use RCA. Put another way, RCA can best be understood in terms of ABC's shortcomings, and vice versa.

RCA and Conventional Cost Accounting. The closest equivalent conventional accounting term to the word "resource" is the word "assets." However, although assets are meticulously tracked on the balance sheet, a conventional system rarely analyzes assets beyond a set of standard financial ratios and calculations—for example, return on assets, current ratios, and inventory turns.

Conventional accounting focuses on outputs. RCA focuses on the manageable process inputs that eventually create financial results reported by conventional systems. Resource management, in the operations/resource perspective, is about beginnings. Conventional cost accounting is about endings, at times, long past. RCA can prevent waste; the traditional approach merely reports unrecoverable waste.

RCA and Advanced Resource Management. RCA implementations are just beginning. Pioneer practitioners like David Keys and Anton van der Merwe suggest that a greenfield site or an atmosphere of serious strategic renewal are best suited to RCA work. This view is based on the maturity of the RCA cost accounting method, dependent upon a vision for organizational design with a strategy already committed to specific capacities, competencies, and technologies, and grounded in committed operational priorities. This in turn assumes deliberate resource commitments.

RCA typically elicits one of two responses in even the most seasoned cost managers: intense curiosity or blatant animosity. Some see the enhancements it brings to resource management as too much bother—especially when they consider how current systems must be modified to blend with yet another new approach. Others believe ABC/M has already adequately addressed resource management. Still others can see that resource management enhancements add value to the quest to understand the nature and behavior of cost and resources. The important point is not who is right and who is wrong, what works and what doesn't: that can only be determined case by case, one organization at a time. Organizations, and the cost managers within them, mature into enhanced methods, each at its own unique paces. The real adventure is the exploration and learning—and the continuous improvement results.

Summary and Lessons from the Field

An important caveat for those who continue to use a conventional cost accounting system's rigid cost types and constrained reporting systems is that one source of cost information (historical/lagging) is not enough. Therefore, trying to make a traditional cost system cough up decision-quality information is a waste of everyone's time. Decision making depends upon different kinds of cost and resource information: detailed and aggregate, historical and predictive, strategic and process, global and local. An executive who explores an existing cost system and finds only one cost flavor—usually retrospective—or cost reporting used only by accountants, needs to assemble a cost management system design team quickly.

Summary points from this chapter include:

- The work of TQM is the work of waste elimination, and it is never done.
- The return on the cost of quality is measurable and significant, but the fruit ripens slowly.
- As a method of managing systems, TOC anticipates the close relationship between cost management and operations revealed by more mature accounting methods like ABC and RCA.
- TQM and TOC methods help managers in conventional cost accounting environments become familiar with the essential links in understanding the relationships of cost, resources, and operations.
- ABC information is only as good as the underlying model design and the data that populates it. Organizations that choose to implement ABC must have financial and nonfinancial managers with an intimate understanding and appreciation of the relationship between resources and operations.
- ABC insights must be accompanied by continuous improvement efforts, or no benefit will accrue; that is, total ABC cost equals total G/L cost.
- RCA principles, especially capacity and resource management, complement ABC models as the next stage of resource accounting and management maturity.

- Beware of project "sprawl." New cost management approaches must be selected according to the needs and readiness of the organization, not by popularity with the competition.
- Discipline management improvement efforts under a unifying system.

The next chapter explores the tactical application of cost and resource management methods. Development of *tactical sense* is key.

Endnotes

1. Organizational readiness is a key factor in project success or failure. Research is beginning to emerge on reasons for failure and how to mitigate risk. For example, CAM-I's research on ABCM projects has resulted in a "Readiness Assessment" to help identify and ameliorate risk. For information, go to: *www.cam-i.org*.

2. A multitude of TQM studies are available. The following are representative of research results. For impacts on:
   - Market share and sales, see Kambize E. Maani, "Does Quality Pay," *Incentive* (February 1990): 20–26.
   - Costs decreases, see CONSAD Research Corporation, "Advanced Technology Program Case Study: The Development of Advanced Technologies and Systems for Controlling Dimensional Variation in Automobile Body Manufacturing" (Gaithersburg, MD: National Institute of Standards and Technology, 1997).
   - Profit, see Y.K. Shetty, "Managing Product Quality for Profitability," *SAM Advanced Management Journal* (Autumn 1988): 33–38.

3. The Pareto principle states 80 percent of problems are generated by 20 percent of the causes. TQM tracks causal factors and attempts to identify the top 20 percent; then improvement methods seek to remedy the chief offenders.

4. Michael Hammer, "Process Management and the Future of Six Sigma," *MIT Sloan Management Review* 43, no. 2 (2002): 27–28.

5. CJ McNair, *The Profit Potential: Taking High Performance to the Bottom Line* (Essex Junction, Vermont: Oliver Wight Publications, 1994): Chapter 8, "The Hidden Costs of Quality."

6. Eric Noreen, Debra A. Smith, and James T. MacKey, *The Theory of Constraints and Its Implications for Management Accounting* (Great Barrington, MA: North River Press, 1995): iii. It is worth noting that Dr. Goldratt's theories and suggested solutions have been well received (if not always acted on) by the accounting profession.

7. Catherine and Joe Stenzel, "ERP System Opportunities and Limitations: An Interview with Eli Goldratt," *Journal of Cost Management* 16, no. 2 (2002): 5–12.

8. Id., 8.

9. Eli Goldratt, course materials from *Overview of the Theory of Constraints for Industry* (Avraham Y. Goldratt Institute, 1995): 1–5.

10. Eli Goldratt, *Necessary But Not Sufficient* (Great Barrington, MA: North River Press, 2000).

11. Eric Noreen, et. al., 12–13.

12. Paul A. Dierks, Gary Cokins, eds., "The CAM-I Glossary of Activity-based Management," *Journal of Cost Management* 15, no. 1 (2001): 34–43.

13. Id.

14. Cooper and Kaplan's most recent exposition of ABC theory and practice is *Cost and Effect: Using Integrated Cost Systems to Drive Profitability and Performance* (Boston, MA: Harvard Business School Press, 1998). A less well-known, but important, predecessor was George Staubus, a pioneer thinker, who wrote, among other books, *Activity Costing and Input Output Accounting* (Homewood, IL: Richard D. Irwin, Inc., 1971). In

addition, as early as 1983, standard reference books (e.g., *Kohler's Dictionary for Accountants*) included definitions for activity accounting terms.

15. Robert S. Kaplan and V.G. Narayanan, "Measuring and Managing Customer Profitability," *Journal of Cost Management* 15, no. 5 (2001): 7.

16. Robert S. Kaplan and Robin Cooper, *Cost & Effect: Using Integrated Cost Systems to Drive Profitability and Performance* (Boston: Harvard Business School Press, 1998): 79.

17. Kaplan and Narayanan, 8.

18. This item and the general content of this section are taken from a three-part series of articles by Anton van der Merwe and David E. Keys, published in the last half of 2001 in volume 15 of the *Journal of Cost Management*:

    - "The Case for RCA: Excess and Idle Capacity," *Journal of Cost Management* 15, no. 4 (2001): 21–32.
    - "The Case for RCA: Understanding Resource Interrelationships," *Journal of Cost Management* 15, no. 5 (2001): 27–36.
    - "The Case for RCA: Decision Support in an Advanced Cost Management System," *Journal of Cost Management* 15, no. 6 (2001): 23–32.

CHAPTER 6

Tactical Management of Costs and Resources

After reading this chapter you will be able to

- Develop a logical process for tactical evaluation and selection
- Develop a sense for when to initiate specific tactics as they support appropriately aligned cost management systems
- Better understand lean manufacturing, reengineering, value engineering, target costing, business life cycle costing, and supply chain management

Organizations advance their vision, mission, and purpose at two primary activity levels: the strategic and the tactical, the global mobilization and the local action. Leadership sets the strategic course by clear communication of focused direction and intentions. The entire organization then executes the work necessary to achieve strategic objectives through tactical use of asset-based resources and competencies. Strategy directs and assigns resources; tactics focus and utilize them. This chapter presents a selection of cost/resource management tactics. Next, Chapter 7 discusses strategic approaches that provide a guidance system for tactics.

Even though most employees have some understanding of *strategy* and *execution*, the terms have become so familiar in the current business lexicon that most people take them for granted. Strategy and tactics are not synonymous. Few companies have mastered managing the connection between the global (strategy) and the local (tactics). Successful companies have leaders who recognize that this connection must be managed, not taken for granted. Strategic drivers, such as client and customer demands and the profit imperative form the context for strategic choices, that in turn lead to selection of tactics best-suited for executing the strategy. (See Exhibit 6.1 for an overview of context, strategy, and tactics.) Tactics are tightly focused to execute specific goals within the overall strategic plan. Although tactics may deliver several strategic advantages, each was developed to achieve a specific strategic advantage, for example, improve quality, contain cost, or speed up cycle time. Successful tactical execution depends upon employees who understand the relationship between the strategic plan and the tactics selected for its execution. This chapter, and Chapter 7, use the following four principles for presenting the interplay between strategy, tactics, and the cost management practices that support them. In elemental form:

- A strategy states *what* will be done.
- A tactic states *how* the strategy will be achieved.
- Resources provide a semifungible foundation of human, physical, and financial *capital* configured into identifiable, competitive competencies.
- Resource-based competencies make *strategic execution* possible.

Analysis of Tactics

Well-designed strategies always integrate resource allocation and cost management as significant elements. Since the profit imperative drives strategic intent, strategic tactics must address cost management implications. This chapter provides a map for the strategic attributes of six well-known management tactics, and demonstrates cost and resource impacts that can

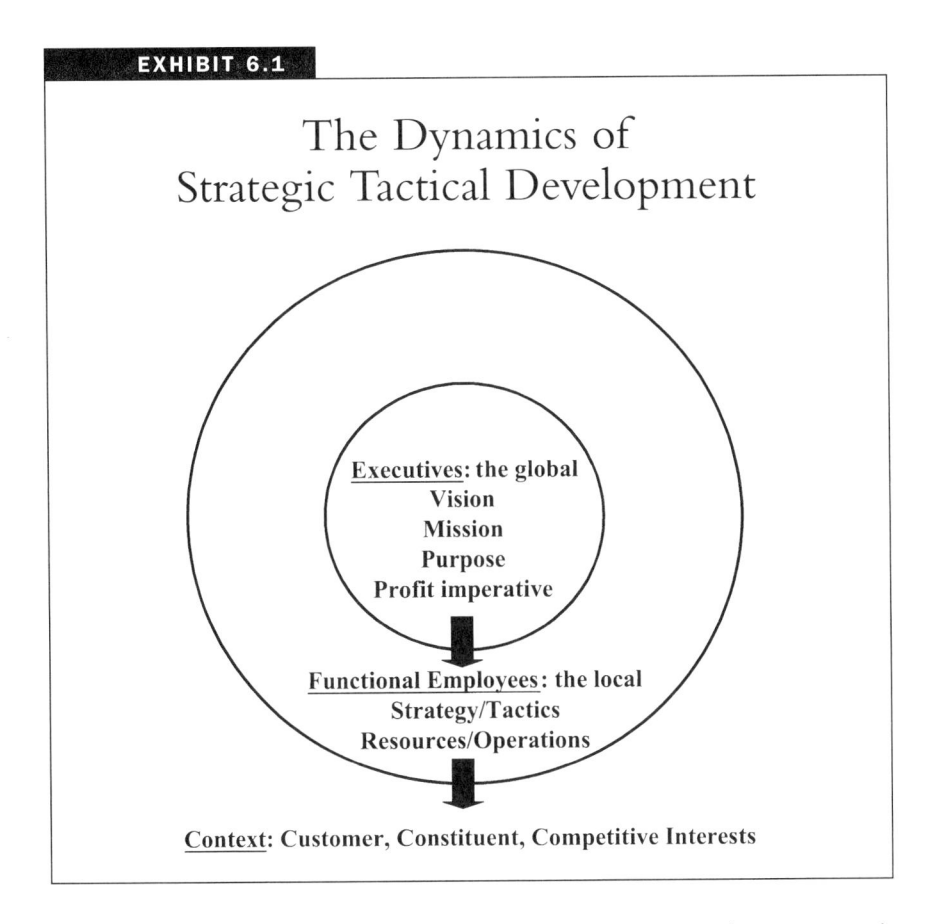

Tactical Management of Costs and Resources

EXHIBIT 6.1

The Dynamics of Strategic Tactical Development

Executives: the global
Vision
Mission
Purpose
Profit imperative

↓

Functional Employees: the local
Strategy/Tactics
Resources/Operations

↓

Context: Customer, Constituent, Competitive Interests

be expected from their appropriate use. The strategic-attribute approach can be applied to any tactic, not just those discussed in this chapter.

Likewise, a sequence of five steps, systematizes the tactics analysis for each chapter section. The five steps support a deliberate process of tactical evaluation and develop a "selection sense":

1. Define what needs to be accomplished. These *clear intentions* are ideally stated as strategic objectives. When it comes to strategic execution, cultivate an *attitude* toward tactics as an array of specialty tools, each designed for a specific strategic objective; discourage "silver bullet" thinking; that is, the search for the "one right tool that will solve all our problems."

2. Develop tactic *selection criteria* based on clearly defined, predetermined strategic *attributes* as they relate to each strategic objective. A strategic attribute is the functional capability the tactic was designed to deliver. Identify primary and secondary strategic attributes for each potential tactic, and clearly differentiate if the strategic attribute works in the best interests of the customer, the organization, or both.

3. *Compare and contrast* viable tactics in terms of cost, human resource requirements, implementation time, and use by competitors.

4. *Select* a tactic based on clearly articulated *connections* between global (strategic intention) and local (tactical execution) alignment, and define expected *results* in measurable performance objectives. Include a set of "abandon tactic" signals.

5. *Test* the performance of selected tactical attributes in an organizational context by means of a limited prototype, by running simulations, and/or by exploring with trusted sources who have used the tactic (not the tactic's salesperson!). Assuming successful test results, *deploy* tactic and measure performance for strategic feedback.

Notice that tactic selection begins with strategy (i.e., clear intention). Strategy creates the context for management tactic selection. Additionally, keep the following definitions in mind.

- *Strategic attribute.* Quality or characteristic of a person, place, or thing; in a tactical cost management context, advantages that contribute to the profit imperative when applied to a process, product, or service.
- *Cost-cutting.* A deliberate reduction of resources usually carried out with insufficient knowledge of process implications, and with disregard for strategic consequences. Cost-cutting is typically used to achieve short-term financial objectives.

Tactical Management of Costs and Resources

> **TIPS & TECHNIQUES**
>
> ### Tactic Selection Steps
>
> Clear intention → attitude → selection criteria → attributes → compare/contrast → select → connections → results metrics → prototype test → deploy → strategic feedback

- *Strategy.* An intention with defined performance outcomes that is stated in cause-effect terms (i.e., if-then), and executed through operational tactics.
- *Tactic.* A method or device for executing a specific strategic objective.

As an example of a business situation that calls for the skillful selection and use of tactics in a cost management context, consider a strategic retreat where a firm's top executives craft objectives for the next eighteen months. As they discuss their strategies, they wrestle with the disconcerting realization that only two of eight objectives for the previous eighteen months met their ROI targets and that two-thirds of strategic initiatives exceeded their budgets.

Strategic Attribute Array

Human beings are born with the capacity to categorize based on familiar patterns—people, places, and objects—and to assign qualities accordingly. In business, revenue and cost are two important organizing categories. Cost/benefit analyses help managers crudely determine the "goodness" of an opportunity. The prudent selection of management tactics that enable specific strategic objectives depends on the identification of more carefully characterized strategic attributes as they align with current and future needs of the customer and the organization. For example, a *rare* work of art, a *well-groomed* puppy, and an *absorbent* sponge may be qualities of some concern to specific products in specific enterprises. However, each of the attributes discussed in this chapter is valuable to some degree to all organizations and each attribute significantly impacts cost management decisions. The strategic attribute array, presented in order of chronological appearance, retraces the evolutionary history of maturing trade and commerce practices.

1. *Profitable.* The wet noodle of all strategic attributes. Whether calculated in barter, currency, or exchange of rights, transactions between entities are engaged with anticipation of profit. The successful management of this attribute *depends* upon the skillful use of all that follow. Profitability is a result predicated on achievement of other preceding strategic attributes. *What profit can we expect?*

2. *Rapid.* If one transaction means profit, the basic logic follows that many transactions yield more profit. Business owners naturally developed an early historical interest in improving performance by increasing the pace that products and services could be made available to paying customers. Business processes (e.g., delivery, design-to-market, production, distribution) depend on speed for market success in most competitive environments. *What cost management benefits might we expect by increasing the speed in our internal-business or customer-related processes?*

3. *Economical.* Synonyms include cheaper, price-competitive, and value-for-money. This strategic attribute is relevant to both the buyer and seller points of view. Once merchants and traders experienced competition, they sought ways to distinguish themselves from their rivals in the eyes of their customers. Price is a perennial differentiation favorite. The Industrial Revolution inaugurated a more sophisticated era with "economies of scale," an

Tactical Management of Costs and Resources

enterprise cost management goal based on large volumes and repetitive processes. Economical tactics apply to internal process management as well as to customer concerns. These tactics make business processes less costly over the long run and impact the customer only secondarily. *How can we make our internal-business or customer-related processes more economical? How would these changes help us better manage our costs?*

4. *Easy, Automated.* Technologically advanced, mechanically enabled performance improvements and innovations attract business because they save the customer time and effort, or improve operations because they save employees time and effort. Other important intuitive aspects of this performance dimension include access, user-friendliness, and storage-related characteristics. (DVD and VCR manufacturers take note!) *How can we automate our internal business or create greater ease of use for our customers? How would these changes help us better manage our costs?*

5. *Reliable.* Doesn't break; durable; is there when you need it. All the speed, economy, and automation in the world fall to ashes if the product/service or internal process breaks down or intermittently becomes unavailable. Enter the Quality Movement. (Computer hardware and software providers take note!) *How can we make our products/services and internal-business/customer-related processes more reliable? How would these changes help us better manage our costs?*

6. *Variety.* A provider makes a wider array of products/services available based on a keen understanding of the target market. Colors, options, accessories, and models are performance improvements/innovations that fit under the umbrella of this strategic attribute. In sharp contrast to the creation of the performance dimensions in the next strategic attribute, the managers of the tactics that

enable variety as a strategic attribute decide what choices are available, not the end user. An attendant method is market segmentation. *How can we create greater variety in our products/services and in internal-business/customer-related processes? How would these changes help us better manage our costs?*

7. *Customized.* The flip side of the variety coin. Organizations using management tactics that capture customer preferences for choices in forms, functions, and accessories have learned the performance power of customization improvement/innovation. Enter the customer-focused era. (Retail clothing manufacturers take note.) Both variety and customization were born of the Quality Movement where attention to customer satisfaction achieved temporary equality with profitability imperatives. *How can we create more customized products/services and internal-business/customer-related processes? How would these changes help us better manage our costs?*

8. *Flexible, Adaptable.* Variety and customization are desirable in the current marketplace. The ownership of flexible, adaptable processes and resources supports profitable variety and customization. Flexibility and adaptability performance innovations consume significant resources in even more mature companies because only the more mature companies employ management tactics designed to leverage this performance dimension. Innovative companies develop more economical ways to be flexible and adaptable. *How can we design more flexible and adaptable internal-business/customer-related processes? How would these changes help us better manage our costs?*

9. *Innovative.* Consumers often value the "newest version," the "latest fashion," and the "next generation." Whether or not innovation means more value, the competitive profile of the current market-driven economy demands that organizations in highly competitive environments create innovative performance advantages both inside company processes and in customer products and services to stay ahead of the competition. (Institutions of higher education take note!) *How can we regularly introduce more innovative products/services and internal-business/customer-related processes? How would these changes help us better manage our costs?*

10. *Humane, Simple, Environmentally Responsible.* Although this set represents an emerging strategic attribute complex that may or may not stand the test of time (and the profit imperative), many international corporations are embracing an increasingly marketable concern for the limited resources of our planet.[1] *How can we limit complexity in our business processes, relate with our employees more humanely, and act more responsibly toward the environment while remaining cost-conscious?*

Any given attribute has a designed-in *performance range*. A grass mower powered by one human pushing is more automated than a scythe or hand clipper; however, its power is puny compared to a John Deere riding lawnmower. When insisting on building in attributes, consider: (1) the real needs of potential customers, (2) the resources required to satisfy those needs, and (3) the longevity of market position for a product that meets those needs. Accurate identification of the exact attributes that a tactic is likely to deliver contributes greatly to targeted use of resources.

Although a diehard proponent of any management tactic will claim that profitability is one of the tactic's strategic attributes, profitability is like "goodness," in that it is only an attribute if it succeeds. The trick is to match a management tactical option with the likelihood of success.

The sections of this chapter highlight primary and secondary strategic attributes for each of the management tactics profiled.

From holistic and developmental viewpoints, as organizations mature and learn to incorporate more recently developed strategic attributes, older, tried-and-true strategic attributes hold their value. Reliability does not replace the importance of speed. Similarly, customization must remain within economical reach of consumers. Imagine Henry Ford telling today's automobile customer, "You can have any color you want, as long as it's black," in light of the extensive array of attributes now expected by consumers. Each strategic attribute requires deployment resources. When management tactics deploy more attributes, organizations consume more resources.

Used as a framework for management thinking, this array of strategic attributes and the five steps in the process of tactic selection, assist in the exploration of selected tactics in light of their potential to partner with cost and resource management. In condensed form, the five steps again are:

1. Determine strategic intention and check "attitude."

2. Identify the desired strategic attributes and determine an acceptable cost for each.

3. Identify candidate management tactics and their primary and secondary attributes.

4. Select the most strategically aligned tactic, formally identify connections to the strategic plan, and set performance metrics for successful deployment outcomes, including or as well as, abandon signals.

5. Test and deploy.

Lean and Agile Management Tactics

Lean and agile are two complementary terms for management tactics that carry significant cost management implications. Lean tactics preceded agile tactics. In the most general terms, lean management practices work to eliminate all forms of waste that occur during product/service production and delivery. Agile management tactics work to eliminate the rigidity of the traditional dependency on economies of scale by increasing product/service delivery flexibility without sacrificing quality or incurring added costs. Lean and agile management practitioners emphasize resource, operations, quality, and continuous improvement perspectives in the design of their tactics.

Lean Management Essentials

One of the most mature subsets of lean management tactics is the Just-in-Time (JIT) production model. JIT is a set of lean manufacturing practices used primarily in repetitive manufacturing processes that work to minimize waste by creating efficient flow processes through linked work centers, eliminating any activity that adds cost without adding value. As materials move through the assembly process across work cells, the right part can be found in the right place at the right time. JIT managers learn to streamline process operations and focus their waste elimination efforts on the interactions of three principal process components: material, space, and human.

Resource flexibility is a key feature of JIT tactics. JIT managers increase the number of multiskilled workers in all processes and select nonspecialized equipment for any process that depends upon tools or machines. Similarly, JIT managers carefully design the physical layout between humans and machines and sets of teams for any given process.

One of the most important features of JIT process management is the integrated "pull" dynamic of process workflow. In contrast to more conventional "push" systems, JIT does not use inventory as a production cushion. JIT management coordinates workflow pull according to eight principles with significant cost management implications.

First, *small lot production* saves space and capital. Work groups can be moved closer together and transportation costs can be reduced. For organizations using TOC methods, JIT helps identify and correct process bottlenecks. Second, JIT management tactics emphasize process *setup efficiency* to minimize human or machine downtime. Third, *lead time* management focuses on the interrelationship and cost management implications of three additional key, time-related elements of process efficiency: human proficiency, product movement, and waiting times. Fourth, the simple, automated *kanban* control system regulates the movement of goods through the production process between work teams, minimizing costs of waiting, downtime, and human oversight of process flow.

Fifth, *uniform production levels* smooth processes during final assembly and permit more accurate output forecasting. The tight internal process management depends upon the sixth JIT management focus, the *supply network*. A few of the ways JIT manages supplier relationships toward greater quality and responsiveness include locating processes near the customer, standardizing delivery schedules and containers, and accepting installment payments rather than payment on delivery.

Finally, *quality at the source* and *total process maintenance* ensure quality while processes become more efficient and cost-effective. Total process maintenance focuses on practices that address breakdowns and breakdown prevention within the production process. Careful records track breakdown costs, frequency, and intervals so that employees can design preventative maintenance schedules and participate in the goal of zero defects.

Tactical Management of Costs and Resources

By reducing inventory and space requirements, JIT practitioners have deployed these tactics of process management to increase capacity, productivity, and product variety; maintain quality; simplify control activities; and lower their costs.

Lean Management Strategic Attribute Profile

Management practitioners who use lean methodologies to eliminate waste while maintaining product/service quality can expect the following strategic attribute performance profile from this management tactic:

- *Primary.* Economical
- *Secondary.* Rapid, easy/automated
- *Largest risk.* Quality

Agile Management Essentials

Agile tactics build upon lean tactics. The consumer electronics industry has joined the automobile industry to meet an increasing need to compete in a market where economies of scale cannot respond quickly enough to changes in competitive innovation. The Japanese originally characterized agile manufacturing in terms of challenges such as the "three-day car," delivering a custom-order car to the dealer in three days or less.

As agile management has spread to other sectors, several agile principles apply to cost managers in all sectors. First and foremost, production economies of scale bear significant setup costs. The second principle for manufacturing and other material-dependent processes, the so-called Lego-block approach to product design, saves significant cost by creating interchangeable parts across production lines and creating the ability to configure the same components in different ways. The third principle calls for including the customer in the product design process.

Agile managers use these tactics without abandoning JIT principles, such as locating close to the customer and supplier.

Agile Management Strategic Attribute Profile

Practitioners of agile management tactics use its methodologies to balance higher process efficiency with job enrichment for employees in expectation of the following strategic attribute performance profile from this tactic:

- *Primary.* Flexible/adaptable
- *Secondary.* Economical, rapid, easy/automated, customized
- *Largest risk.* Disruptive innovation by competition

Reengineering

Reengineering is a method that fundamentally, and often totally, redesigns processes. A true management child of the 1980s, reengineering is arguably an offspring of the Quality Movement and a loose collection of methods called "process value analysis." These tactics expose the working dynamics of resources/costs within processes, to drive out nonvalue-added costs and modify processes accordingly. Looking back across more than fifteen years since its inception, reengineering was one of the first formalized attempts to unravel and optimize the intricacies of organizational design—now an area of intense management interest. In essence, reengineering champions took a look at the "can of worms" that dysfunctional business processes had become and said, "Don't Automate [the processes], Obliterate [them]."[2] In other words, start from scratch and *build* a process/organizational design that works *significantly* more efficiently and effectively. At that time, executives were rapidly computerizing and automating anything that moved, but automating inefficient processes is nonsense.

In 1993, Michael Hammer, with coauthor James Champy, wrote *Reengineering the Corporation: A Manifesto for Business Revolution.*[3]

Tactical Management of Costs and Resources

Since then, the Hammer and Champy publishing efforts have diverged. Hammer relentlessly pursued "the process enterprise," and Champy focused on organizational process improvements through leadership and better management."[4]

Champy subsequently wrote *Reengineering Management: The Mandate for New Leadership* in 1995, probably in response to a pervasive middle management resistance to reengineering in the early 1990s.[5] This resistance can be summed up in a question: If the last reengineering project laid off three of your close colleagues, what will your attitude be toward the next reengineering round? The reengineering Achilles' heel is forgetting about people. Michael Hammer himself took some of the blame for the false start, saying, "I wasn't smart enough about that. I was reflecting my engineering background and was insufficiently appreciative of the human dimension. I've learned that's critical."[6]

Another practice further undermined early reengineering experiences. Under the name *reengineering*, some executives implemented significant downsizing initiatives and lapsed into a *cost-cutting* mania. For executives influenced by fifty years of financial metric predominance, reengineering probably looked like a good tool to make costs go away. Some costs did indeed go away, but in the process of reducing costs, process capabilities were undermined, and valuable people were fired, often only to be rehired as contractors. The cost-cutting shortcuts inappropriately superimposed on reengineering principles fouled the workings of a valid method.

As reengineering and the "process enterprise" found more solid footing, enhancements included the addition of strategic planning, more training, cultural change techniques (read: overcoming resistance), supportive software, and other supplemental methods, such as ABC/M. For example, in the period 1995–1996, Levi Strauss "put the brakes on its $850 million reengineering effort after management created turmoil by demanding that 4,000 workers reapply for their jobs as a part of a reorganization into 'process groups.' Levi Strauss ultimately stretched out its reengineering timetable by two years, promised not to discharge anyone as a result of the overhaul and allocated an extra $14 million for a two-year 'education' effort to calm employees."[7]

Reengineering Essentials

Reengineering developed as an attempt to "make a difference" in process management. Although its roots predispose practitioners toward technical process myopia, it is a rapid and powerful management tactic for improving process performance when the people issues are carefully managed. Neglect the human dimension and employees predictably obstruct implementation. Reengineering proponents claim that the tactic can produce significant cost savings; however, it is difficult to prove that other efforts (e.g., parallel initiatives in TQM, ABC/M, natural attrition) do not account for a portion of professed impacts.

Michael Hammer's more current work on the "process enterprise," with its emphasis on process ownership, has expanded reengineering advantages to include a more holistic view of the organization. However, the enduring tactical characteristics aimed at process redesign remain:

- *Fundamental.* Aimed at core competencies and entrenched ways of doing business.
- *Radical.* Disregards existing structures versus paying attention to fixing existing processes.
- *Dramatic.* Quantum improvements versus marginal or incremental changes.

Reengineering achieves these three tactical characteristics when four essential elements[8] of the reengineering methodology guide the work. These four do not reflect later significant evolutions in attendant leadership and process enterprise considerations. See chapter endnotes.

1. *Mobilization.* Create a business process map, determine process priorities, and appoint process owners and reengineering team.
2. *Diagnosis.* Understand customers and current processes, identify weaknesses, and determine targets for redesign.
3. *Redesign.* Fundamental, radical, dramatic business process redesign, followed by prototype design, tests, learning, and improvement iterations.
4. *Transition.* Initial release (i.e., rollout) followed by succeeding releases, reaping the benefits, and finally institutionalizing.

Reengineering Strategic Attribute Profile

Reengineering practitioners who use the tactic to balance higher process efficiency with job enrichment for employees can expect the following strategic attribute performance profile from this management tactic:

- *Primary.* Easy and automated—from the *customer* viewpoint
- *Secondary.* Rapid, flexible/adaptable, economical
- *Largest risk.* Employee resistance

Value Engineering

The terms *value engineering* (VE) and *value analysis* (VA) are synonymous for a management tactic with significant cost management implications, especially in the design phase of a product or service. General Electric was one of the first firms to use value engineering, initially applied to purchasing processes in 1947.[9] Rooted in the engineering discipline by way of common goals, VE connects directly to TQM customer and quality objectives and indirectly to the ABC/M focus on what the customer will pay for (i.e., value). VE, TQM, and ABC/M share two common objectives: eliminate waste and extraneous functions; realize high quality at the lowest possible cost.

Used successfully, VE drives growth by (1) presenting a superior value proposition to customers, and (2) cost reductions that contribute to a greater profit margin. Value engineering tactics particularly attract product designers and target-costing practitioners. VE tactics chiefly seek to design functional product/service qualities that deliver the most value to customers based on well-understood customer preferences. After design and development work, VE deploys its value analysis elements that focus on production cost management and monitor cost structures during the manufacturing cycle.

Robin Cooper and Regine Slagmulder point out that, "Target costing and value engineering can be viewed as concurrent activities as can kaizen costing and value analysis."[10] The authors go on to emphasize that, "It would be wrong to view VE as just another cost-reduction program. VE is primarily about product functions and only secondarily about cost. The motivating force behind VE is to ensure the product achieves its basic function in a way that satisfies the customer at an acceptable cost. Consequently, VE programs are the domain of the product engineer, not the accountant."[11] Even so, VE has significant impact on cost structure, where the leading indicators, customer value and manufacturing efficiencies, are assumed to lead to improvement of lagging financial results.

Value Engineering Essentials

VE tactics come in a number of formats. Cooper and Slagmulder use a three-part classification to describe the varied approaches: (1) product-direct application, (2) comparative tear-down approaches, and (3) miscellaneous limited, but focused, applications of VE tactics such as the checklist method, the one-day cost-reduction meeting, mini-VE, and the VE reliability program. The authors succinctly describe the first two categories that they consider most fundamental. (Emphases in the first paragraph are added.)

[Product-direct] VE can be applied directly to proposed products at different stages of the product design process. These different approaches are called "Looks." *Zero-look* VE is the application of VE principles at the *concept proposal stage*, the earliest stage in the design process. Its objective is to introduce new forms of functionality that did not previously exist. *First-look VE* focuses on the major elements of the product design and is defined as *developing new products from concepts*. The objective is to enhance functionality of the product by improving the capability of the existing functions. *Second-look VE* is applied during the *last half of the planning stage and the first half of the development* and product preparation stage. The objective of second-look VE, unlike that of the zero- and first-look, is to improve the value and functionality of existing components, not create new ones. Consequently, the scale of changes is much smaller than for zero- and first-look VE.

Comparative applications of VE consist of tearing down other products to identify new ways to reduce costs. Tear down is defined as *a comparative VE method through visual observation of disassembled equipment, parts, and data arranged in a manner convenient for such observation*. There are numerous approaches to tear down. The six dominant techniques are dynamic, cost, material, static, process, and matrix tear down. The first three methods are designed to reduce a product's direct manufacturing cost. The next three are intended to reduce the investment required to produce the product through increased productivity.[12]

All VE tactics aim to achieve two simultaneous performance goals: cost reduction and customer-driven quality improvements. In the spirit of Total Quality, VE practitioners usually apply VE techniques to VE processes as well. Cross-functional information exchange is another hallmark trait of VE.

A common VE pitfall relates to pricing. Although consumers want variety, innovation, and customization, when push comes to shove *cheaper* (i.e., more economical) often wins out as long as a product is reliable. The engineering discipline sometimes fails to take this into account. This stems from a misunderstanding of what cheaper means to the consumer. It is not simply price. The value of consumer *time* is a more subtle addition to the price tag. Specifically, value engineering can make errors in assuming consumer willingness to pay for an array of product bells and whistles. Designing in 1,000 capabilities costs the developer money that the customer may not want to pay for the sake of the 980 functions that will never be used. VE practitioners would do well to repeat the following mantra: The customer will pay the price for only those features that the customer needs. Successful VE practices depend upon good information about customer cost/benefit expectations.

Even price cutting has risks, as it may not entice more buyers who vigorously avoid extensive functionality requiring considerable time investment to learn. Naturally, technology products are vulnerable to this pitfall: Think software applications and set-top boxes. The only way to get most consumers to invest money in using new product/service functions is to make using them very, very easy. Think ease of user interface. Spending less time to acquire a new skill acts like a credit/discount to the monetary price, and therefore, makes the investment cheaper. Standard economic models do not even approach explaining this kind of interdependent dynamic. Repeat the VE mantra.

Value Engineering Strategic Attribute Profile

Value engineering tactics assume that well-understood customer-value imperatives dictate the quality of product design that in turn is aligned with effective production process design that then leads to reduced costs, increased customer satisfaction, and greater profits. Depending on the specifics of the design objectives, VE tactics address many different strategic attributes in the array. From the customer perspective, VE can help organizations adaptively create strategic advantages that include more economical, easy/automated, reliable product/service performance attributes. However, from the organizational perspective, the strategic strength of VE lies in innovation directly connected to actual customer preferences. Balancing innovation and profitability takes great skill because the VE process itself is expensive, as is the discovery of customer value perceptions.

- *Primary.* Innovative
- *Secondary.* Variety, customized, flexible/adaptable
- *Largest risk.* Implementation costs that erode profit

Target Costing

Target costing (TC) is a direct answer to the faults of cost-plus pricing and a direct contributor to the profit imperative. Informed by market conditions, TC tactics use engineering-based principles to manage costs and resources. Target cost management tactics aim to enable prices that yield a specified level of profit when employed during product/service planning and development stages or redesign efforts. Robin Cooper and Regine Slagmulder have a long history of experience in TC development and tactical application. They define TC as a "structured approach to determine the cost at which a proposed product with specified functionality and quality must be produced in order to generate the desired level of profitability over its life cycle at its anticipated selling price. It is as much a tool of profit management as it is of cost management."[13]

Japanese manufacturers were among the first to use TC tactics in their quest for profitable manufacturing process innovation. In conjunction with the TQM practices discussed in Chapter 5, and the lean and agile tactics discussed in this chapter, aligned target costing tactics allowed the Japanese to penetrate Western markets quickly and profitably. North American manufacturers partially closed the competitive gap created by the Japanese when they started to utilize TC tactics. That said, some firms that adopt TC tactics make a big mistake when they use TC as an isolated cost reduction tool. As an integrated tactic that strategically orchestrates (1) customer-preference information, (2) market dynamics, (3) product development, and (4) production management, target costing becomes a dangerous method when used for conventional cost-cutting purposes. Using TC tactics with incomplete information in any of these four areas produces risk.

Target Costing Essentials

Cooper and Slagmulder define the essentials of target costing: "At the heart of target costing lies a deceptively simple equation: Target Cost = Target Selling Price − Target Profit Margin."[14] This deceptively simple equation belies the work and focus required to design and produce a product to a targeted cost. Four questions need to be answered, one by one, before a target price or cost can be established.

1. *What do customers want?* The Quality Movement established customer focus. Pushing products into the marketplace without adequate customer inputs became a risky proposition. Based on preselected market segments and internal capabilities, a firm must discover what customers truly value. Firms discover customer preferences through sales and market history, focus groups, surveys, and other methods that determine which products/services have a reasonable chance of success. The discovery process includes ascertaining what competitors are already doing or may do in the near future.

2. *What and how much can be sold?* Few things in business are harder to do than set a price on an undefined product or service with unknown demand. In this situation, the strengths of TQM blend

with TC to clarify product definition, design, and market. Design decisions focus on the level of quality and on fitness specifications. Serious market research, not just conventional sales forecasting, assists in answering volume questions. Finally, target costing practitioners investigate how the new or redesigned product/service aligns within an existing product/service line.

3. *What are the possible cost structures and the pricing constraints based on our profit expectations?* This is where the cost rubber meets the pricing road. Creating a cost structure begins in the design or redesign phase of a product or service. Recall that about 80 percent of cost structure is determined at this stage. Production costs represent the downstream results of design work; therefore, marketers, designers, and producers need to coordinate from the beginning of the product's/service's life cycle. Supplier cost structures for components and support services also need to be included.

4. *How can new product/service risk be mitigated?* The answers to questions 1, 2, and 3 mitigate risk. Life cycle costing tactics, discussed later in this chapter, work with TC to expand the view of product/service economic timelines. Many companies set return-on-investment hurdle rates for products and services. Fewer firms terminate a product or service when hurdle rates are consistently missed. Target costing tactics deliberately guide management through resource investment and disciplined design planning to improve the risk/benefit ratio.

Many small and medium companies have neither resources nor expertise to gather comprehensive market and customer data, but they can still make use of target costing tactics through *product-level* and *component-level* target costing as developed by Cooper and Slagmulder.

Product-level TC depends on internal production and engineering staff to manage toward cost reduction without jeopardizing customer satisfaction. Product-level target cost managers focus on functions, features, and service levels. Even the smallest organizations can calculate their current product-level costs, set strategic objectives for cost improvement, and track progress by matching these efforts to actual costs. Supply chain management of component costs complements product-level TC at the parts procurement level.

Naturally, more benefit accrues from TC work at all three tactical levels—market, product, component—but work at any level usually yields improvements. However, risk increases when only one or two TC levels are used because managers work with incomplete information.

Finally, an obvious cost-related question: Which resource expenditures should be included in TC analyses? Conventional cost accountants would answer, "All variable costs." However, as pointed out in the first three chapters, conventional variable costing has serious shortcomings. A better approach uses ABC product-cost analyses that include all costs directly related to the product in question. The complexity and cost of this ABC application can be limited by the scope of the inquiry.

Target Costing Strategic Attribute Profile

Target costing is designed for profit management through better cost and pricing management. Thus, TC addresses all three of the income statement's major sections: revenue, expenditures, income/loss. Heavily market and customer-driven, TC methods inherently integrate an appropriate quality level based on the customer preferences that drive its tactical dynamics. TC is roll-up-the-sleeves cost and profit management with crystal-clear objectives and no fancy talk. It directly serves the profit imperative by leveraging several cost-focused strategic attributes:

Tactical Management of Costs and Resources

- *Primary.* Economical
- *Secondary.* Reliable, innovation-supportive
- *Largest risk.* Using without the necessary discipline or market information; losing a sense of changing conditions in the profit "forest" during lengthy, focused analysis of the target cost "trees"

The most reliable TC practitioners have learned to adopt a just-the-facts, scientific attitude to keep the work as realistic as possible. They keep a record of past TC efforts against actual results, to temper enthusiasm. The profit forest/cost trees analogy refers to the discipline required to also watch the big picture as it changes in the market while deliberately following target costing method detail. Getting lost in the details of a target costing initiative is a real danger. Target costing takes time, and the more time and energy invested, the harder it is to let the product go. But conditions change, competitors make moves, and TC practitioners must monitor factors beyond internal cost and process to make certain effort is going into the most promising products/services.

Life Cycle Cost Management

The most common experience in managing products and services follows a familiar sequence: careful concept analysis followed by design and preparation for the launch, then scrupulous shepherding of the new offering, and in short order, the fledgling blends into the indistinguishable, aggregated mass of the income statement. Ad hoc or cumbersome attempts to terminate or redesign an offering often end in either no decision or an uninformed judgment from the top.

The macroeconomic perspective of life cycle cost management (LCCM) can change this situation for the better. The typical LCCM initiative focuses on products and services, but the same tactics apply to managing the life of a brand, a technology investment, a customer relationship, the progress of a major initiative, and even to the life cycle of an entire business or industry.

Like target costing, life cycle cost management is conceptually simple but requires rigorous design and implementation discipline. Ideally, LCCM practitioners blend their efforts with target costing tactics to create a broader scope for product/service management. Target costing focuses on design and production; life cycle costing takes that information and adds a birth-to-death perspective. Together, TC and LCCM are the guardians of profitable innovation.

Life Cycle Cost Management Essentials

A life cycle runs from birth to maturation to death, or in product/service terms, from idea to design to test and production to the marketplace to the time when management revitalizes or abandons the idea. Some products/services have several incarnations, like the American Motors/Chrysler Jeep, or the Harley Davidson motorcycle. Life cycle analysis tactics can either precede or coevolve with TC to provide a go/no-go signal prior to innovation or renewal investments. All products/services need monitoring and adjustment at critical points in their lifespan, particularly when profit objectives change. LCCM practitioners deploy many specific tactical nuances dedicated to accumulating, analyzing, and altering costs over the life cycle. LCCM tactics also justify investments, affect interim cost reduction, and identify "hidden" life cycle costs.[15] Exhibit 6.2 depicts six key life cycle stages.

Cost management permeates the life cycle by:

- Creating a cross-functional consensus for the LCCM design.
- Keeping senior management honest by providing "just the facts."
- Producing preliminary life cycle cost estimates to assure that all relevant costs are included (i.e., SG&A as well as production).

EXHIBIT 6.2

Product/Services Life Cycle

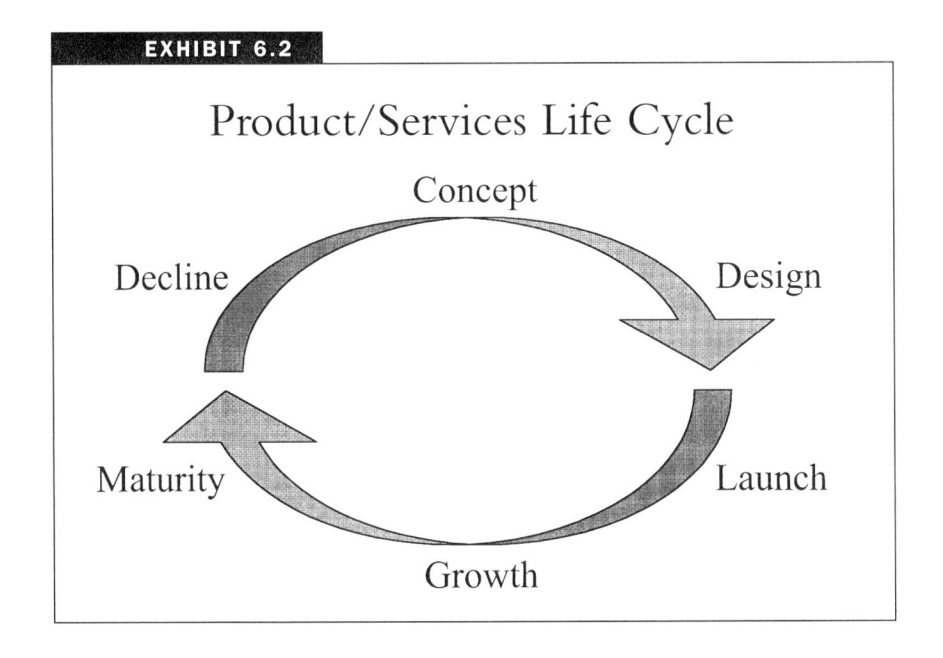

Concept → Design → Launch → Growth → Maturity → Decline

- Comparing actual ROI and/or recalculation of ROI at appropriate intervals (not done in most conventional environments).
- Leading cost reduction activities.
- Monitoring and reporting production cost and product/service profitability.
- Signaling alerts to profit erosion.
- Managing costs during phase-out and termination.

Traditionally, the income statement aggregates an organization's bundle of products and services along business segments and product/service lines. But just as a household budget can accumulate a significant negative position by overspending in several small categories, small losses on products/services can also add up to a disturbing negative position. Three disciplines that ameliorate or even prevent embarrassing situations like this include:

1. Reliable profitability information for actual performance of each product/service (ABC/M).
2. Timely management of information coordinated across all products and services with attention to synergies or conflicts between different offerings.
3. Rigorous target and life cycle costing.

When applied together, these three disciplines may not guarantee profitability but they provide management with early insight to risks, explicit cost/profit goals, signals that cost reduction efforts are needed, and information to "manage out of" the product or service before it significantly erodes total profit.

LCCM also minimizes premature bailouts based on early nonprofitable status reports. LCCM prepares managers to expect a profit learning curve that includes start-up costs and time to penetrate markets as natural parts of the life cycle. An ABC/M analysis will help managers assign LCCM costs where they belong: to the new product/service, rather than spreading costs across all products, as in conventional overhead/absorption accounting.

Life Cycle Cost Management Strategic Attribute Profile

Like target costing, LCCM focuses equally on profit management and cost management. Both approaches operate at the nexus of the diverse functions and energies that combine to launch a new product, implement an ERP system, or revitalize a brand.

- *Primary.* Economical
- *Secondary.* Innovation-supportive
- *Largest risk.* Use without the necessary discipline or market information; failure to compare actual to estimate and/or failure to act on LCCM information to alter cost and profit structures

In summary, life cycle cost management creates predictive advantage for any strategic intention that involves the management of costs over the long term. It does so by evaluating revenue-generation against cost and guiding cost reduction activities. LCCM is a powerful organizing tool, well worth the investment when aligned with appropriate long-term strategic cost management intentions.

Supply Chain Costing and Interorganizational Cost Management

Some time ago, cost management burst through the confines of individual organizations and began connecting cost and resource management efforts across and between organizations. *Outsourcing*, the strategic purchasing of ongoing external production capabilities and other services, was the first wave. Gradually, alliances deepened between customers and suppliers. Where once internal company cost information was secret and closely guarded, organizations started to share analyses and data openly with customers and suppliers in hopes of attaining mutually beneficial changes in cost structures. Richard Schonberger captures some of the early lessons. First, he cites what he calls, "a lesson from Japan, circa 1980: Don't have too many suppliers." Next, he cites, "a lesson from the United States, circa 1985: Don't have too many part numbers [i.e., components]."[16] Lean and agile manufacturing approaches developed during this time advocated both outsourcing and supply chain management to optimally utilize internal resources and manage costs.

More recently, progressive companies use systems thinking throughout the life cycles of products/services and customer/supplier relationships to form affiliations that create opportunities to manage costs strategically. A term has emerged to describe supply chain cost management efforts: Interorganizational Cost Management (ICM). Robin Cooper and Regine Slagmulder describe ICM as interdependent cooperative relationships, and define it as "a structured approach to coordinating the activities of firms in a supplier network so that total costs in the network are reduced."[17]

Supply Chain Costing and ICM Essentials

Cooper and Slagmulder provide a concise synopsis of the ICM worldview and describe how target costing and value engineering blend with supply chain tactics:

> Target costing lies at the heart of interorganizational cost management. It has two primary objectives. The first is to identify the cost at which a given product must be manufactured if it is to earn its target profit margin at its expected or target selling price. The second is to decompose the target cost down to the component level. The firm's suppliers then are expected to find ways to deliver the components they sell at the target prices set by their customers while still making adequate returns. When the suppliers also use target costing to discipline their product development processes, *chained target costing systems* emerge. Chained target costing is an important element of interorganizational cost management because it transmits the competitive pressure faced by the firm at the top of the supply chain to the other firms within the chain. It aligns the cost management programs of the firms in the chain by indicating to the suppliers where the buyer expects cost reduction to occur.
>
> Target costing systems, whether stand-alone or chained, operate at arm's-length as the cost reduction efforts of the buyer and supplier are undertaken in isolation. However, this isolation limits the effectiveness of the overall cost management process because each firm confines its analysis to local savings. Interorganizational cost management overcomes this limitation by creating formal mechanisms for the design teams of the firms in the supply chain to interact. These interactions enable

the product and its components to be designed in ways that reduce costs throughout the supply chain. Value engineering, an organized effort to find ways to achieve the product's functions in a manner that allows the firms to meet their target costs, lies at the heart of these interactions.[18]

ICM and supply chain tactics focus on design and production phases similar to target costing and value engineering. Importantly, though cost management is the primary driver of supply chain collaborations, other important advantages arise in this interorganizational paradigm. The adage, "two heads are better than one," applies; ICM facilitates creativity and innovation as diverse expertise and viewpoints come together. Internal administrative and operational process improvements also frequently emerge as part of the interorganizational cross-fertilization.

In *Supply Chain Development for the Lean Enterprise*, Cooper and Slagmulder offer four questions to investigate the activity level of ICM within an organization. These questions should be asked of both accountants and purchasing staff.

1. Does your firm set specific cost-reduction objectives for its suppliers?

2. Does your firm help its customers and/or suppliers find ways to achieve their cost-reduction objectives?

3. Does your firm take into account the profitability of its suppliers when negotiating component pricing with them?

4. Is your firm continuously making its buyer-supplier interfaces more efficient?[19]

Only a mature Stage III or Stage IV CMS can support such goals by accurately targeting and tracking cost reductions and cost structure changes. In addition, an advanced CMS enables two additional aspects of great import to ICM alliances: better demand forecasts and improved capacity/inventory management.

Supply Chain Costing and ICM Strategic Attribute Profile

Supply Chain and ICM tactics exemplify the trend toward attribute blending and integration as business methods evolve to more comprehensive models. Note how many strategic attributes these tactics possess. Compare the attribute profiles of earlier methods. Remember that these tactics (and strategic systems in the next chapter) are presented in a rough chronology of their development.

- *Primary.* Economical for customers and all members of the supply chain.
- *Secondary.* Easier/automated, reliable, rapid, innovative, flexible/adaptable.
- *Largest risk.* All attributes are at risk when an organization attempts to implement supply chain and ICM tactics *without* also applying the principles of lean and agile manufacturing. Failure can also quickly develop when the good of the whole supply chain partnership is sacrificed to the avarice of one or two members.

Supply chain and ICM execution involves many functions across participating organizations. The work must be planned and coordinated if it is to succeed. Eight major steps (see Tips & Techniques: "Steps to Adopting ICCM") are recommended over an extended timeline. This is no overnight fix, but rather an integrated process and relationship improvement effort.

Summary and Lessons from the Field

The more intelligent an organization becomes, the more it utilizes a greater range of management methods and tactics, with greater knowledge that *blending* methods and tactic works best. This means creating a strategy, intention, or focus as an overall umbrella to guide selection

> **TIPS & TECHNIQUES**
>
> ## Steps to Adopting ICCM
>
> 1. Identify the parts of the product [service] that are going to be externally sourced.
> 2. Determine the appropriate level of the buyer-supplier relationship for each externally sourced item.
> 3. Rationalize [the] supplier base.
> 4. Develop the appropriate supplier relationships.
> 5. [Increase] the efficiency of the buyer-supplier interface.
> 6. Develop the necessary skills in the techniques of ICM.
> 7. [Extend] lean supply and ICM both upstream and downstream in the firm's supply chains.
> 8. [Extend] lean supply and ICM to internal suppliers.
>
> Adapted from Robin Cooper and Regine Slagmulder, *Supply Chain Development for the Lean Enterprise: Interorganizational Cost Management*, Portland, OR: Productivity, Inc., 1999, pp. 24–25.

and execution of the right management tactics, in the right degree, with the right method-partners. Only a "learning organization" can develop this kind of competence. An organization that fails in the long run is the one that seeks the single right answer and punishes those who deviate from simple, short-term, cost-obsessed solutions.

The path to value is a precarious road. Efforts to create successful, profitable customer and supplier partnerships carry no guarantees of success. New product/service failures are expensive and waste precious time and resources. Chapters 5 and 6 show an array of management tactics and approaches that can support better cost management and mitigate risk in new ventures and in improvement efforts. Tactic selection sense requires the ability to:

- Articulate clear intentions before choosing tactics.
- Choose a management tactic based on the capacity of its strategic attributes to execute strategic intent.
- Link capital allocation and performance expectations to strategic planning and supportive management tactics.
- Blend management tactics to suit the unique set of needs for each initiative.
- Whenever possible, test run a management tactic in a simulation or prototype effort; proof of concept saves time and resources.
- Keep in mind that strategies and management tactics are created anew in every organization; they cannot be copied.
- Allocate appropriate resources. Tactical deployment takes resources. That means people, space, equipment, and above all, executive participation.

Endnotes

1. For example, see Arie de Geus, *The Living Company* (Boston: Harvard Business School Press, 1997).

2. Michael Hammer, "Reengineering Work: Don't Automate, Obliterate," *Harvard Business Review* (July–August 1990): 104–112.

3. Michael Hammer and James Champy, *Reengineering the Corporation: A Manifesto for Business Revolution* (New York: HarperBusiness, 1993).

4. For example, see
    - James Champy, *X-Engineering in the Corporation: Reinventing Your Business in the Digital Age* (New York: Warner Books, 2002).

- Nitin Nohria and James Champy, *The Arc of Ambition: Defining the Leadership Journey* (Cambridge, MA: Perseus Books, 2001).
- Michael Hammer, "Process Management and the Future of Six Sigma," *MIT Sloan Management Review* 43, no. 2 (Winter 2002): 26–32.
- Michael Hammer, *The Agenda: What Every Business Must Do to Dominate the Decade* (New York: Crown Publishing, 2001).
- Michael Hammer, *Beyond Reengineering: How the Process-Centered Organization Is Changing Our Work and Our Lives* (New York: HarperBusiness, 1996).

5. James Champy, *Reengineering Management: The Mandate for New Leadership* (New York: HarperBusiness, 1995).

6. Joseph B. White, "Re-Engineering Gurus Take Steps to Remodel Their Stalling Vehicles," *The Wall Street Journal* (November 26, 1996): section A, pp. 1, 13.

7. Id., 13.

8. From materials provided at a lecture attended by C. Stenzel, given by Michael Hammer, March 2, 1994, Minneapolis, MN.

9. Dr. Richard Schonberger cites the GE effort in his book *Let's Fix It! Overcoming the Crisis in Manufacturing* (New York: The Free Press, 2001): 186. Dr. Schonberger notes that "SAVE International [originally, Society of American Value Engineering] is the umbrella organization for the value engineering discipline, value-eng.com."

10. Robin Cooper and Regine Slagmulder, "Target Costing for New Product Development, Parts 1, 2, and 3," *Journal of Cost Management* 16, nos. 3–5 (2002)

11. Id.

12. Id.

13. Id.

14. Id.

15. For detailed discussions of life cycle management, see *The Handbook of Cost Management*, John Shank, ed. (New York: WG&L, RIA Group, 2002).
16. Richard J. Schonberger, *Let's Fix It! Overcoming the Crisis in Manufacturing* (New York: The Free Press, 2001): 185.
17. Robin Cooper and Regine Slagmulder, *Supply Chain Development for the Lean Enterprise: Interorganizational Cost Management* (Portland, OR: Productivity, Inc., 1999): xxii.
18. Id., xxii, 1–2.
19. Id., 3.

CHAPTER 7

Strategy-Based Systems and the Future of Cost Management

After reading this chapter you will be able to

- Enhance your use of strategic vocabulary
- Develop a sense for aligning tactics with strategic systems
- Understand three of the most common strategic management systems: strategic cost management, value-based management, and strategic performance measurement and management
- Use incentives to support strategic achievement

Analogies for strategic planning call on many images; for example, sailing a large ship, winning a team sports event, and navigating an aircraft instrument panel. Always the analogy involves something sizeable and complicated, with dynamic components subject to changing variables. Anyone who has sailed a ship, flown an aircraft, or played a team sport knows the feeling of being on the outer edge of control. Organizational life operates under similar dynamics. An unexpected gust of competitive wind can upset balance. A sudden storm of disruptive technology can cloud the business landscape. The unanticipated departure of a key employee can injure a winning sales or operations team. In positive contrast, there is the exhilaration of sailing with a well-coordinated crew, the adventure of flight, and the thrill of a game well played. The business parallels are obvious.

Weathering adverse conditions is much easier when an organization has a vision, strategy, and directional course for the enterprise. Employees can be replaced, competition can be countered, and technologies can be developed. But if executives do not chart a clear course, articulate it well and often, and change that course when necessary, resources whither and waste, performance targets lose their meaning, and the workforce becomes distressed. "Where there is no vision, the people perish." (Prov. 29:18.)

The approaches discussed in this chapter stand at the forefront of current management maturity. Within each comprehensive framework, cost management remains a core practice but becomes integrated into strategic context. In spite of the healthy array of comprehensive (i.e., organization-wide) approaches available, a significant number of executives—especially in public companies—continue to manage with a short-term, financial focus. This is no secret. The reasons why are equally evident. The prime suspects include:

- *Investor and analyst focus on financial measures.* EPS, share price, P/E ratio, and so on
- *Executive compensation keyed only to financial results.* Revenue growth, EVA, RONA
- *Stock option prevalence.* That is, the compensation expense that, until recently, rarely appeared on the income statement

Recent events have called into question short-term practices and the myopic focus on financial measures. The bursting dot-com bubble, eroding confidence in accounting firms, big business accounting shenanigans, and increasing regulatory strictures may exert the necessary pressure to force a level of disclosure capable of changing counterproductive practices.

The strategic systems explored in this chapter may facilitate improved business practices. While investigating these systems, it is important to understand some key definitions.

- *Incentive.* Etymologically stemming from the word "incantation," any item that incites action; in a business sense, any item that incites action *and aligns* the behavior of individual employees with broad organizational intentions.
- *Management Control System.* "The formal, information-based routines and procedures managers use to maintain or alter patterns in organizational activities." [1]
- *Shareholder/Stakeholder.* Throughout this book, but especially in this chapter, shareholder refers to any person who owns stock in the organization; stakeholder refers to any person who benefits, or suffers, in any way from the success or failure of the organization.
- *Strategic Cost Management (SCM).* The "application of cost management techniques so that they simultaneously improve the strategic position of a firm and reduce costs. Strategic cost management can be applied in service and manufacturing settings and in not-for-profit environments."[2]

Strategy: A Rose with Many Names

The term *strategy* is so generic that managers often do not bother to confirm a common understanding of strategic process. Frequently, executives in strategic planning sessions tacitly assume everyone around the table understands strategy in the same way. More often, the truth is that in a roomful of executives there are as many descriptions of strategy as there are people in the room. It is probably fair to say that many executives could not name the school of strategic thought they adhere to, although they regularly create strategic plans.

Strategic planning and success depend more upon a common strategic vocabulary than on any specific strategic theory. Without this commonality, disjointed management tactics conflict with one another, projects proliferate, and employees get confused. Confused employees create confused customers.

A clear strategy, communicated widely and articulately, has the opposite effect. Tactical choices align with overall strategic direction. Limited resources are efficiently conserved. People at all levels make decisions within clear guidelines, knowing which actions contribute to success and which do not. Customers and clients who sense organizational and employee confidence are more likely to purchase products and services.

Many Models

In an article titled, "Reflecting on the Strategy Process," Henry Mintzberg and Joseph Lampel categorize strategic management into ten schools.[3] This forms a fairly comprehensive as-is picture of strategic approaches. Rather than push the merits of a single school of strategic thinking, they describe the strengths and weakness of each and recommend a deliberate, three-step approach to any strategic practice:

1. Choose the appropriate strategy for specific conditions.

2. Blend relevant constructs from two or more schools.

3. Avoid overdependence on any single strategic perspective.

The authors also insist that the chief responsibility of executives is to formulate strategy and discover what works in practice. This is ongoing creative work. Their article recommends blending all ten schools into a new perspective: strategy formation as a single process.

Obviously, strategic thinking has grown beyond the confines of the familiar SWOT analysis—strengths, weaknesses, opportunities, and threats. Therefore, executives should forget about finding the "perfect" strategy and become facile in creating and evolving a dynamic strategic process aligned with specific organizational conditions and requirements. If this begins to sound much like blending cost management methods and tactics, it is.

This brief discussion of strategy sets the context for the remaining sections in this chapter, because more mature businesses use some form of strategy as their management paradigm than any other framework for

> **TIPS & TECHNIQUES**
>
> ## Ten Schools of Strategy Formation
>
> | School | Intended Message | Associated Homily |
> |---|---|---|
> | 1. Design | Fit | "Look before you leap." |
> | 2. Planning | Formalize | "A stitch in time saves nine." |
> | 3. Positioning | Analyze | "Just the facts, ma'am." |
> | 4. Entrepreneurial | Envision | "Take us to your leader." |
> | 5. Cognitive | Cope or create | "I'll see it when I believe it." |
> | 6. Learning | Learn | "If at first you don't succeed, try, try again." |
> | 7. Power | Promote | "Look out for number one." |
> | 8. Cultural | Coalesce | "An apple never falls far from the tree." |
> | 9. Environmental | React | "It all depends." |
> | 10. Configuration | Integrate, transform | "To everything there is a season." |
>
> Excerpted from Table 1 in "Reflecting on the Strategy Process," Henry Mintzberg and Joseph Lampel, *MIT Sloan Management Review*, (Spring 1999), pp. 21–30.

organizational coordination. However, strategy is not the only framework for managing an organization. Some companies do very well with strong vision and cultural values.[4] Others consider themselves process-oriented companies in the spirit of the "process enterprise." Human service organizations are frequently mission-driven. In process, vision, and mission contexts, strategic planning may not be emphasized at all. The critical point remains: The primary context for setting the direction of the organization and its activities must be clearly articulated and widely communicated. Whether the organization sets direction based on strategy, vision, mission, value creation, process, or even the budget, everyone must speak the same language.

A last word of historical caution. As this is written in mid-2002, pundits and analysts are trying to decide whether the global economy is in recession, recovering, or already mended. The signals are mixed and volatile. In the confusion, a disturbing number of organizations have reengaged the predictable slash-and-burn cost-cutting tactics typical in uncertain business climates. During good economic times, there is plenty of time for strategy and performance management. When the financial measurements deteriorate, managers rivet their attention on the short term and revert to counterproductive cost cutting. A manager with a cost-cutting hatchet is more likely to destroy significant value than to save significant costs. Cost reductions for their own sake (e.g., indiscriminant layoffs, cutting all department budgets by x percent) disable value creation; in contrast, strategically grounded resource and cost management creates value.

Giving Cost Management a Strategic Context

Referring again to the four-stage model of cost management system development in Exhibit 1.3 in Chapter 1, note that product, customer, operational, and strategic information categories do not even surface until the Stage III system. Following a predictable development sequence, Stage III organizations grow beyond the financial report-driven cost management system by learning, step by step, the value of capturing more managerially relevant information.

First, as they learn the value of managerial information, Stage III organizations introduce more operationally oriented resource accounting systems, like ABC, to complement the external reporting focus of the traditional cost accounting system. Next, once employees become accustomed to the timeliness of operational resource accounting information, they begin to see the need for more immediate operational feedback and control. ABC matures to ABM. Finally, as organizations learn the difference between leading and lagging indicators across these independent information systems, "strategic performance" becomes a meaningful and manageable next step.

Strategic insight motivates organizations moving toward Stage IV to integrate the stand-alone systems to provide internal and external constituents with a balanced performance database that reports up-to-date, relevant information on cost, customer, operations, and strategy from a single management system. Stage IV organizations frequently utilize a form of cause-effect "strategic mapping," to explicitly chart the path of strategic execution.[5] In a Stage IV CMS, resource management is deliberate and purposeful. The purpose of this book is to provide executives and managers with the cost management background necessary to move a Stage II organization forward. Typically, informed *nonfinancial* managers lead the way out of Stage II stasis.

Migration from Stage II, to III, and then to IV comes only through a process of learning and development. Organizations cannot skip steps by implementing an off-the-shelf enterprisewide software system. "Relevant information" means something to employees only when they have learned how to apply it. Jumping from Stage II to Stage IV puts an organization at risk of resembling "a golfer buried in a sand trap near the green who attempts to sink the ball in the hole with a single shot, [and finds itself] reburied in Stage II."[6]

Strategic Cost Management

Executives design organizations—intentionally or not—to display a particular profile: a mission-driven entity, an economic profit machine, a complex adaptive living system, a military operation, or a competitive

TIPS & TECHNIQUES

Questions to Ask *about* Your Accountant

Two-thirds of accounting graduates in the United States take jobs with corporations. Ten to fifteen years ago, bookkeeping skills and closing the books on time were enough. This is no longer true. Financial professionals are now expected to be the *strategic partners* and *internal business advisors* for corporations. Bookkeeping skills remain important but transparent. The demands of an advanced CMS linked to strategy that utilizes the tactics and systems described in Chapters 5, 6, and 7 require a top-notch financial professional or an accountant who is willing to work to become one. Here are yes/no questions to ask *about* your accountant to ascertain whether he or she is up to the challenge. The more yes answers, the better.

YES/NO

Grade C Profile

____Focuses on the financial internal well-being of the corporation.

____Proficient in budgeting, asset management, and standard costing.

____Provides accurate historical financial information.

____Closes the books on time and provides timely financial reports.

____Adept at using appropriate technology.

Grade B Profile (Includes all C competencies)

____Focuses on financial and operational internal well-being of the corporation.

____Provides accurate financial and operational information.

____Capable of decision-quality forecasting and simulation.

____Astutely analyzes and suggests actions for global and local issues.

TIPS & TECHNIQUES CONTINUED

____Develops approaches and recommendations that lead to significant improvements.

____Participates in process improvement efforts; works well on teams.

____Helps design information systems.

Grade A Profile (Includes all C and B competencies)

____Focuses on internal and external (i.e., customers, suppliers) corporate well-being.

____Consistently exhibits leadership competencies.

____Is an excellent verbal, written, and quantitative communicator.

____Has excellent interpersonal and team-building skills.

____Is instrumental in shaping and evolving organization strategy.

____Leads continuous performance improvement efforts.

____Leads design and implementation of knowledge management IT systems.

Advanced Profile (Includes C, B, and A competencies and then some)

____Focuses on holistic corporate well-being, including community and environmental impacts.

____Advocates long-term financial health versus short-term extractive gains.

____Exhibits leadership in the business community.

____Exhibits leadership in social and environmental concerns.

____Is considered a role model for others regarding integrity.

athletic team. Strategic Cost Management (SCM) practitioners see, direct, and guide the organization as a cost structure designed for generating value through strategies supported by appropriate resource allocations. Recalling that SCM is defined as the "application of cost management techniques so that they simultaneously improve the strategic position of a firm and reduce costs," organization design ideally mirrors the strategic cost structure. For example, if the firm is primarily driven by R&D efforts, significant portions of both resources and authority reside strategically in R&D functions in the classic architectural principle of "form follows function." In other words, strategy structures and integrates all cost management techniques.

In short, SCM is an updated name for Advanced Cost Management. Using cause-effect logic, SCM deploys any of the suitable cost management tactics and concepts discussed in all previous chapters of this book. Cost and resource managers who reach the SCM milestone understand conventional cost accounting *and* advanced cost management methods well enough to create a highly visible and transparent system of strategic cost structures for resource allocation and cost management. SCM means never having to say "either/or"; for example, "Either we cut costs to meet profit targets, or we spend money to achieve strategic objectives."

Strategy assumes integration. From the top down, executives must orchestrate strategic execution through integrated processes and activities. Most executives are in organizations where processes and information systems already exist. Thus, design and implementation of a Stage III or IV CMS must take existing functions and IT platforms into account. Without exception, SCM and strategic integration rely heavily on coordinated information technology.

The relevant point is that connecting an advanced cost management system to existing business and financial processes is a work of management art, as much as technology. Specifically, SCM practitioners strategically select and utilize the same management tactics such as those discussed in Chapter 6—supply chain management, target costing, and life cycle management—to enhance or replace conventional systems. Similarly, within an SCM context, ABC/M is capable of organizationwide impact to cost structures. When methods and tactics such as these are strategically applied, they support improved management of processes, products, services, customers, suppliers, resources, and capacity.

Strategic Cost Management and Financial Management

As its name implies, Strategic Cost Management approaches resource management from both cost and strategy perspectives. Cost provides the financial emphasis. Strategy provides activity alignment and integration structure. This combination makes it possible for SCM practitioners to directly impact financial results through intentional resource allocations based on management's strategic choices. Within cost and financial systems, the SCM method improves budgeting (ABB), transfer pricing decisions, product costing and pricing, and the measurement of waste. These financial aspect improvements are a direct result of more complete resource information and a common set of management priorities for decision making across functions.

From an information systems perspective, nearly all ERP systems now contain cost and performance management modules. These modules use the same cost database for financial and cost management reporting; therefore reconciliation—total cost to total cost—is practical, in characteristic Stage IV CMS fashion. While the financial module facilitates firmwide and segment profit reporting, the cost module addresses internal management concerns related to customer, product, and supplier profitability. These functions describe the basics of an integrated Stage IV CMS information technology appropriate for supporting SCM.

In a business environment ruled by the interests of the profit imperative, managers will predictably pay more attention to the information from the system that is used to determine incentives and bonuses. The incentives typical of conventional accounting systems push managers to make decisions based on GAAP profit, or in public companies, on share price measures. In contrast, Stage III and IV companies that take an SCM view typically use an ABC/M system to report more accurate and timely information about the contributions that strategic activities make to the profit imperative. Unlike GAAP accounting, ABC/M points directly to opportunities for process and activity improvement. These are the concrete achievements that directly contribute to profitability, and thus a superior incentive basis.

Unfortunately, many Stage III companies still ask employees to serve two masters when they pay incentives based on the GAAP system, while they attempt to manage activity and process improvements with SCM tactics. The key insight here is that SCM tactics *lead* to profitability, whereas financial accounting reports results. Executives need to resolve any conflicts or mixed messages between systems. Diligent attention to incorporating decision support and incentive logic is essential, especially during ERP implementations.

Nonfinancial Strategic Cost Management Focus Points

Strategic cost management practitioners direct resource allocation and cost structure control both inside and outside of organization boundaries. Therefore, applications cover a lot of ground. Some of the more common management applications include:

- Supply chains and the lean enterprise
- Internal markets—for example, streamlining transactions, creating pseudo-profit centers

- Capacity and supply-demand analyses
- Organizational design studies based on cost and resource structures
- Product design and development, using target costing and value engineering
- Product mix and pricing
- Value-chain management
- Customer profitability
- Brand or product line support

Frequently, ABC/M is the cost management method of choice for working with these analysis objectives within the SCM context.

All SCM initiatives address market and competitive positions, promote improved cost frameworks, and work to align human behavior throughout the organization. With so many possible applications, prudent SCM practitioners regularly perform a strategic audit of all current and planned cost management initiatives to confirm that each supports the organization's strategic intentions, that projects are not redundant, and that insights are quickly and widely shared. Organizations new to this practice can use the strategic audit to refocus the entire cost management system and realign its components with strategic intent.

Refocusing cost management means abandoning the "easy" answers like across-the-board cuts, and turning to more intelligent tactics such as ABC/M, resource consumption accounting, and supply chain management.

Methods of Strategic Cost Management Financial/Nonfinancial Integration

"I must meet strategic goals for which I have inappropriate resources, but I must use those inappropriate resources according to budget directives that prevent me from applying the resources I have toward meeting strategic goals." This catch-22 statement could be uttered by any manager constrained by conventional cost accounting and budgeting practices. For example, a Fortune 500 retailer intending to implement a performance measurement system allocated a sizeable sum to the initiative—the lion's share to IT and software implementation. Knowledgeable (and frustrated) project leaders wanted to apply some of the funds to data research and analyses and to consulting support. They were unable to do so because IT "had the budget." Conventional budget systems frequently include such constraints and controls.

Strategic cost management makes sure that resource allocation follows a clear logic and has the consensus of those charged with implementation. Again, ABC/M is arguably the chief cost management method in the SCM arsenal, because it focuses on connecting resources to activities and, subsequently, to cost objects identified as strategic points of interest. Executives are capable of delivering appropriate resources (e.g., people, space, money) only when the management system they use integrates strategic planning, budgeting, and resource allocation activities. Organizations that emphasize financial objectives and incentives based on them develop a budget-driven culture; organizations that employ fiscal control systems that adapt and blend with the actual business environment cultivate a strategy-driven culture. The strategy-driven culture collects and integrates nonfinancial information necessary to deploy the strategy and connects it to financial results.

Strategic Cost Management Capabilities Assessment

Strategic Cost Management has high potential for integrating an array of tactics because it functions inside and outside the walls of the organization. SCM creates significant management value in terms of customer and supplier relationships. When coordinated under an SCM umbrella,

ABM methods can provide clear cause-effect insights into customer profitability, especially when combined with statistical methods. SCM practitioners investigate the profitability of customer relationships in terms of the cost of customer-focused strategy. In other words, SCM helps identify the costs that are incurred but typically go unrecognized in customer analyses. New strategies bring new activities with unexpected and sometimes unconventional costs. ABM translates strategic innovations into activity cost elements and cost drivers so that profitability can be more accurately determined.

Similarly, SCM utilizes ABM to investigate and compare the costs of different customer relationship profiles by size, complexity, required service-after-sales, and other distinguishing features. Sometimes the costs incurred serving a customer can significantly undermine the profit that customer's purchases bring the organization. Fire the customer? ABM can discover the actual costs behind these high-cost relationships and help managers negotiate and control the costs of serving various customer types. Here are some examples of customer cost-to-service activities that detract from customer proceeds, but remain invisible in conventional profitability accounting.

- Rebates
- Pricing schemes
- Special customer services at zero incremental price to customer: breakpacks, small-order size, desktop delivery, software support, special packaging, special labeling, warehousing, contingent sales inventory
- Expanded product line and product customization
- EDI order entry errors by customers[7]

Incentive structures help explain why organizations usually do not understand or manage customer profitability. Where incentives are based on sales revenue growth, executives pay attention to the top line of the income statement and hope for the best in terms of costs associated with that growth. Likewise, when compensation depends on profit or price/earnings measurements, executives attend to the bottom line of the income statement. Sales growth and aggregate profitability are the most common bases for incentive calculation; both points of focus omit product-specific cost (COGS) and expense (SG&A), the main containers of major cost drivers.

Last, some SCM practitioners believe that the flexibility of the SCM financial/nonfinancial information system creates important diagnostic opportunities for mapping profitability for the next round of strategic planning.[8] Each strategic cycle attempts to enhance profitability. Profitability maps show the most important areas of analysis for decision-support information gathering and reporting before and during each strategic cycle.

For example, ABC information could be used to characterize the relationship between resource expenditures and revenue generation. Very high- and very low-profitability products, services, and customers are obvious starting points for profit probability mapping. Similarly, some organizations may choose to map new, or proposed, product, service, or customer profitability performance against well-understood business offerings and customer relationships. The same logic can be applied to important but poorly performing products, services, or customers. This kind of ABC-generated profitability mapping guides managers to make profitable decisions in line with organizational strategy.

Value-Based Management

The path to value creation is an uncertain road. Commerce and trade have been interested in value for centuries, but in the last part of the twentieth century, value concepts became explicitly defined. ABC/M and TQM were among the first formal methods designed to eliminate

Strategy-Based Systems and the Future of Cost Management

waste and focus attention on value-added and nonvalue-added activities and processes. More recently, the term *value proposition* has been popularized.[9]

Financial reporting, the stock market, and the profit imperative place the focus on value in activities that create *shareholder* value. But owners are not the only constituents with value expectations. What do customers really value? What do they *really* want? How can managers positively distinguish the organization's value proposition from the competitor in the eyes of the customer who buys the product/service that leads to revenue and profit? Should we be as concerned about value propositions for internal constituents (i.e., employees) as we are about customers and shareholders? Is there any profit to be gained by managing employee value propositions? How do all the converging interests of those concerned with an organization's success or failure work together to create mutually satisfying value? The answers to these questions lie in how each organization uniquely chooses to define, create, and measure value.

In its most fundamental sense, James Knight defines value-based management as a "systematic approach to creating shareholder value."[10] Paul Sharman believes that cost management falls under the larger umbrella of value-based management: "Value-based management (VBM) is the super-system of measurement and management, within which cost management is subordinate."[11]

So, like strategic cost management, value-based management is a conceptual umbrella that coordinates a variety of tactics and systems to accomplish its ends. Unlike the Balanced Scorecard, discussed in the next section, no one has yet come up with a widely accepted model for a VBM model.

Value-Based Management and Financial Management

Value-based management usually targets shareholder value and directs all organizational energy toward maximizing shareholder wealth. Although the validity of this singular focus is questioned, shareholder wealth is the current VBM focus. The cost of capital also figures prominently in VBM calculations. The biggest risk in using a VBM approach is that it may encourage the financial measurement myopia that operationally mature resource managers try to avoid. This risk is greatest when value is measured only in monetary terms. Many VBM proponents counter that valuation in monetary terms is the whole point, and creating shareholder value focuses the organization and drives success for all constituents. Arguably, the profit imperative has made VBM, in some form, the current predominant business model. However, many value-based managers have learned that shareholder value propositions depend upon other predecessor value-proposition relationships.

Customers grow ever smarter and more savvy, hence, identifying and meeting their shifting expectations has become a necessary part of the game. Even notoriously price-sensitive customer constituents will not always be swayed by price tags alone. The equation is a simple one: Fulfill customer expectations at a price that the customer is willing to pay.

Nonfinancial Value-Based Management Focus Points

Value must also be measured in nonfinancial terms. Although shareholder value creation is a necessary goal under current business paradigms, financial capital management falls short when other value dimensions remain unattended.

A long, complex process of market research, product/service design, employee performance, resource allocation and utilization, and other leading-indicator activities determine share price and profit. Therefore, shareholder value creation must be managed from strategy first, then executed through enabling processes and activities, then carried out by people who believe that their value propositions are also being met. The cause-effect relationship of various VBM models is emerging as:

satisfied employees → satisfied customers → profitability → increased shareholder wealth.

The causal links in any value proposition chain will feature these four steps with varying degrees of emphasis. The steps preceding profitability focus on the nonfinancial elements that support shareholder value creation. Shareholder wealth is a downstream result.

Methods of Value-Based Management Financial/Nonfinancial Integration

One of the best known approaches for value creation is the Stern Stewart Economic Value-Added (EVA) model that uses the following equation to create shareholder value:

EVA = NOPAT − [capital times the cost of capital] where NOPAT = net operating profit after tax.

To address nonfinancial and nonshareholder elements, EVA-type methods sometimes include a stewardship perspective. Typically, this is interpreted as the care and nurturing of assets not one's own, like the biblical "good steward." Some of the best VBM models cascade financial and nonfinancial measurements throughout the organization, all aligned toward the profit imperative, but cognizant of nonfinancial drivers.

Strategic cost and performance management models frequently use VBM approaches. ABM and EVA act as complementary partners in cost and value management. Organizations enhance their economic value added by integrating activity-based profitability maps into EVA concepts. Stated simply, any justifiable economic investment must earn at least the cost of its capital as follows:

$$ABC - EVA = \text{Revenue} - [ABC\ \text{Cost} + (\text{Capital Employed} \times \text{Cost of Capital})]^{12}$$

This EVA/ABC arrangement means that the organization must determine the capital deployed for each cost object and identify a risk-adjusted rate for that capital.

Value-based models make good candidates for the high-level objectives within the Balanced Scorecard's financial perspective discussed later in this chapter. "EVA's contribution as a financial metric is to go beyond accounting net income by recognizing an explicit capital charge for a business. Whether companies use ROI, ROCE, EVA, or some other value-based metric as the high-level financial objectives, they have two basic strategies for driving their financial performance: growth and productivity."[13]

Strong VBM methods like EVA are worthy candidates for measuring financial capital and explicitly managing the financial aspect. VBM systems work best when blended with other methods that more thoroughly address employee well-being, customer and supplier profitability, intellectual capital, brand value, and process management dimensions.

Value-Based Management Capabilities Assessment

By this point in the discussion, it should be increasingly clear that as cost management methods mature, they become less rigidly structured and more amendable to synergetic blending with complementary methods. SCM and VBM in particular are conceptually flexible enough to accommodate a wide array of supportive approaches. The most important caution is to be sure to consider the value propositions for *all* significant stakeholders, not just shareholders. Employee stakeholder benefits include greater job security, increased compensation that includes non-salary types such as more valuable stock options, autonomous decision making, and opportunities for promotions and other forms of job enrichment.

The greatest challenge to VBM practitioners is to keep a balanced focus on financial and nonfinancial information. Pressures from institutional investors and other short-term-focused stakeholders to create immediate, short-term value often compromise the long-term value propositions for employees and customers, as well as for society at large.

Performance Measurement and Management Systems

As discussed in this section, performance measurement and management systems are control paradigms designed to comprehensively coordinate all organizational resources, processes, operations, and strategic decisions into an integrated management system. Performance management paradigms come in many flavors (and brands), but they all share three common characteristics:

1. Financial information and cost management systems serve as one element in a balanced, linked set of financial and nonfinancial information resources.

2. Continuous improvement as measured by the system is part of daily management life for all employees, activities, and functions.

3. The performance management system aligns all employees, business units, and constituents by means of a few, carefully articulated central management objectives.

Measurement changes behavior. When organizations reach a level of high resource management maturity and insight, executives begin to value clarity and consensus about central management objectives. This focus permits leadership to decentralize authority and decision making throughout a well-informed, strategically aligned workforce. Performance management systems leverage information resources by establishing a formal architecture for the organization's financial and nonfinancial information intelligence. A key goal for the performance system architecture is to balance financial and operational/nonfinancial information.

Most organizations base their performance management information architectures on strategy and value creation, and build them from basic information categories: financial, process, customer, supplier, and sometimes research, innovation, and employee data. Less frequently, information categories include advanced components such as community health and environmental impact. Performance management systems emphasize organizational priorities through various IT architecture designs, using information access, performance measure accountability, and results visibility to signal preferred actions and to direct employee attention. Ideally, this information is conveyed immediately and widely through Internet access and Web sites. Four central management focuses guide the performance information system design: budgetary compliance, process improvement, value creation for identified constituents, and strategic accomplishment.

Budget-centered performance management systems use a conventional information system design that parallels the arrangement of organizational structure in either a classic corporate/divisional/departmental hierarchy (see Exhibit 7.1a) or a more advanced framework such as activity-based budgeting—ABB—(see Chapter 5). Corporate develops and assigns responsibility for performance measurements that focus on the primary budgetary accountabilities at each organizational level or activity focus.

Financial measurements typically dominate traditional performance management systems because the organizations that employ a Stage II

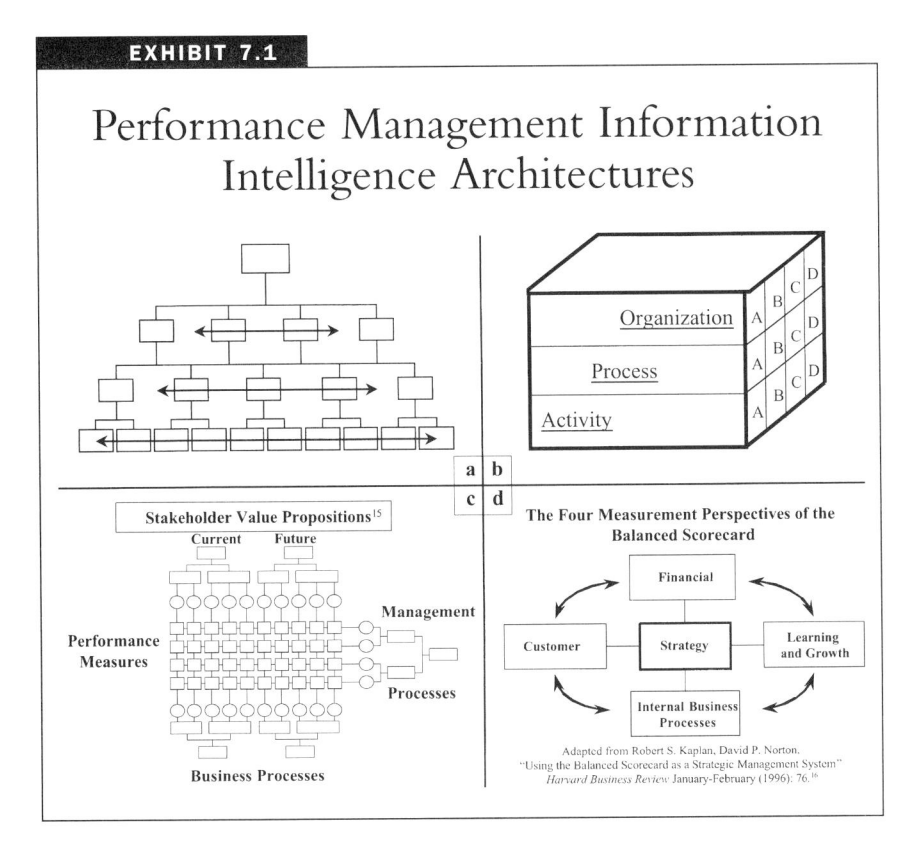

Strategy-Based Systems and the Future of Cost Management

EXHIBIT 7.1

Performance Management Information Intelligence Architectures

a	b
c	d

Stakeholder Value Propositions[15]
Current / Future

Performance Measures

Management
Processes

Business Processes

The Four Measurement Perspectives of the Balanced Scorecard

Financial — Strategy — Customer — Learning and Growth — Internal Business Processes

Adapted from Robert S. Kaplan, David P. Norton, "Using the Balanced Scorecard as a Strategic Management System" *Harvard Business Review* January-February (1996): 76.[16]

---

architecture depend upon the budget and conventional accounting systems as the primary means of control. Traditional systems frequently measure success against the budget. Even advanced budgeting methods, such as ABB, cannot achieve strategic balance or execution on their own. Consequently, this section addresses three performance measurement systems that attain a more balanced and comprehensive management perspective. First, *process-centered* performance management systems use an information intelligence architecture that captures the interdependent dynamics across three broad measurement layers:

1. The overall *organization*
2. The *processes* that support it
3. The *activities* that support the processes (see Exhibit 7.1b)[14]

Process-centered architectures measure the performance of each of these three levels with appropriately chosen metrics for organization, process, and activity. In this model, perspectives A, B, C, and D might be Financial, Customer, Quality, and Supplier. Process-centered systems work well in organizations that need rapid continuous process improvement to remain competitive. Process-centered systems measure success in terms of *process metrics.*

Second, *value-centered* performance management systems use an information intelligence architecture that maps value chains throughout the organization. Greg and Raymond Reilly articulate value creation performance management with their Measure Network (see Exhibit 7.1c).[15] The concept that "stakeholders value propositions," not strategy, holds central position in this approach. Strategic planning is viewed as one of several management processes. Manager, employee, shareholder, customer, and supplier stakeholders manage interdependent value-creating activities by mapping performance measurement *value chains* across an organizational *metric pool.* Appropriate *measurement sets* reflect the concerns of each stakeholder group, as well as common points of attention. Organizations choose value creation-centered performance management architectures when competitive success depends upon continuous innovation and product/service value enhancement.

Third, *strategy-centered* performance management systems measure strategic success. The Balanced Scorecard, developed by Robert Kaplan and David Norton, currently stands as the most widely embraced strategic performance management control system. With strategy front and center, organizations select performance measurements that align with strategic objectives in four measurement perspectives: Financial, Customer, Internal Business Process, and Learning and Growth (see Exhibit 7.1d).[16] This deceptively simple measurement architecture demands that managers apply and tailor metrics from each perspective to all levels of the organization, including business units, processes, employees, and functions. The Balanced Scorecard (BSC) and other strategic performance management systems measure success in terms of how well each of these organizational elements performs in the four measurement perspectives. Employees design all measures in all four perspectives to test the organization's strategy. Consequently, organizations that depend upon innovation and/or rapid strategic renewal frequently choose a strategy-centered information architecture to guide performance management.

IN THE REAL WORLD

Higher Education Measurement Perspectives

The authors assisted the University of Minnesota's Carlson School of Management (CSOM) in their implementation of a strategic performance measurement and management system. Faculty from eight academic departments, along with wide representation from administrative and program functions, developed an organization-wide set of measures for managing the school's activities. Early in the project, there was significant resistance to "corporatizing" CSOM's performance management system. "Don't give us any Balanced Scorecards!" warned the faculty. As project facilitators, the authors sat up and took notice. Developing measurement perspectives that reflected the school's mission was of paramount importance. With this mission-driven outlook in mind, CSOM faculty and staff developed the following five measurement perspectives:

1. Teaching
2. Research
3. Outreach
4. Employee fulfillment
5. Financial consequences

> **IN THE REAL WORLD CONTINUED**
>
> Faculty leaders explored how "strategy" and CSOM's Strategic Plan would mesh with these five measurement perspectives. The collaborative nature of the school's governance structure provided the context for an answer. Each degree program (e.g., Undergraduate, MBA, PhD), academic department, and administrative function (e.g., IT, Financial Services) would support and enable the school's strategy by designing a few critical measures in the appropriate measurement perspectives, and then manage toward them with incremental targets and long-term goals for excellence. The performance management system was named CSOM's Portfolio of Academic Excellence.
>
> This example of performance measurement and management in a noncorporate setting points out the importance of creating language and frameworks that match the culture of the organization.

Performance Management and Financial Management

Before an organization chooses to adopt a formal process, value, or strategy-centered performance management system, it should deploy a mature operationally focused cost management system. Implementation of a decision-quality CMS is not only a necessary developmental step, but also a critical component of any performance measurement system. In short, when organizations develop and integrate ABM or similar product and customer costing methods to complement financial reporting, operational, and strategic information, cost management information flows in an informative, logical manner.

The ABM or other product/customer costing and operational control system becomes the foundation of the budget for the entire organization for resource assignments in all organizational units. Conventional accountants and other financial professionals have carefully and successfully schooled nonfinancial managers to believe in the importance of the information contained in budgets and in financial statements. However, managers require operational information to run the business. The specific structural design of a Stage III cost management system that provides nonfinancial managers with financial and operational information will more than likely suggest the most compatible performance measurement and management methodology.

Nonfinancial Performance Management Focus Points

When an organization with a Stage III cost management system wants to move into the realm of formal performance management, the key nonfinancial measurement focuses will be dictated by the organization's most important nonfinancial relationships. The strategy-centered Balanced Scorecard methodology gives organizations four measurement perspectives: Financial, Customer, Internal Business Process, and Learning and Growth. Implemented variations on the Balanced Scorecard suggest additional or alternate perspectives, such as Employee, Supplier, and Regulatory. Specific contexts, especially in noncorporate organizations, clearly dictate a deviation from the four classic BSC perspectives. Here Balanced Scorecard proponents often create a fifth perspective when they believe that a particular relationship deserves extra management attention. For example, when city governments adopt performance management, some have added a fifth perspective called Community.[17] However, executive teams must avoid recklessness and carefully consider the risks and benefits of multiple measurement perspectives. Performance management is an exercise in choice and decision making designed to force executive management to select only those relationships that are most important to business success.

Product manufacturers and service providers that maintain competitive performance profiles by means of their efficient, effective processes often create a process-centered performance management architecture. The nonfinancial perspectives of most process-centered performance measurement architectures are generally less constrained than the branded Balanced Scorecard. Specifically, process efficiency and overall organizational success depend on continuous improvement at the activity level in process-intensive businesses (again, see Exhibit 7.1b). The process-centered architecture makes organizational needs and successes visible for the front-line, hands-on activity-level employee. Employees understand what to do—now—in their daily activities. Many organizations that have not reached the strategic level of management maturity cannot imagine how an entire measurement set could be developed for a learning and growth perspective outside the financial realm. Growth sounds logical, but learning? Why measure learning? Strategic organizations acquire knowledge through the measurement of strategy, and they adapt their processes and activities based on what they learn. Nonstrategic organizations are better off measuring and learning to manage more fundamental nonfinancial information perspectives related to operations, process, and resource management first. An alternate approach can also have good results. An organization can combine this focused work by using a performance measurement and management system to explore and develop their strategic planning. In other words, systems like the BSC can actually help develop strategy where it is weak or nonexistent.

Value-centered performance management architectures offer a flexible framework for nonfinancial performance measurement needs across a wide range of organizational maturity. When a mature organization develops a strategy based on a specific value-creation formula, executives can use tightly focused nonfinancial and financial performance measurements to create value chain maps to inform and link employees at all levels. Value-centered performance management also works well for some less strategically mature organizations that can clearly identify the primary value-creating activities that keep them competitive. For organizations in this category, the discipline of the value-centered performance measurement mapping process helps employees manage nonfinancial performance parameters and reveals new opportunities for value enhancement.

Methods of Performance Management Financial/Nonfinancial Integration

Performance measurement and management has developed in a pattern that parallels ABC/M, although the pace of performance management has been accelerated by the comparatively greater availability of supportive software applications for performance management. The parallels exhibit three main points of commonality:

1. Development of *meaningful categories* to capture quantitative information; for example, resource, activity, and cost object constructs in ABC and measurement perspectives in performance measurement and management.

2. Development of *management principles* to affect changes using the quantitative information; for example, activity-based management, and the Balanced Scorecard's management processes (described in the next paragraph and depicted in Exhibit 7.2).

3. Efforts to *map strategic or process execution* and to statistically validate findings. For example, ABC/M frequently partners with TQM's process mapping; and more recent BSC enhancements call for strategic mapping.

All performance measurement and management proponents enjoy demonstrating the obvious value of linking financial and nonfinancial measures. However, demonstrating relationships is easy compared to improving performance and creating synergies. More than other models, the BSC has steadily evolved measurement and management integration, based on central management objectives supported by financial and nonfinancial information. The BSC provides principles and practices that are useful in any performance management approach. The Balanced Scorecard is the most widely practiced performance management methodology to date. It has been designed to continually focus on ways to achieve faster and better strategic execution.

Paralleling its four measurement perspectives, the Balanced Scorecard directs performance management practices with four formal management processes: Translating the Vision, Communication and Linkage, Business Planning, and Feedback and Learning (see Exhibit 7.2).[18] For less than $25, any motivated management team can read all about basic BSC measurement and management perspectives in Kaplan and Norton's 1996 book, *The Balanced Scorecard*, where they outline what to measure, how to implement, how to manage once the BSC is up and running, and how to create rapid strategic renewal. Organizations that choose to manage performance benefit by adapting these four deliberate management processes to the central focus of their performance management system.

In their second book, *The Strategy-Focused Organization*, Kaplan and Norton admit their own learning curve in their preface: "We proposed the Balanced Scorecard as the solution to [the] performance measurement problem. But we learned that adopting companies used the Balanced Scorecard to solve a much more important problem than how to measure performance in the information era. That problem, of which we were frankly unaware when first proposing the Balanced

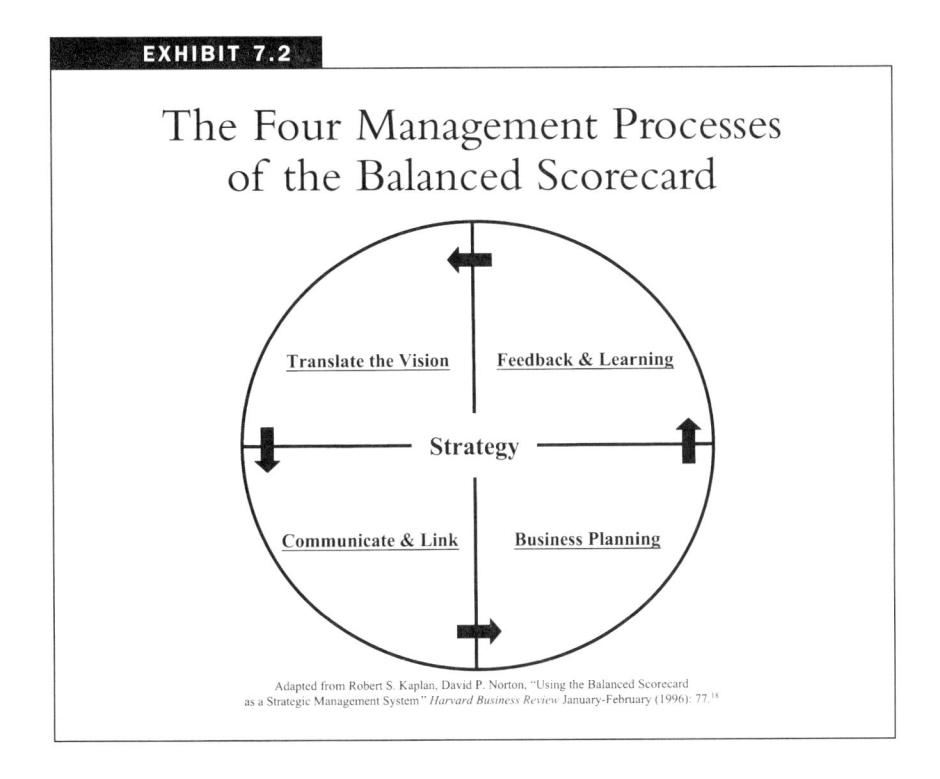

> **EXHIBIT 7.2**
>
> ## The Four Management Processes of the Balanced Scorecard
>
> Translate the Vision | Feedback & Learning
>
> Strategy
>
> Communicate & Link | Business Planning
>
> Adapted from Robert S. Kaplan, David P. Norton, "Using the Balanced Scorecard as a Strategic Management System," *Harvard Business Review* January-February (1996): 77.[18]

Scorecard, was how to implement new strategies."[19] The execution of strategy is the central purpose of *The Strategy-Focused Organization*, using strategic mapping, incentives, and other concrete paradigms.

Just as strategy occupies the position of central focus in the Balanced Scorecard, so process and value provide the focal point for the second and third system types depicted in Exhibit 7.1. Process and value-centered systems have yet to concisely and commonly codify their underlying principles. However, the four BSC management processes easily translate to process and value terminology, and they remain just as valid. In BSC language, "Translating the vision" easily becomes "Translating the value proposition" or "Translating process improvement goals."

The BSC "Communication and Linkage" performance management process carries the high-level translation of the central management objective into the common language and vocabulary of the organization regardless of system type. The work becomes more detailed, local, and customized to each organization in the Balanced Scorecard's third management process, "Business Planning." Even so, the system type affects the vocabulary of the work more than its principles. Finally, the "Feedback and Learning" process renews the entire performance management process cycle, in any of the three system types, by using performance measurement information to correct and enhance the central management objectives.

In all these management processes, business units and employees work cross-functionally to establish key performance measures to support the organization-level performance objectives. If the organizational culture or its managers lack the maturity to work cross-functionally, performance management will initially prove to be an exercise in frustration. Consensus-building activities create winners and losers. Key measures mean that some things are simply more important than others. Performance measurement creation is an exercise in restraint and discretion. A performance management process calls executives and employees to set and accept ambitious long-term stretch targets to drive continuous improvement. In the course of the work, parochial and territorial ambitions must blend with the greater vision. The planning of central management priorities should be synchronized with the annual budgeting process so that business units can actually follow through on their linked accountabilities.

In *The Strategy-Focused Organization*, Kaplan and Norton recommend five more management principles. These, too, can be applied to other performance management methods and their terminology.[20]

1. Translate the strategy to operational terms using strategy maps and Balanced Scorecards.
2. Mobilize change through executive leadership and the governance process.

3. Align the organization to the strategy through explicit business unit and shared services synergies, facilitated through corporate guidance.

4. Make strategy a continual process and encourage strategic learning.

5. Make strategy everyone's everyday job by raising strategic awareness, constructing personal scorecards, and designing balanced paychecks.

Performance Management Capabilities Assessment

All organizations measure and manage performance in some form. All organizations must meet a few basic entrance requirements before joining the growing number that use performance management as the central management paradigm. Organizations stuck in Stage II need not apply. When financial reporting alone drives decision making, nonfinancial operational information is largely ignored. Spend the money creating an operationally focused cost system that tracks product and customer costs first.

Similarly, executives in Stage III organizations who expect that an ERP system installation will create a ready-made performance management system also need to spend a little money first and read a good book—*The Balanced Scorecard Step-by-Step.*[21] The how-to description given in this book can give any management team a good blueprint for the hard work behind creating a customized performance management structure. Otherwise, the organization will spend a boatload of money on software that nobody will use because it does not contain the information that they need.

Incentives

The importance of incentives cannot be overemphasized. The form that incentives take—monetary or nonmonetary—depends on the preferences of the workforce profile; therefore, this section does not recommend a specific type of incentive. The most effective incentives are designed with active employee participation and consensus. (See "Incentives for Californians and Midwesterners.") Monetary incentives can cause extensive strategic damage. Think of executives who manage *only* to the financial measures that determine how *they* get paid. On the other hand, carefully crafted incentives can promote just the right behavior. Perhaps the most important aspect of designing incentives is an appropriate view of the workforce.

Influencing behavior is the core purpose of incentives. Daniel Goleman recommends paying for performance under a human competency paradigm. Incentive distribution under a human competency paradigm means that managers and executives, in particular, are rewarded for having, acquiring, or developing "emotional intelligence" competencies that have been shown to impact bottom-line performance.[22] When correctly integrated and deployed, incentives not only support, but accelerate, success. The Balanced Scorecard is the only strategic management model described in this chapter that explicitly integrates incentives into the fabric of its management system. In *The Strategy-Focused Organization*, Kaplan and Norton devote an entire chapter, "The Balanced Paycheck," to incentive discussions. (Italics appear in the original text.)

> Finally, each of the successful [BSC] organizations linked *incentive compensation* to the Balanced Scorecard. Most executives opted for a team-based, rather than an individual-based, system for rewarding performance. They used the business unit and division scorecards as the basis for rewards, an approach that stressed the importance of teamwork in executing strategy.[23]

Incentives are critical success factors that must be aligned with all organizational tactics and systems. Whatever the context, incentives must not be designed in a void. Create the strategy, the core processes,

Strategy-Based Systems and the Future of Cost Management

> **IN THE REAL WORLD**
>
> ## Incentives for Californians and Midwesterners
>
> Buck Knives, a brand-name manufacturer located in San Diego, California, developed a productivity incentive program in the early 1980s. Framed with strict quality and industrial engineered work standards, the program tracked savings in monetary terms, and shared gains fifty-fifty between the company and its employees. All full-time employees, from the lowest to highest paid, earned an incentive share based on one and the same formula. In the interest of customizing the incentive to the desires of its people, company owners sought an annual employee vote to determine how much of the incentive pool would be paid in cash bonuses and how much would be applied to extra time off, beyond industry-standard vacation and sick days for all employees. The extra time off was then scheduled around significant holidays for the entire company.
>
> This method lead to a marked opinion split between the majority of employees who were "native" Californians (i.e., lived in the state from at least high school age on), and "transplanted" employees, predominantly from the Midwest, who had moved to California after approximately age thirty. The natives consistently voted overwhelmingly (~90 percent of votes) for as much extra time off as the company would allow. In contrast, the Midwesterners exhibited solidarity in their consistent desire to have the incentive paid 100 percent in cash bonuses. The democratic one-vote-per-person approach led to as much as a dozen extra days off every year.

or the key value propositions first, then design the incentives—with one exception: *executive* incentive leadership. Executive incentive leadership must proceed with five important incentive practice insights. First, the priorities that executives openly communicate (with or without explicit incentives or incentive expletives) have a way of immediately focusing employee attention and influencing employee behavior. Second, executives can guide the incentive structure by aligning their own pay schemes with openly communicated priorities and performance targets, and by publicly announcing their own results. The classic example of how *not* to strategically align incentives is to base executive bonuses primarily on sales revenue growth that quickly erode the profit imperative. Even worse are executive bonuses that are paid without any explicit and public performance measures. Executives need to demonstrate that they have some "skin in the game" by participating equitably and publicly in incentive rewards, not dominating them regardless of harm to the organization's resources and morale.

Third, like performance measurements, executives must assure financial/nonfinancial balance in incentive design. Rewarding exclusively on financial performance is not recommended, although studies indicate that companies continue to put the heaviest proportional weight on financial outcomes.[24] Fourth, employee incentives are an exercise in patience. Kaplan and Cooper recommend that executives use caution when constructing incentives and delay linking incentives to newly implemented balanced scorecards. This advice applies to all tactics and systems for three reasons:

1. Initial performance system designs often go through several subsequent iterations as learning and insight accrue. Switching incentives to match performance system changes often causes confusion and even anger.

2. Performance data integrity may be an issue in the first year or more. Compensating on bad data has obvious problems.

3. "Unintended or unexpected consequences" sometimes result from premature incentive implementation.[25]

Strategy-Based Systems and the Future of Cost Management

Fifth, from a resource management perspective, executives must implement incentive designs deliberately and with clarity about the resources they are committing. Incentives cost something in terms of money, time, and employee goodwill. Putting resources in the wrong place doesn't just cost money, it frustrates employees and sends them confusing signals for behavior. Incentive systems compensate clearly identified stakeholders in ways that align owners and employees at all levels of the organization under a common strategic purpose. Consequently, employees must clearly understand three sets of variables regarding performance and compensatory incentive rewards:

1. The measured performance variables for the job.
2. How their behavior affects the measured performance variables.
3. How the measure performance variables translate into individual rewards.[26]

Incentives simply fail to enchant or motivate employees when they cannot see a clear cause-and-effect relationship between these variables. The long-term success of strategically aligned incentive systems depends upon creating a clear cause-and-effect line of sight for all employees.

Summary and Lessons from the Field

Taken as a whole, performance measurement and management toward articulated objectives is heady work. However, a small set of principles can help organize the effort.

- Make sure everyone in the organization speaks the same strategic (or process, or vision, or mission) language.
- Indiscriminate, short-term cost cutting destroys value.
- Strategic cost management is the nexus of resources/costs and value creation.

- As cost management methods mature, they are less rigidly structured and more amendable to synergetic blending with complementary methods.

- First things first. Organizations must establish mature operational resource-based costing systems before adopting an advanced performance management system.

- Performance management disciplines executives to achieve consensus and limit the focus of organizational attention to only its most important relationships.

- Incentives of the right kind, at the right place and time, for all employees are essential.

Looking Ahead: Emerging Trends in Resource and Cost Management

A recent survey of the top North American cost and performance management experts reveals a strong awareness and sensitivity to human, social, and environmental dimensions, as well as an urgency to address them. Beyond continuing technical methods and software development, the consensus expressed in the opinions of these thought leaders came in response to an innocent question: If Henry Ford, Frederick Taylor, or Adam Smith showed up in your office and asked for an update on the state of twenty-first-century cost management, what would you tell him?[27] The experts made the following points independently and repeatedly.

The Human Dimension Matters Most

The source of value in organizations depends most on the employees who deliver goods and services. The command-and-control hierarchy is outmoded. Empty incentive tactics become far less effective as more employees choose to align their work contributions with more humane environments. Technical advantage can be duplicated; human relationship cannot.

Value Creation—Not Just Shareholders Anymore

As discussed earlier in this chapter, value creation is the dominant management focus of the most successful comprehensive cost and organizational management paradigms. Although value creation originally meant shareholder wealth creation, the meaning has expanded to include all organizational constituents. If there is any one point of agreement among the experts, it is the importance of value creation and management. There is also agreement that shareholder value creation cannot be managed in isolation from other organization stakeholders—employees, customers, suppliers, the community.

Cost Management Information—Not Just Numbers Anymore

The experts surveyed can usually be found with sleeves rolled up, crunching numbers, and designing reports that communicate insights. To do this, they maintain high awareness of the quality of cost management information. All the numbers knowledge in the world is worth little if it cannot be effectively communicated and then acted on. Executives constantly ingest and interpret information about resources. Cost management information must facilitate the rapid assimilation of dynamic inputs based on a clear understanding of the nature and behavior of cost. When a CMS design stays true to this mission, executives' decisions hit nearer the mark.

Visualize and Build the Organization

Organizational design is a critical factor in support of strategic execution. The command-and-control structures of the 1950s and 1960s move too slowly in a world of instant information and local action. The experts named organizational design as one of the next big strategic enablers. Excellent tactics and strategies outpace cumbersome organizational structures that slow adaptation to changing market forces and hinder rapid, agile strategic execution. Part of strategic execution includes creating or reconfiguring organization structure and committing appropriate resources to accomplish strategic objectives. Flat, decentralized organizations where autonomous workers respond directly and rapidly to customers and clients do not need three echelons of vice presidents. They just get in the way.

Intangible Resources

Highly valuable resources called intangible assets go by many other names: intellectual property, knowledge capital, organizational intelligence, and human capital. Truth be known, they have high visibility when we look in the right places: people, brand names, information systems, skills, and competencies. They are now the most important drivers of value creation, and the necessary focus of resource and cost management.

Open the Books: Alliances and Resource Transparency

Until very recently, financial professionals regularly and with good intent, withheld relevant cost and financial information from the majority of nonexecutive employees and from most external constituents unless they were creditors or shareholders. Perhaps this practice still exists as an outdated belief from the days of Scientific Management when organizations used centralized control structures to manage the behavior of uneducated employees. In a competitive environment that depends more and more on knowledge workers, withholding relevant information results in asymmetrical employee understanding. As discussed in

Strategy-Based Systems and the Future of Cost Management

Chapter 6, effective supply chain management also requires information sharing across organizations.

The terms *profit-conscious professional* and *productive citizen* are not mutually exclusive. In fact, these roles are critically interdependent. Living up to both means staying informed, remaining alert, and conducting local activities with an eye on short- and long-term outcomes. And the primary responsibilities of a cost manager? They remain the same. Recent events make it startlingly clear that it is *not* short-term financial gain. When all the layers of the onion are peeled away, surely one prime directive remains: Carry out short-term actions that assure the long-term well-being of the organization, the people in it, and the community where it resides, because all their fates and well-being are interconnected.

Endnotes

1. Robert Simons, *Levers of Control: How Managers Use Innovative Control Systems to Drive Strategic Renewal* (Boston: Harvard Business School Press, 1995): 5.

2. Robin Cooper and Regine Slagmulder, "What is Strategic Cost Management?" *Management Accounting* (January 1998): 14, 16.

3. Henry Mintzberg and Joseph Lampel, "Reflecting on the Strategy Process," *MIT Sloan Management Review* (Spring 1999): 21–30.

4. The vision paradigm is explicated in James C. Collins and Jerry I. Porras, *Built to Last: Successful Habits of Visionary Companies* (New York: HarperBusiness, 1994).

5. Robert S. Kaplan and David P. Norton, *The Strategy-Focused Organization* (Boston: Harvard Business School Press, 2001): 83–86.

6. Robert S. Kaplan and Robin Cooper, *Cost & Effect: Using Integrated Cost Systems to Drive Profitability and Performance* (Boston: Harvard Business School Press, 1998): 26.

7. Robert S. Kaplan and V.G. Naraynan, "Customer Profitability Measurement and Management," *Journal of Cost Management* 15, no. 5 (2001): 8.

8. Robin Cooper and Regine Slagmulder, "Developing Meaningful Profitability Maps: Cascading Cost/Benefit Trade-offs," *Management Accounting* (December 1998): 16–17.

9. Michael Treacy and Fred Wiersema, *The Discipline of Market Leaders: Choose Your Customers, Narrow Your Focus, Dominate Your Market* (Cambridge, MA: Perseus Publishing, 1996).

10. James A. Knight, *Value-Based Management: Developing a Systematic Approach to Creating Shareholder Value* (New York: McGraw-Hill, 1998).

11. Paul Sharman, "Cost and Performance Management in the Age of Global Change," *Journal of Cost Management* 14, no. 5 (2000): 42.

12. Robin Cooper and Regine Slagmulder, "Integrating Activity-Based Costing and Economic Value Added," *Management Accounting* (January 1999): 16–17.

13. Kaplan and Norton, 83–84.

14. Paul Sharman, "Using Performance Architecture to Create Economic Value," *Journal of Cost Management* 15, no. 6 (2001): 11–16.

15. Gregory P. Reilly and Raymond R. Reilly, "Using a Measure Network to Understand and Deliver Value," *Journal of Cost Management* 14, no. 6 (2000): 5–14.

16. Robert S. Kaplan and David P. Norton, "Using the Balanced Scorecard as a Strategic Management System," *Harvard Business Review* (January–February 1996): 76.

17. Paul Niven, "Examining the Endurance of the Balanced Scorecard," *Journal of Cost Management* 15, no. 3 (2001): 23.

18. Kaplan and Norton, "Using the Balanced Scorecard," 77.

19. Kaplan and Norton, *The Strategy-Focused Organization*, vii–viii.

20. Id., 9.

21. Paul R. Niven, *Balanced Scorecard Step-by-Step: Maximizing Performance and Maintaining Results* (New York: John Wiley & Sons, Inc., 2002).

22. Joe and Catherine Stenzel, "Measuring Leadership Attributes that Matter: A Conversation with Daniel Goleman," *Journal of Strategic Performance Measurement* 4, no. 1 (2000): 9.

23. Kaplan and Norton, *The Strategy-Focused Organization*, 13.

24. Id., 254–255. Note: Balanced Scorecard research showed the following weight ranges for the BSC measurement perspectives: financial 40 percent weight, customer measures 15 to 20 percent weight, internal business process metrics ~25 percent weight, and learning and growth metrics 15 to 20 percent weight.

25. Kaplan and Cooper, 266–267.

26. Robert S. Kaplan and Anthony A. Atkinson, *Advanced Management Accounting* 3rd ed. (Upper Saddle River, NJ: Prentice Hall, 1998): 681.

27. In 2000, in their role as editors-in-chief of the *Journal of Cost Management*, the authors carried out extensive conversations with the journal's board of advisors, in the interest of creating a vision for the publication for the twenty-first century. Most of the board members' views were published in the September/October 2000 issue of the journal. All quotes and references in this section are based on this work. See *Journal of Cost Management* 14, no. 5 (2000).

Suggested Readings

Chapter 1

Don Hansen and Maryanne Mowen, *Management Accounting*, 3rd ed. (Cincinnati, OH: South-Western Publishing Co., 1994).

G. Foster Horngren and S. Datar, *Cost Accounting: A Managerial Emphasis*, 9th ed. (Englewood Cliffs, NJ: Prentice Hall, 1997).

Robert S. Kaplan and Robin Cooper, *Cost & Effect: Using Integrated Cost Systems to Drive Profitability and Performance* (Boston: Harvard Business School Press, 1998).

Catherine Stenzel and Joe Stenzel, "The Reconciliation of Finance and Operations: A Conversation with Brian Maskell," *Journal of Strategic Performance Measurement* 3, no. 5 (1999): 21–26.

Chapter 2

H. Thomas Johnson and Robert S. Kaplan, *Relevance Lost: The Rise and Fall of Management Accounting* (Boston: Harvard Business School Press, 1987 and 1991).

Peter M. Lenhardt and Stephen D. Colton, "Dispelling Two Myths of Modern Cost Management," *Journal of Cost Management* 14, no. 5 (2000): 21–23.

Chapter 3

Ron Bleeker, "Key Features of Activity-Based Budgeting," *Journal of Cost Management* 15, no. 4 (2001): 5–20.

Marc J. Epstein, *The Effect of Scientific Management on the Development of Standard Cost Systems* (New York: Arno Press, 1978).

Lawrence P. Grasso, "Is It Time to Revisit Zero-Base Budgeting?" *Journal of Cost Management* 11, no. 2 (1997): 22–29.

Don Hansen and Maryanne Mowen, *Management Accounting*, 3rd ed. (Cincinnati, OH: South-Western Publishing Co., 1994). This textbook, or any good management accountant text, provides detail on all the conventional cost accounting methods discussed in this chapter.

Jeremy Hope and Robin Fraser, "Beyond Budgeting," Chapter D1 in *Emerging Practices in Cost Management: 2001–2 edition*, James B. Edwards (Valhalla, NY: WG&L/RIA, 2001).

Michael F. Latimer, "Linking Strategy-Based Costing and Innovation-Based Budgeting," *Strategic Finance* (March 2001): 39–42.

J. Lehr McKenzie and Gary L. Melling, "Skills-Based Human Capital Budgeting: A Strategic Initiative, Not a Financial Exercise," *Journal of Cost Management* 15, no. 3 (2001): 30–36.

Chapter 4

Eliyahu M. Goldratt, *Necessary But Not Sufficient* (Great Barrington, MA: North River Press, 2000).

H. Thomas Johnson and Robert S. Kaplan, *Relevance Lost: The Rise and Fall of Management Accounting* (Boston: Harvard Business School Press, 1987 and 1991): 125–126.

Robert S. Kaplan and V.G. Narayanan, "Measuring and Managing Customer Profitability," *Journal of Cost Management* 15, no. 5 (2001): 5–15

CJ McNair, "The Hidden Costs of Capacity," *Handbook of Cost Management*, Section E5. (New York: Warren, Gorham & Lamont/RIA Group, 1997).

CJ McNair, *The Profit Potential: Taking High Performance to the Bottom Line* (Essex Junction, VT: Oliver Wight Publications, 1994).

Jeanne W. Ross and Cynthia M. Beath, "Beyond the Business Case: New Approaches to IT Investment," *MIT Sloan Management Review* (Winter 2002): 51–59.

Chapter 5

Ron Bleeker, "Key Features of Activity-Based Budgeting," *Journal of Cost Management*, vol. 15, no. 4 (2001): 5–20.

Barry J. Brinker, ed. *Guide to Cost Management* (New York: John Wiley & Sons, Inc., 2000).

Robin Cooper and Robert S. Kaplan, *Cost and Effect: Using Integrated Cost Systems to Drive Profitability and Performance* (Boston: Harvard Business School Press, 1998).

Suggested Readings

CJ McNair, *The Profit Potential: Taking High Performance to the Bottom Line* (Essex Junction, VT: Oliver Wight Publications, 1994).

Catherine and Joe Stenzel, "The Reconciliation of Finance and Operations: A Conversation with Brian Maskell," *Journal of Strategic Performance Measurement* 3, no. 5 (1999): 21–26.

Joe and Catherine Stenzel, "The Next Generation of Quality: A Conversation with Dr. A. Blanton Godfrey," *Journal of Strategic Performance Measurement* 2, no. 6 (1998): 5–11.

A series of articles by Anton van der Merwe and David E. Keys, published in the last half of 2001 in volume 15 of the *Journal of Cost Management*.

- "The Case for RCA: Excess and Idle Resource Capacity," *Journal of Cost Management* 15, no. 4 (2001): 21–32.

- "The Case for RCA: Understanding Resource Interrelationships," *Journal of Cost Management* 15, no. 5 (2001): 27–36.

- "The Case for RCA: Decision Support for an Advanced Cost Management System," *Journal of Cost Management* 15, no. 6 (2001): 23–32.

Reginald Tomas Yu-Lee, *Explicit Cost Dynamics: An Alternative to Activity-Based Costing* (New York: John Wiley & Sons, Inc., 2001).

Chapter 6

Robin Cooper and Regine Slagmulder, *Supply Chain Development for the Lean Enterprise: Interorganizational Cost Management* (Portland, OR: Productivity, Inc., 1999).

Michael Hammer, *Beyond Reengineering: How the Process-Centered Organization Is Changing Our Work and Our Lives* (New York: HarperBusiness, 1996).

MIT Sloan Management Review, Fall 2001 issue, focuses on various *life cycle perspectives* and includes articles on technology life cycles, outsourcing choices based on an organization's place in its life cycle, and even CEO selection to fit the company's place in its own life cycle.

Richard Schonberger, *Let's Fix It! Overcoming the Crisis in Manufacturing* (New York: The Free Press, 2001).

Suggested Readings

Chapter 7

Robin Cooper and Regine Slagmulder, *Supply Chain Development for the Lean Enterprise: Interorganizational Cost Management* (Portland, OR: Productivity, Inc., 1999).

Robert S. Kaplan and Anthony A. Atkinson, *Advanced Management Accounting*, 3rd edition (Upper Saddle River, NJ: Prentice Hall, 1998), Chapter 13, "Incentive and Compensation Systems," and Chapter 14, "Formal Models in Budgeting and Incentive Contracts."

Robert S. Kaplan and David P. Norton, *The Balanced Scorecard: Translating Strategy into Action* (Boston: Harvard Business School Press, 1996).

Robert S. Kaplan and David P. Norton, *The Strategy-Focused Organization: How Balanced Scorecard Companies Thrive in the New Business Environment* (Boston: Harvard Business School Press, 2002).

James A. Knight, *Value-Based Management: Developing a Systematic Approach to Creating Shareholder Value* (New York: McGraw Hill, 1998).

Henry Mintzberg, B. Ahlstrand, and J. Lampel, *Strategy Safari: A Guided Tour through the Wilds of Strategic Management* (New York: The Free Press, 1998).

Paul Niven, *The Balanced Scorecard Step-By-Step* (New York: John Wiley & Sons, Inc., 2002).

Michael E. Porter, *Competitive Advantage: Creating and Sustaining Superior Performance* (New York: The Free Press, 1985).

MIT Sloan Management Review, Spring 1999 issue, which is almost entirely devoted to articles on strategic management.

Robert Simons, *Levers of Control: How Managers Use Innovative Control Systems to Drive Strategic Renewal* (Boston: Harvard Business School Press, 1995).

Michael Treacy and Fred Wiersema, *The Discipline of Market Leaders: Choose Your Customers, Narrow Your Focus, Dominate Your Market* (Cambridge, MA: Perseus Publishing, 1996).

Index

A

ABC. *See* Activity-based costing
ABC/M. *See* Activity-based costing, management
Absorption, 54
  overhead and, 52–56
Activity drivers, 163
Accountability, 13, 139
Accounting:
  backflush. *See* backflush accounting
  cost, 2, 16, 24
    applications, 37–38
    conventional, 33–58, 98, 113, *also see* traditional
      activity-based costing and, 167–169
      capacity management, 119
      employee headcount control, 125–128
      expense item management, 122–123
      inventory perspectives, 116–117
      pricing perspectives, 131–132
      product/service development, 135–136
      project evaluation, 137–138
      resource consumption accounting and, 175–176
      Theory of Constraints and, 158
      total quality management and, 151–153
    performance, 36
    resource consumption. *See* resource consumption accounting
    resource optimization, 35
    predictive, 40–41
    structures, 59–100
    terminology, 33–58
  financial, 2, 5, 68, 74, 86, 91, 94, 96, 102, 106–114
  government and fund. *See* government and fund accounting
  management, 3, 16, 17, 24
    shortcomings, 26
  managerial, 2
  operational resource. *See* operational resource accounting
  organizational structure and, 60–68
  profit-center, *See* profit-center accounting
  resource. *See* resource accounting
  resource consumption. *See* resource consumption accounting
  responsibility. *See* responsibility accounting
  traditional, 3, *also see* conventional
    absorption and overhead, 52
    strategy and, 39
Activity-based budgeting. *See* budget, activity-based
Activity-based costing, 159–172
  activity based budgeting and, 85–86
  contrasted with conventional accounting, 167–169
  core principles and management objectives, 161–165
  defined, 162
  Economic Value-Added and, 236
  general ledger and, 159–161
  software, 165
Activity-based management, 164
  contrasted with conventional accounting, 162–164
  cost management advantages and shortcomings, 166–172
  operations and, 165–166
  reengineering and, 195–196

265

Index

strategic cost management and, 228–232
value engineering and, 197
Advertising, 123–124
Agile manufacturing, 191–194, 209
Allocation, 55, 85
Assets, 17

B

Backflush accounting, 104
Balanced Scorecard, 240, 244
  incentives and, 250
  linking financial and nonfinancial information, 245–249
  management perspectives, 246, 247
Balance sheet, 5, 89, 94
Blended approaches, xii
Bottleneck in Theory of Constraints, 156
Break-even analysis, 104
Brimson, Jim, 115
Budget, 59, 61
  alternatives to conventional, 81–89
    activity-based, 85, 164–165
    continuous, 83
    flexible, 83
    human capital, 86
    innovation-based, 87
    responsibility-based, 83
    zero-based, 84
  attributes of effectiveness, 88
  beyond budgeting, 88–89
  categories:
    main, 76
    interrelationships, 77
  conventional limitations, 71, 81–89
  mistakes, 82
  relationship to cost management system, 71
  standard costs and, 68–80

C

CAM—I. *See* Consortium for Advanced Manufacturing—International
Capacity:
  actual, practical, theoretical, 104
  management, 118–121
    activity-based accounting and, 120
    resource cost accounting and, 120, 173–174
  quality availability, 120
Capital, 92
Capital budgets, 21, 92
Capital investment, 92–97
  analysis methods, 95–96
    accounting rate of return, 95
    internal rate of return, 96
    net present value method, 96
    payback period, 96
Capital spending, 27
Chart of accounts, 61, 68, 85, 161
COGs. *See* Cost of goods sold
Common wealth, 108, 123
Consortium for Advanced Manufacturing—International, 88
Consumption ratio, 55
Control, 14–30
  budgets and, 70–73, 82, 88
  forecasts and, 89
  operations/resource context, 111–114, 141–142
  performance management systems, 28–29
Cooper, Robin, v, 8, 23, 42, 71, 162, 165, 198, 202, 209–212, 252
Cost, 2
  actual, 46
  assumptions, 41
  behavior, 4, 35, 40–41
  budgeted, 46
  center. *See* cost center
  controllable, noncontrollable, 47
  current-actual, 47

266

Index

direct, 5, 46
discretionary, nondiscretionary, 45, 85
driver. *See* cost driver
expense/expenditure distinctions, 3, 39–40
expense accounts, 48
fixed, 5, 42
of goods sold. *See* cost of goods sold
indirect, 5, 46, 85
object. *See* cost object
opportunity. *See* opportunity cost
overhead. *See* overhead
pool. *See* cost pool
of quality. *See* cost of quality
resource and, 101–102
semi-fixed, 5, 44–45
semi-variable, 5, 44–45
standard. *See* standard cost
step-fixed, 5, 44–45
step-variable, 5, 44–45
structure, 14
sunk, 47
types, 4, 40–58
  absorption, 52
  defined, general, 41
  evolution, 44
  overhead. *See* overhead
  variable, 5, 42
  visibility, 27
Cost accounting, 2
  conventional, 33–38
  operations relationships, 22–24
  historical, 24–26
Cost accumulation
  methods:
    job-order costing. *See* job–order costing
    process costing. *See* process costing
Cost center, 61
Cost driver, 42–43, 55, 109
Cost & Effect, 8, 23
Cost management, xiii, xiv
  characteristics, 10–11, 22
  development. *See* Four-stage model
  objectives, 2–14
  purpose, 4
  relevance, 27–28
Cost management system, 4
  budget and, 97
  forecasts and, 90
Cost object, 161
Cost of goods sold, 3, 20, 54, 74, 122, 163
Cost pools, 163
Cost of quality, 152–154

D

Decision packages. *See* budget, zero-based
Decision support, 86, 112, 138, 166
Depreciation, 94, 97
Discounted cash flow, 27

E

Economic Value-Added, 235–236
Enterprise resource planning, 10, 106, 117, 123, 157, 165, 249
ERP. *See* enterprise resource planning
Expenditure, 3, 39–40, 68
Expense:
  common categories, 122
  operating, 3, 39–40,
Expense item management, 121–125

F

Forecasts, 89–92
  sales relationship to standard cost, 77
  sales relationship to activity-based budgeting, 85
Four-stage model, 8–10, 106
  activity-based costing and, 167
  cost management system design, 44
  cost management system objectives and, 10–14
  connections between financial and management focus, 20–21
  performance management, 28–29, 243, 249
  Stage II, 110

strategy and, 222–223
supply chain/interorganizational costing and, 211

G
Goldratt, Eliyahu, 154–157, 159
Government and fund accounting, 67

I
Incentives:
  responsibility accounting and, 65
Income statement, 5, 89
Interorganizational cost management, 209–214
Inventory management, 114–118
Investment center, 62

J
Job-order costing, 67
Johnson, H. Thomas, 72, 106, 117
Just-in-time:
  forecasts and, 90
  lean manufacturing and, 191–194
  production, 104, 114, 118

K
Kanban, 104–5, 114, 118
Kaplan, Robert, v, 8, 23, 42, 106, 117, 162, 165, 240, 246, 250, 252

L
Lagging indicators, 109–110, 124
Leading indicators, 109–110
Lean manufacturing, 191–193, 209
Life cycle cost management, 205–209
Life cycle management, 134

M
Materials requirement planning, 90, 105, 117, 132
McNair, CJ, 22, 121, 154
Measure Network, 240
MRP. *See* materials requirement planning

N
Nonvalue-added, xiii

O
Operational resource accounting, 102–143, 103
  contrasts with financial accounting, 106–114
  capacity management, 119–121
  employee headcount control, 128–131
  expense item management, 123–125
  inventory perspectives, 117–118
  pricing perspectives, 133–134
  product/service development, 136–137
  project evaluation, 139–140
Operations:
  activity-based management and, 165–166
  cost accounting relationships, 22–24
  historical, 24–26, 106–108
  focus, 10–14
  organizational activities, 104
  resource consumption accounting and, 175
  Theory of Constraints and, 157
  total quality and, 150–151
Opportunity cost, 61
  capital investment and, 94
Organizational design, 112, 255
Outsourcing, 209
Overhead, 72
  absorption and, 52–56
  activity-based costing and, 163
  material, labor, and, 48
    standard costs and, 74
  predetermined overhead rate, 55

P
Pareto principle, 148
Performance management, 237–253
  Balanced Scorecard. *See* Balanced Scorecard

Index

budget-centered, 238
control system, 28–29
financial management and, 242–243
incentives and, 249–253
integrating financial and nonfinancial information, 245–249
nonfinancial management and, 243–249
  measurement perspectives, 240–241, 243
  process-centered, 239, 244
  strategy-centered, 241–242, 244
  value-centered, 240, 244–245
Period expenses, 21
Prediction, 62
Price, 104
  variance, 104
Pricing, 131–134
  cost-plus, 131
  transfer, 131
Process-based cost management, 145–180
Process costing, 68
Process mapping, 145
Product/service development, 134–137
  activity-based management and, 169–170
Profit, 2
  operations/resource context, 111–114
Profit Center, 61
Profit-center accounting, 60
Profit imperative, 2, 156, 182
Profitability, 17, 44
  customer:
    activity-based management and, 170–172
Project evaluation, 137–140
Purchase-price variance, 75, 105

Q

Quality movement, 29, 118
  Quality at the Source, 105, 114, 192
  reengineering and, 194

Total Quality Management *See* Total Quality Management
forecasts and, 90

R

RCA. *See* resource consumption accounting
Reengineering, 194–197
Relevance Lost, 72, 106, 107
Resource, 101–102
Resource accounting, 60, 83
Resource-based cost management, 145–180
  emerging trends, 254–257
    human dimensions, 254
    intangibles, 256
    organizational design, 255
    stakeholder value-creation, 255
  Theory of Constraints and, 158–159
  Total Quality Movement and, 153–154
Resource consumption accounting, 172–176
  activity-based cost management and, 172–175
  conventional cost accounting and, 175–176
  core principles and management objectives, 172–174
  cost management advantages and shortcomings, 175–176
  operations and, 175
Resource drivers, 163
Resource pools, 174
Resource management, 107–110
  customer profitability and, 170–172
  incentives and, 253
  product/service profitability and, 169–170
Responsibility accounting, 60–61, 63
  principles, 65–66
Responsibility center, 60–61, 64–66, 83
  activity-based management and, 161
Return on investment, 27, 107, 136

Index

capital investment and, 94–95
Economic Value-Added and, 236
Theory of Constraints and, 156
ROI. *See* return on investment

S

Sales, general and administrative, 3, 20, 21, 67, 122, 134, 169–170
  activity-based costing and, 163
Scientific management, 63, 71
Sector, 66, 66–68
Segment, 67, 67–68
  analysis, 67
  reporting, 67
SG&A. *See* Sales, general and administrative
Standard cost, 47, 62
  behavioral implications, 75–76
  budgets and, 68–80
  cost management advantages and shortcomings, 175–176
  defined, 74–75
  history, 71
Standard price, 77
Standard sales volume, 78
Standard Industrial Classification, 67
Strategic cost management, 223–232
  activity-based management and, 228–232
  defined, 219
  financial management and, 227–228
  nonfinancial management and, 228–230
Strategy, 39, 217–257
  attributes, 183–191
  Balanced Scorecard and, 246–247
  budgets and, 78, 82, 87, 89, 92
  implementing new, 246–247
  models, 220
  operational accounting, 107
  performance measurement and, 244
  resource accounting and, 102
  tactics. *See* tactics

Statistical process control, 149
Supply chain:
  costing, 209–214
  forecasts and, 90
Systems thinking, 155

T

Tactics:
  analysis of, 182–185
  defined, 182–183
  strategy and, 102, 182–216
Target costing, 133, 201–205
Theory of Constraints, 145, 154–159
  activity-based management and, 159, 164, 167
  core principles and management objectives, 155–157
  cost management advantages and shortcomings, 158–159
  operating expenses and, 158–159
  operations and, 157
Throughput in Theory of Constraints, 156, 158
TOC. *See* Theory of Constraints
Total Quality Management, 145, 148–154, 157
  activity-based management and, 159, 164, 167
  core principles and management objectives, 148–150
  cost management advantages and shortcomings, 151–153
  operations and, 150–151
  reengineering and, 196
  value engineering and, 197
TQM. *See* Total Quality Management
Transfer pricing, 104, 131–132
Turney, Peter, 86

U

Unexpired costs, 17

Index

V
Value, xiii, 5
  cost/resource relationships, 141
  shareholder, 5
Value-based management, 232–237
  financial management and, 234
  nonfinancial management and, 234–237
Value creation:
  expense item management and, 121, 123
  stakeholder, 255
Value engineering, 197–201
Value management, 98
Value proposition, xiii
Value management, xiii
Variance, 56, 62, 75
  Accounts, 74

W
Waste, 121, 136, 150